White servitude in Colonial America

An economic analysis

DAVID W. GALENSON

Department of Economics
University of Chicago
and
Division of the Humanities and Social Sciences
California Institute of Technology

CAMBRIDGE UNIVERSITY PRESS

Cambridge
London   New York   New Rochelle
Melbourne   Sydney

Published by the Press Syndicate of the University of Cambridge
The Pitt Building, Trumpington Street, Cambridge CB2 1RP
32 East 57th Street, New York, NY 10022, USA
296 Beaconsfield Parade, Middle Park, Melbourne 3206, Australia

First published 1981

Printed in the United States of America

Library of Congress Cataloging in Publication Data
Galenson, David W.
White servitude in colonial America.
Revision of the author's thesis (Ph.D. –
Harvard University, 1979) with the title:
The indenture system and the colonial labor
market.
Bibliography: p.
1. Indentured servants – United States –
History. I. Title.
HD4875.U5G34 1981   305.5′6   81–7682
ISBN 0 521 23686 X   AACR2

To my parents

White Servitude in Colonial America is based on the author's dissertation, "The Indenture System and the Colonial Labor Market: An Economic History of White Servitude in British America," which was awarded the David A. Wells Prize for the year 1979–80 by the Department of Economics of Harvard University.

Contents

Contents

Preface

White servitude was one of the major institutions in the economy and society of colonial British America. Indentured English men and women constituted the principal labor supply for many of the early British settlements in the New World, and their successors continued to make up an important part of white immigration to the British colonies in America throughout the seventeenth and eighteenth centuries. Yet those bound immigrants who arrived in the West Indies or the Chesapeake in the first half of the seventeenth century performed a very different role in the colonial labor market than did the indentured servants who came to British America in the middle of the eighteenth century. This book provides a description of the evolution of the economic function of white servitude in colonial America based on an examination of detailed evidence about the population of bound immigrants, and analyzes the sources of this process through the use of an explanatory framework designed to provide an understanding of the determinants of the major changes that occurred over time in the composition of colonial labor forces. In this way, this book is intended to produce both a thorough portrayal and an explanation of the causes underlying a dramatic episode of early American history in which hundreds of thousands of European men and women of the seventeenth and eighteenth centuries voluntarily sold themselves into bondage for a period of years in order to become part of the earliest stream of immigrants from the Old World to the New.

Slavery played no part in the plans of the early colonizers of British America. The use of bound white laborers preceded the use of black slaves in every British American colony, and it was only after an initial reliance on indentured servants for the bulk of their labor needs that the planters of the West Indies and the southern mainland colonies turned to slaves. Knowledge of why colonial planters substituted slaves for servants is critical to an understanding of the causes of the growth of black slavery in North America. This knowledge can be gained only through the comparative study of both of these systems of labor. As a result of its direct importance for the history of the nineteenth century and its indirect importance for the history of the twentieth, slavery has long been one of

Preface

the central concerns of American historians. Indentured servitude has received considerably less attention, and its history remains more obscure. This book is therefore also intended to contribute to our knowledge of the causes of the growth of slavery in colonial America by illuminating the closely related and relatively neglected decline of white servitude.

This study is a revised version of my dissertation, "The Indenture System and the Colonial Labor Market: An Economic History of White Servitude in British America," submitted to the economics department of Harvard University in 1979. I have accumulated many debts to people and institutions both during the preparation of the dissertation and during the subsequent period of revision.

The computations in the study were supported by grants from Harvard University, the National Science Foundation (Grant G3-3262), the National Bureau of Economic Research, and the University of Chicago. An Arthur H. Cole Grant from the Economic History Association assisted in the collection of data. A John E. Rovensky Fellowship from the Lincoln Educational Foundation helped to support my research in England, as did a Jens Aubrey Westengard Scholarship from Harvard. I am grateful to all these institutions for their support. None should be associated with any of the views expressed in this study.

In all the places I worked I benefited from access to excellent research facilities. I am grateful to the staffs of the Bristol Record Office; the British Museum; the City of Liverpool Libraries; the Corporation of London Records Office, London Guildhall; the Greater London Records Office, Middlesex Section; the Institute of Historical Research, London; the National Register of Archives, London; the Public Record Office, London; the Scottish Record Office, Edinburgh; the Somerset Record Office, Taunton; the Maryland Hall of Records, Annapolis; the Virginia State Historical Society, Richmond; and to those of the libraries of the California Institute of Technology, the Cambridge Group for the History of Population and Social Structure, the University of Chicago, Harvard University, and the University of London, for their assistance.

Seminars at a number of universities gave me the opportunity to present preliminary versions of parts of this study for criticism and discussion. Sections of the study were also presented at the 1976 Cliometrics Conference at Madison, Wisconsin, the Seventh International Economic History Congress at Edinburgh in 1978, the 1979 annual meetings of the Organization of American Historians at New Orleans, the 1980 Cliometrics Conference at Chicago, the 1980 annual meetings of the Economic History Association at Boston, and the 1980 annual meetings of the Social Science History Association at Rochester.

Preliminary versions of parts of this study have appeared in *Annales de*

Démographie Historique, Explorations in Economic History, the Historical Journal, the *Journal of Economic History,* the *Journal of Political Economy,* the *Journal of Southern History,* and the *William and Mary Quarterly.*[1] I am grateful to each of these journals for permission to reproduce some of the material from those articles here.

Photographs of Crown–copyright records in the Greater London Records Office (Figures 3.1, 3.2, and 3.3) appear by permission of the Controller of H.M. Stationery Office. Photographs of documents in the Corporation of London Records Office (Figures D.1 and D.2) are reproduced by permission of that office.

I have accumulated too many debts to individuals over the course of the five years spent in preparing this study to acknowledge fully here. I have recorded some of these elsewhere. Of too many others I can only say that I hope those people who helped me by suggesting sources and references, by guiding me through the intricacies of libraries and archives, by writing or correcting my computer programs, or by reading, discussing, and commenting on drafts of papers or chapters are aware of my appreciation.

Yet some of my debts dominate. Robert Fogel, as the chairman of my dissertation committee, gave constructive advice and critical comments that always focused directly on the central issues of my study. His questions always led me to probe more deeply into both evidence and interpretations. Stanley Engerman, the second member of my thesis committee, first suggested the subject to me, and remained closely involved with every subsequent stage of my investigation. His contributions to this study and to my education have been great, and are not easily measured or acknowledged. His many comments on my work and discussions of issues involved with it were invariably a source both of encouragement and of intellectual challenge. Richard Freeman, the third member of my thesis committee, generously provided assistance and enthusiasm for the work of a student outside his own principal field of interest.

Three of my former teachers of economic history- Paul David, Peter McClelland, and Peter Temin- continued to take an interest in my research, and each made significant contributions to this later work. Russell Menard brought my attention to a number of important issues and sharpened my perceptions of colonial history. Lance Davis's incisive comments on my dissertation and subsequent discussions provided me with detailed criticisms that resulted in considerable improvements in the manuscript.

A number of my colleagues in the economics department at the University of Chicago, including Andrew Abel, Gary Becker, Donald McCloskey, Frederic Mishkin, Melvin Reder, Sherwin Rosen, Theodore Schultz, and George Stigler, read my work and gave me the benefit of their high standards of criticism. Among those elsewhere, Lois Carr, K. G. Davies, Richard Dunn, Morgan Kousser, Peter Laslett, John McCusker, Jacob Price, Roger Schofield, Richard Sheridan, and Lorena Walsh were particularly helpful in commenting on preliminary versions of part or all of the manuscript and in providing advice on sources. Noel Currer-Briggs generously provided me with a copy of his manuscript of transcriptions of the Bristol servant registrations of 1654–86.

Mary Carnell, Myrtle Tuzar, and Marye Allen typed a succession of drafts of the manuscript cheerfully and efficiently.

My sister, Alice Galenson, has encouraged me in my work for as long as I can remember. Her encouragement has always been given when I needed it most, and it has always helped.

My parents, Marjorie and Walter Galenson, have always set high intellectual and personal standards for me, and have always had faith in my ability to achieve them. I have seen this study as an affirmation of the interests and values we share, and it is dedicated to them.

D.W.G.

Part I

Introduction

1

The significance and origins of the colonial indenture system

Throughout the American colonial period many Europeans were enabled to emigrate to the New World by entering contracts of servitude called indentures. These constituted promises on the part of the emigrant to work for a designated master or his assigns during a fixed period of time in return for passage to a specified colony, maintenance there during the time of the contract, and specified freedom dues at the conclusion of the term. The contract could be sold by the master at any time during its term. The indenture did not make the servant a slave, for it was the servant's labor, rather than his person, that was temporarily owned by the master; at the end of the time stated in the contract, the servant became free. Yet indentured servitude did involve a stricter obligation than most forms of labor contract because the system provided for the enforcement of the agreement by requirement of specific performance of the work described in the contract.

The indenture system initiated the use of bound labor in British America. The basic elements of the system were in use by the Virginia Company by 1620 and may have been worked out earlier, so that indentured servitude was in existence almost within a decade of the first settlement at Jamestown.[1] Wherever slavery ultimately developed, indentured servitude had earlier been in use. To British colonial planters in the early seventeenth century, the indenture system offered the most accessible supply of bound labor. In those colonies in which abundant land and the availability of a profitable staple crop made the demand for labor grow rapidly there was a high demand for servants. As a result, for many regions it became true that, as John Pory reported from Virginia in 1619, "our principall wealth . . . consisteth in servants."[2]

Quantitatively, indentured servants played a major role in early British migration to the New World. Although their total numbers are not subject to precise estimation, an indication of their significance is given by Abbot Emerson Smith's judgment that between half and two-thirds of all white immigrants to the American colonies after the 1630s came under indenture, or Wesley Frank Craven's estimate that 75 percent or more of Virginia's settlers in the seventeenth century were servants.[3]

The quantitative importance of the indenture system was greater than that of slavery in both the early settlement of British America and the development of its economy. The Chesapeake colonies of Maryland and Virginia prospered through the use of white servants in the seventeenth century, and when black slaves came in significant numbers, as U. B. Phillips noted, they were "late comers fitted into a system already developed."[4] It is in this sense that Eric Williams wrote in his history of slavery in British America that "white servitude was the historic base upon which Negro slavery was constructed."[5] Estimates based on probate inventories suggest that as late as the second half of the 1670s servants made up 80 percent of all Maryland's bound labor and thus outnumbered slaves in the colony by a ratio of four to one.[6]

Yet although the indenture system was established and developed on a large scale before the arrival of slavery, the importance of white servitude in British America declined over time, whereas once established, in many areas the importance of slavery grew. Although these processes have not been precisely dated for many regions, the general outlines are clear. Few white servants emigrated to the West Indies after the middle of the eighteenth century. In the last twenty-five years of the seventeenth century servants fell from four-fifths of Maryland's bound labor to only a quarter, and their share continued to fall thereafter.[7] Although white servitude survived the colonial period, and apparent isolated cases of indenture in the United States can be found as late as the fourth decade of the nineteenth century, it appears that by the time of the American Revolution the indenture system had ceased to be quantitatively important in any part of British America.[8]

Unanswered questions remain concerning almost every phase of the indenture system's history, and most aspects of its operation. This study attempts to provide full responses to some of these, and partial answers to others, both through the adduction of new evidence and a reexamination of existing work. One portion of the analysis is aimed at establishing the characteristics of a large group of indentured servants. Among the variables considered are their age, sex, occupational structure, and literacy. A second section analyzes the functioning of the transatlantic market for servants. The results of these investigations are examined for trends to derive some indications of how the role of the indenture system in the colonial labor market changed over time, and why it ultimately disappeared. A third section places this evidence within a theoretical framework to suggest a possible explanation of the causal forces behind the introduction, evolution, and disappearance of the indenture system.

White servitude: English origins and colonial adaptations

In 1583 Sir George Peckham wrote a pamphlet entitled *A True Reporte, of the late discoveries, and possessions, taken in the right of the Crowne of Englande, of the Newfound Landes, By that valiaunt and worthye Gentleman, Sir Humfrey Gilbert Knight.*[9] Because the pamphlet was intended to obtain subscriptions for a colonizing expedition to Newfoundland, it stressed the importance and feasibility of founding British colonies in North America. In the concluding section, designed to show "that the Planting there, is not a matter of such charge or diffycultie, as many would make it seeme to be," Peckham wrote:

I say & affirme that God hath provided such meanes for the furtheraunce of this enterprise, as doth stand vs in steed of great treasure: for first by reason that it hath pleased God of his great goodnesse, of long time to holde his merciful hand over this Realme, in preserving the people of the same, both from slaughter by the sword, & great death by plague, pestilence, or otherwise, there is at this day great numbers (God he knoweth) which live in such penurie & want, as they could be contented to hazarde their lives, and to serve one yeere for meat, drinke, and apparel, onely without wages, in hope thereby to amend theyr estates; which is a matter in such like journeis, of no small charge to the Prince.[10]

This passage may have been the first statement of the principle on which the colonial indenture system was later founded and operated, namely, the voluntary exchange by an English man or woman of labor servitude to a designated master during a fixed period of time for passage to the New World and maintenance there during the term of the contract. But any actual connection between this statement and the initiation of indentured servitude in the seventeenth-century American colonies remains unclear. Although many elements necessary for an explanation of the origins of the indenture system have long been available, they have sometimes been seen as conflicting observations in relation to the historical basis of the indenture system. However, with only minor modifications, they are quite consistent with each other. This has become particularly clear in the light of recent research in English social and economic history, for recent findings have pointed to a likely synthesis of the elements already available and have provided additional evidence to fill some existing gaps.

Some historians have depicted the colonial indenture system as a novel institution. In this view, the system was the result of improvisation, and considerable ingenuity, on the part of the colonizers of North America.[11] Although the problem – how to people a new world – was unprecedented, the economic opportunity was a great motivator, and a novel solution was devised to recruit a labor force to exploit the riches of North America.

Others have seen the indenture system as less a new departure than the adaptation to a new environment of a traditional institution, that of apprenticeship.[12] In this light, the novelty of the institution was much less: "That a man should become a bondservant by legal contract was not strange, for the ancient institution of apprenticeship was known to all."[13] What is not clear is how the extension of the institution to unskilled workers was regarded by contemporaries, for apprenticeship was defined as an arrangement by which youths were trained in specific crafts, and normally involved a minimum term of seven years.[14]

It now appears that both these positions contain elements of the true explanation of the origins of the indenture system. To see this more clearly, it is helpful to consider some important aspects of the society from which the colonizers came. The motives of those who founded the colonies of North America have received considerable attention from historians. Although many specific motives have been identified, one theme, concerning the form the colonies were to take, dominated much of the contemporary literature on colonization. One of its early statements appears in the pamphlet quoted above, Peckham's *True Reporte* of 1583. Peckham appended to the pamphlet a copy of the "Articles of Assurance," a description of the social and economic structure of the colony he envisaged, based on a plan drawn up a year earlier by Sir Humphrey Gilbert. Gilbert's plan has been referred to by a biographer as a "framework for a colonial Utopia,"[15] yet the model from which the idealized society was taken is clear. For a consistent theme that ran through much, if not most, English colonizing literature of the late sixteenth and early seventeenth centuries was the desire to reproduce English society in the New World. Although most colonizers aimed at creating a purified version, or perhaps re-creating that of an earlier, manorial era, the society and social structure they wished to implant in the wilderness were those of England. This has been recognized by many historians.[16] Perry Miller, for example, suggested this in terms relevant to this discussion when he wrote of an early governor of Virginia who "intended, he said, to create in Virginia a society 'like our natiue country,' and England was a society of gradations."[17]

Not only was seventeenth-century England a society of gradations, but its preindustrial economy was based on agriculture, and its social institutions were highly developed and attuned to the problems of allocating a labor force efficiently to agriculture. The results of recent research on the social structure of traditional England tend to suggest that the indenture system, although modified in form, can be seen as a geographic extension of one of the most pervasive institutions of seventeenth-century England.

Indentured servants were initially sent to the New World to provide agricultural labor.[18] In this they were the equivalent not of English apprentices but rather of English servants in husbandry, or farm servants.

Peter Laslett has estimated that between a quarter and a third of all families in Stuart England contained servants, most of whom, female as well as male, were engaged in agricultural labor.[19] A recent study has estimated that during the seventeenth and eighteenth centuries, between one-third and one-half of all hired labor in English agriculture was performed by farm servants, and that in a typical parish more than half of hired full-time agricultural workers were servants.[20]

Typically, in preindustrial England, boys and girls born in a cottage would leave home for service sometime after the age of 10. These servants in husbandry, as they would then be called, usually remained in the position of servant until marriage.[21] This period was normally divided between a number of different households, for one characteristic of farm servants was their frequent, typically annual, mobility.[22] In this they differed from those who entered training in industrial crafts, true apprentices, who usually spent the entire period of life-cycle service in a single household. Recent research has indicated that the actual number of apprentices has been exaggerated by historians.[23] It may be a consequence of this that the quantitative importance of servants in husbandry has often been underestimated. Peter Laslett has recently estimated that, although those in service – apprentices and servants in husbandry – may have made up between 10 and 15 percent of the population of seventeenth-century England, apprentices alone may have accounted for less than 1 percent.[24] Service in husbandry seems also to have been a common feature of many other traditional societies.[25] Servants in these systems lived in the house of their masters much as additional children, and indeed the word used by English contemporaries to describe the extended group living together under one roof was "family."[26]

The system under which farm servants worked in England was well defined by custom. Servants lived in the house of a master who provided them with room and board in addition to wages. Although their contracts were usually verbal rather than written,[27] they were legally enforceable, as both legislation and a considerable body of litigation, consisting of complaints by both masters and servants, attest.[28] The normal duration of the contracts was one year, but cases can be found in which servants bound themselves for either shorter or longer periods.[29]

Although the indenture system differed from the system of service in husbandry chiefly in the distance the servants traveled upon leaving home, this was a sufficiently important economic difference to necessitate several modifications in the institution. These had a considerable impact on its operation, for each change tended to make the indenture system more rigid and formal than its English counterpart. The most fundamental change, from which the others apparently followed, was in the duration of the normal term of service. As noted above, the English servant in husbandry typically served a short term, rarely remaining more than a year or two in one place. Longer terms were needed for those servants sent to the American colonies because of the considerable expense of transporting them.[30] The reason for this is straightforward. The indenture system provided a link between English labor supply and colonial demand. The link was effected through the indenture, which was a credit mechanism by which the servant, unable to borrow elsewhere the money necessary for the passage fare, borrowed against the future returns from his labor. The indenture was thus a promise to repay the loan, and the security on the loan was the servant himself. The length of the term depended on the amount of time necessary for repayment.[31]

These longer terms, dictated by the need of the lender to recover his large initial investment, had legal precedents in the English system of service in husbandry and even more commonly in apprenticeship. But in the colonial indenture system the terms raised greater problems of enforcement than had existed in England. These problems were aggravated by the high marginal productivity of labor in many parts of the land-abundant colonial economy, as the high wages of free labor and the relatively easy availability of land in many colonies, particularly in the early seventeenth century, provided strong economic incentives for servants to breach their contracts by running away. As a result, the adaptation of the English institution to the American colonies produced an additional body of colonial legislation aimed at preventing servants from deserting their masters. This may have had a significant effect on the daily lives of the colonists, for one preventive measure used in all colonies from early times was the requirement that anyone traveling had to have a pass.[32]

Yet although the requirement of obtaining a pass to travel may have been an annoyance to colonists, the effects of the adaptation of the English system of service may have cut much deeper into colonial society than to just the level of convenience. Both the need for a large body of legislation to prevent servants from running away and the fact that running away was the most frequent cause for the appearance of servants before colonial magistrates suggest the introduction of a new adversary status – or at least the aggravation of the existing one – into the relationship between master and servant. Unlike their counterparts in England, colonial indentured servants were no longer considered additional children. The mechanism used to secure the investment in their voyage to the colonies had made them into property. To be sure, servants were valuable property in the early colonies, but they were no longer additional members of a family, as servants had been in England.[33]

An important difference between the colonial indenture system and English service in husbandry was that colonial masters were free to sell their servants for the remaining term of their contracts whenever they pleased. Edmund Morgan has pointed out that this shocked some seventeenth-century Englishmen,[34] and it did constitute an anomaly in an English context. In fifteenth-century England it had been acceptable to sell the service of apprentices freely as the master's property, but by the seventeenth century apprentices could be sold only with the permission of the master's guild. By the time of the first settlement at Jamestown, binding an English apprentice with intent to sell him was considered an abuse.[35] There can seldom have been a need to sell farm servants in England, because of both the short terms of their contracts and the ease with which these could be terminated – since wages were generally paid to servants at frequent intervals according to their productivity,[36] neither the master nor the servant normally acquired a sizable net investment in the contract; the amount of money owed by one to the other was rarely large. As has been seen, this was not the case for indentured servants in the colonies, for their contracts represented large investments to their masters in the form of debts owed to them by their servants. Convenience provided a strong incentive to make these contracts transferable, for servants were rarely bound in England by the person they were to serve in the colonies. The distances and costs involved made it impractical in most cases for planters to travel in England to recruit their own workers, so that by the standard form servants were bound to serve an English agent or his assigns to make it possible to transfer the contract upon the servant's arrival in the colonies. This, of course, had the effect of making the indenture negotiable not only initially but also at any subsequent time before its expiration, and an English servant in Virginia now discovered that his master could sell him "like a damnd slave."[37]

Although some aspects of the indenture system diverged from contemporary English practices, it did embody, as seen earlier, important elements of continuity. The system is perhaps best viewed as the adaptation, with such changes as were dictated by economic necessity, of an institution basic to the English agricultural economy. Instead of moving from one village to another to enter service, after 1607 English youths frequently moved to another continent. In functional terms the indenture system was thus primarily a geographic extension of the system of service in husbandry.[38]

Yet, it might be objected, a voyage to the New World in the seventeenth century, which took from two to three months, was not a routine event; surely an institution that required transatlantic passage must have been regarded quite differently by contemporaries than one that involved only a local journey. Some caution is required in dealing with this objection, for most contemporary discussion of the indenture system resulted from public interest in a larger issue, the question of whether emigration to the colonies was beneficial to England. As a result, most contemporary literature dealing with the indenture system is strongly biased.[39] However, even allowing for this, examples can be found to demonstrate clearly that Englishmen of the seventeenth century could naturally conflate the two systems of colonial indenture and English service in husbandry. An example appears in a description of Maryland written in 1666 by George Alsop, a former indentured servant. Demonstrating an unquestioning belief in what R. H. Tawney called the "functional view of class organization," Alsop wrote: "Then let such, where Providence hath ordained to live as Servants, either in England or beyond Sea, endure the prefixed yoak of their limited time with patience."[40] Similarly, William Wood wrote of New England in 1635 that "there is as much freedom and liberty for servants [there] as in England and more too," and an anonymous author of Carolina in 1666: "Let no man be troubled at the thoughts of being a Servant for 4 or 5 years, for I can assure you, that many men [in England] give mony with their children to serve 7 years, to take more pains and serve nothing so well as the Servants in this Plantation will do."[41] It should be noted that these writers were all favorable to the indenture system, and were trying either directly or indirectly to attract recruits to it. Yet what is important for this discussion is their unselfconscious conflation of the status of servants in England and the colonies. Alsop and Wood do this explicitly, the anonymous Carolinian implicitly by arguing that colonial servants were better placed even than English apprentices who, unlike the lower status servants in husbandry, had to pay for access to their more desirable places.

Development and forms of colonial indentured servitude

The argument outlined here might seem to lead to the conclusion that the indenture system was an important source of social and economic continuity in the British colonization of North America. It did represent as direct a transplantation of a common English institution as was possible under the economic circumstances. Yet it would appear that the adaptations produced a fundamental change in the institution, as the rigidity introduced as a result of economic imperatives destroyed relationships basic to the English system of service in husbandry, and resulted in a system in which men were traded and sold as objects. Thus, although the indenture system appears to have been the solution to the problem of how to move the English system of service in husbandry across the Atlantic, the form it took was quite different from that of the institution on which it was modeled. An examination of the actual development of the system suggests how quickly the economic sources of the differences molded the new institution.

Significance and origins of the colonial indenture system

The characteristic form of the indenture system emerged from early experimentation with a variety of different arrangements by the Virginia Company. The company's purpose was the simple one of maximizing its profits, and the succession of formulas it tried were all intended to do this by recruiting a labor force for Virginia that would work for the company's benefit. In devising schemes with which to attract settlers, the company met with no interference from the British government, for from the first there was an understanding that emigration to America was to be handled privately, without intervention by – or expense to – the king.[42]

The company's initial plan was to treat migrants as "adventurers," or investors. Prospective settlers in Virginia in 1606 were each promised a share of stock in the company, toward a division of the company's profits that was to occur at the end of five years. In return, the settlers were to live in Virginia at the company's expense and to work there wholly for the company.[43]

Profits five years in the future apparently proved inadequate to motivate the colonists, and the company's early attempt to use military discipline to make communal production profitable was equally a failure. The subsequent development of the form of immigration characteristic of the indenture system was closely connected to other changes that marked the company's gradual surrender of its control over the colony's economy. An obvious need to give settlers stronger positive work incentives led to tentative economic reforms as early as 1609, when small amounts of land were given to individuals for private gardens, and in 1613 somewhat larger plots were granted to settlers to farm on their own account. This reform led to a new system, established by 1616, under which newly arrived colonists could be rented from the company for employment as laborers on private farms.[44]

In 1618 a reorganization of the colony's government produced a ratification of the movement toward individual enterprise, as earlier settlers were granted sizable plots of land on which they were to pay rents to the company. In conjunction with this change, the company offered to transport new settlers to Virginia and establish them there as sharecroppers; the company would give the tenants land and provide them with food and capital for an initial period in return for half their output. At the end of seven years of tenancy, the farmer would be freed from the agreement, and would be given 50 acres of his own land.[45]

As part of the same thrust to increase Virginia's population, the company arranged with the City of London to have one hundred poor children sent to Virginia in 1618 at the City's expense. The terms of the contract drawn up by the City's Common Council indicate that the children were to be treated as apprentices and placed on land as tenants for freedom dues at the end of their seven-year terms. These children, and others in the following four years, were sold to the free settlers of the colony. In a parallel enterprise, in 1619 the company began to send young women to Virginia to be sold to planters as wives upon payment to the company of the cost of their passage.[46]

These transactions of 1618 and 1619 clearly foreshadowed the indenture system. The first documented example of the system's characteristic form on a significant scale occurred in 1620, when the Virginia Company sent to the colony "one hundred servants to be disposed amongst the old *Planters.*" The cost of passage was advanced by the company, and the servants were transferred to individual planters upon reimbursement of these costs. This marked the full development of the transaction that became prevalent for English indentured servants, as colonial planters obtained the services of the immigrant for a specified time upon payment of a lump sum to the importer.[47]

One other common feature of the indenture system had also been introduced by the company before this time. From about 1618, the company had provided an additional incentive for planters to transport servants to Virginia on their own account by the promise of a "headright," or grant of land, for each individual brought into the colony. By 1619, the size of these grants had been set at 50 acres.[48]

Although pioneered by the Virginia Company, the characteristic form of the indenture transaction was quickly borrowed by private planters and merchants, and the headright was soon adopted by other colonies as a means of encouraging the importation of new settlers. As a result, the indenture system remained in use throughout the British settlements in America long after the dissolution of the Virginia Company in 1624.[49]

Fundamentally, indentured servitude was an institutional arrangement that was devised to increase labor mobility from England to America.[50] The settlement of the New World made available for cultivation vast amounts of new land, and in those regions in which crops could be found that would both exploit this resource and satisfy the demands of the large English market, the result was a marginal productivity of labor in agriculture considerably above that found in England. As will be seen later in this study, the marginal productivity of labor in many parts of colonial America was sufficient to allow many bound English workers to repay the cost of passage to the colonies in as little as four years. Yet when English colonization of the Americas began, the problem existed of how workers unable to afford the high cost of the fare out of their own savings could borrow the necessary funds. The requirements of the situation, with the need for the emigrant to repay the funds after traveling across the Atlantic Ocean, posed enormous problems of enforcement for any potential British lender, and it is not surprising that existing British financial institutions were inadequate to the task. As was seen in the preceding description of the Virginia Company's early experiments, the initial solution was for a firm active in colonial production to advance the cost of passage to workers who would then become employees of the firm until this loan was repaid. The problems of supervision and motivation caused by this scheme soon led the company to rent out the workers it transported to private producers. This modified system was short-lived, as the company apparently quickly perceived the advantages of simply selling the workers it imported to individual planters for the period necessary for repayment of the loan, specified in the workers' contracts. By doing this, the company unambiguously transferred all costs of supervision and enforcement of the contract to the planters, including all risks, such as the possible escape or death of the servant. Once the principle of outright sale of the contract had been established, a large firm no longer had any significant advantage in the transportation of servants, for there was no longer a need for supervision of large numbers of agreements for any extended period in the colonies, and the period during which the transporter extended credit was reduced to the time between the signing of the contract in England and its sale in the colonies, principally the two to three months during which the servant was in transit to the colonies. The cost of entry into the servant trade was low, and the industry quickly became one in which many merchants participated.

Yet the form of the indenture bargain was not limited to a single type. At least three distinct methods existed by which people became servants. The distinctions ceased to matter once the servant had been bound, for legally all white colonial servants were treated the same by both statute and custom, but the differences in form did have implications for the operation of the trade in servants. The first type to develop was that already described, in which a servant entered an indenture before leaving Europe. The contract generally was sold to a new master when the servant arrived in the colonies, but the basic dimensions of his servitude, particularly the length of term, were fixed by the contract. A variant of this form developed to deal with cases in which prospective servants arrived in the colonies without written indentures. On arrival they were sold as servants, and to provide some protection for these people each colony developed its own legislation specifying the "custom of the country." An important element of this legislation was the regulation of the term to be served by those arriving without indentures.[51]

During the eighteenth century a third form of arrangement appeared. Under the redemptioner system, the emigrant crossed the Atlantic under a promise to pay his fare on arrival in America. He might sometimes have made partial payment before sailing. After arrival, a period of time, usually two weeks, was allowed for the servant to raise the balance of the fare. If he failed to raise the money, he was sold into servitude by the ship's captain for the balance due. The length of the term for which he was bound was therefore determined by the size of his debt.

The redemptioner system apparently originated in the transportation of Germans to the British colonies, and although the arrangement was used to some extent in the British servant trade in the eighteenth century, most British servants in the colonies had arrived under indenture or were bound by the custom of the country, whereas most Germans apparently came as redemptioners. Although the reason for this has never been fully explained, some elements of a possible answer can be suggested. The differences in form could have resulted in part from differences in the requirements of the emigrants. Whereas virtually all British servants emigrated individually, it was more common for Germans to emigrate in families.[52] The redemptioner system's routine provision for partial payment of fares in advance might have better suited German families who had raised some capital from the liquidation of the assets accumulated by the parents than young English men and women who emigrated as servants, few of whom had worked long enough to have much savings. The redemptioner system might also have been more flexible in adapting to a situation in which a family wanted to spread the costs of transportation more evenly among a group of people. Thus the adjustment of the length of contracts after the servants' arrival in the colonies may have made it easier, in binding the family as a group rather than individually, to make the terms of the family members less unequal in length than would have been the case under the indenture system, so that the members of a family could be freed closer to a single date.[53] The redemptioner system's allowance for a period after arrival in the colonies during which the servant could attempt to raise the balance of the fare was also probably more useful to emigrants who traveled in large groups over time to a single destination, as the Germans tended overwhelmingly to flow to Philadelphia, where many individuals or families might expect to find friends or relatives to give or lend them the fare to cancel their debts.

These considerations involving the needs of the emigrants are all possible components of an explanation of the prevalence of the indenture form among British emigrants and the redemptioner agreement among Germans. An important analytical difference between the systems might have resulted from differences in the typical situations of German and English emigrants upon embarking for America. For there was a difference in the allocation of risk under the two systems. Under the indenture system, the economic risk in the trade was borne primarily by the merchant who bound the servant in England for future sale in the colonies. Because the merchant normally took personal title to the contract, he was a speculator in the servant's labor and would personally absorb any profits and losses resulting from changes in the value of the contract between the times of agreement in England and sale in the colonies. In contrast, under the redemptioner system the principal risk was transferred to the servant. Except in the case of death of the servant in transit, the merchant or ship's captain was guaranteed a fixed sum for his passage.[54] Any changes in the value of the servant's labor between the time of his departure from Europe and his subsequent arrival in the colonies would accrue to him personally in the form of a longer or shorter term of servitude. Thus, whereas under the indenture system the term to be served was fixed before the servant's departure and the sum received by the merchant upon delivery varied, under the redemptioner system the reverse was the case, as the merchant's receipts were fixed and the servant's term varied.

A possible cause of this difference could have been the differences in the typical conditions of servant supply in the two cases. Unlike English servants, German redemptioners normally entered their agreements outside their native country.[55] Thus the Germans entered agreements with captains in Dutch ports, where their alternative opportunities for work were poor and the cost of returning to Germany substantial. The presence of whole families in many cases must have reinforced the tendency for the redemptioners' choices to be restricted at the time of entering the agreement for transportation. The same factors did not affect English servants, for their alternative opportunities were not restricted in the same way by language barriers or the need to support a family. The shift of the risk from merchant to servant may therefore have been a consequence of the lower opportunity cost to the Germans of entering the indenture system at the time of making their agreements.[56]

Further investigation of the differences among these variants of colonial servitude lies beyond the scope of this study and will not be pursued here. The principal focus of this investigation will be on servants of the first type, those who traveled to the colonies after signing an indenture. Although much remains unknown about the relative numbers of servants who emigrated under each of the three arrangements at particular times, this appears to have been both the longest lived and quantitatively the most important of the contributors to the colonial indenture system.

Principal sources of evidence and plan of the study

In the early decades of the twentieth century, the colonial indenture system was the subject of a number of major historical investigations, each of which examined its operation in a single colony.[57] The most comprehensive monograph to date on the system in all parts of British America was written during the 1930s and published in 1947.[58] Since then, colonial white servitude has not been the subject of large-scale study.

Some recent authors have made contributions dealing with particular aspects of the system, but these have been narrow in scope. Because of this relative neglect, in 1974 K. G. Davies suggested in his history of *The North Atlantic World in the Seventeenth Century* that the indenture system was due for a reconsideration.[59]

This study attempts such a fresh examination. It is based principally on the systematic analysis of a collection of six separate data sets, each composed of English legal registrations of large numbers of individual indentured servants. These have not previously been subjected to thorough analysis. The registrations, however, are not a new source to historians. As will be noted in the course of this study, several of the collections have been used when they were relevant to historians' studies of particular regions, and a few have even served as the principal sources for separate, smaller investigations. Yet all these uses of the data have been partial, both in their use of only one or two of the collections and in their consideration of only some of the variables on which the data contain information. This study uses all known servant registrations made in England during the American colonial period that survive in sizable collections, and considers virtually all the important variables in each. This approach allows comparisons of results across samples in addition to the multivariate analysis of the evidence of particular samples.

For an investigation that seeks to understand long-run changes in economic conditions there are numerous obvious advantages to this approach, and these need not be enumerated here. Yet some questions do nonetheless arise. The central one, ubiquitous in historical research, concerns the representativeness of the sample. To what extent can findings about the people contained in the sample be applied to the larger population of indentured servants from which they are drawn? Although no definitive answer to this question can be offered, a number of relevant considerations can be noted. First, the registrations span a long period of time–the earliest is from 1654, the latest from 1775–and they come from England's three major ports in the period, London, Bristol, and Liverpool. It must nonetheless be pointed out that their distribution across both time and space is very uneven. However, that they are not a random sample in these respects does not necessarily mean that they are biased with respect to certain other important variables. As will be seen, although some considerations of the possible effects of bias can be usefully undertaken, for many of the variables analyzed there is no way to test this issue directly. A systematic presentation and analysis of the available evidence can at least serve to establish the characteristics of the sample, and in some cases the plausibility of the results obtained can be checked by reference to other types of evidence.

Together, the six sets of registrations cover a total of 20,657 servants. It is relevant to the present discussion to know what proportion of the whole immigrant servant population these represent. The available estimates are tentative in the extreme, but some rough outlines may be drawn from them. One estimate of the magnitude of the servant migration is that of Carter Goodrich, who estimated that half the total white immigration to the thirteen mainland colonies was made up of servants.[60] This was extended by Abbot Emerson Smith, who estimated that between one-half and two-thirds of all white immigrants to all the British colonies after the 1630s were servants.[61] Estimates of net white migration to the British colonies for the period 1650–1780, with a description of how they were made, will be presented later in this study.[62] Although these figures are rough, they show that net white migration to the British colonies totaled approximately 600,000 during this period. Smith's estimate would therefore imply a total net migration of servants from 1650 to the end of the mainland's colonial era, the period spanned by the servant registrations used here, in the range from 300,000 to 400,000. The servant registrations on which this study is based might therefore represent between 5 and 7 percent of the total servant population from the relative period.

These proportions are not sufficiently high to warrant strong assertions concerning the representativeness of the registrations in the sample for the whole servant population. Yet once again it should be emphasized that they represent all known registrations of their kind that survive in significant numbers. Earlier studies based on one or two of the six samples used here have obviously relied on smaller shares of the total. More registrations may be discovered in the future, and these might serve to fill some existing gaps in the geographic and temporal coverage of the records currently available. Yet is it unlikely that new discoveries will ever raise the proportion of the total population covered to the point where it will no longer be necessary to worry about the representativeness of the surviving sample. As in most historical studies, the question of representativeness will ultimately remain unanswered. The procedure in this study will therefore be that followed by others in similar circumstances, simply to make the sample of the particular type of data to be analyzed as large as possible. Systematic analysis will then give us firm information about those included in the sample and, pending the discovery of additional data, will provide the best available basis for generalization about the larger population.

The remainder of this study is divided into four sections. The following section, titled "Characteristics of the servant population," provides a quantitative description and analysis of some important demographic and economic characteristics of the 20,657 immigrants covered by the servant registrations that form the major primary sources for this investigation. Chapter 2 considers the age and sex distributions of the servants, Chapters

3 and 4 deal with the occupations of the male servants, and Chapter 5 analyzes the servants' literacy. This section provides information about the distribution of these variables for the servants in each of the samples analyzed and considers differences in the distributions across samples, thus identifying trends that occurred over time in the composition of the servant population.

The third section, "Migration and the transatlantic market for indentured servants," uses the evidence of the servant registrations to analyze the migration of the servants. Chapter 6 provides an overview of the colonial destinations of the servants, giving a quantitative indication of changes over time in the relative importance of different colonial regions as servant importers. The chapter also explicitly relates the individual characteristics of the servants to their colonial destinations. This serves to establish differences in the typical sex, age, and occupational composition of the servants bound for the different servant-importing regions at a given time, as well as changes in the typical characteristics of servants bound for each region over time. Chapter 7 examines the market for servants that linked the colonies with Great Britain. Using an economic model of the market as an interpretive framework, empirical estimates indicate how the transatlantic trade valued the servants' labor, by means of an analysis of the lengths of the terms for which the servants were bound. These estimates provide information about both the way in which the particular characteristics of individual servants affected their expected productivity in the colonies and the nature of the choices the servants faced in binding themselves to serve in America.

The fourth section of the study focuses explicitly on the role of the indenture system in the colonial labor market. Chapter 8 combines the results of the previous section with other evidence to provide a quantitative view of the ways in which indentured labor interacted with free and slave labor in the colonies, and to construct a description of how the role of white servitude evolved in those regions in which it was quantitatively important. Chapter 9 then presents an economic model of labor supply to the American colonies designed to explain the determination of the composition of colonial labor forces by the three available types of labor – free, servant, and slave. This model is used to examine the composition of the labor forces of a number of major colonial regions, and to isolate the factors responsible for some significant changes in their composition. The chapter also uses the evidence of the servant registrations to test an implication of the model concerning the relationship between the quantitative importance of slavery in a colony and the skill composition of the colony's servant population.

Significance and origins of the colonial indenture system

A concluding section summarizes the results of this investigation concerning both the American colonial experience and the indenture as a form of labor contract, and briefly surveys the role of bound labor in the history of the Americas.

Part II

Characteristics of the servant population

2

The age and sex distributions of the indentured servants

This section is devoted to a quantitative description of the characteristics of the population of indentured servants from the evidence available in the servant registrations. One basic element of this is the population's demographic structure. This chapter provides an overview of its distribution by sex and age.

Composition by sex

Although the sex of the servants was not recorded independently in most registrations, it can be inferred from their names. Table 2.1 presents the sex distributions of the servants in each of the six samples of registrations. The initial observation concerning the distributions has to do with the obvious imbalance between men and women. Women did not make up as much as one-third of the servants in any of the samples examined. Thus the greatest proportion of women in any single sample was the 30.8 percent of the total registered in London during 1683–86, whereas the lowest was the 5.5 percent of the London registrations of 1718–59. In total, women comprised only 18.4 percent of the servants in all the samples. This supports the familiar finding that the indentured servants bound for colonial America were predominantly men.[1]

Previously, less has been known of possible trends in the sex composition of the servant population over time. Table 2.2 presents the results obtained by aggregating the registrations across samples by decade. This yields a series from the pooled samples of the servants' sex distributions by decade. With the exception of the first decade of the eighteenth century, the observations divide temporally into two relatively homogeneous groups. The first is made up of the five seventeenth-century decades covered, in which women made up between 21 and 25 percent of total registrations. The second group includes the six eighteenth-century observations after 1710, in which women made up less than 10 percent of registrations in five decades and a maximum of just over 15 percent in one. The observation that does not fit into these groups comes from the Liverpool registrations made in the first eight years of the eighteenth

Characteristics of the servant population

Table 2.1. *Sex distributions of indentured servants by sample*

Sample	Men		Women	
	No.	%	No.	%
Bristol, 1654–86	8,173	76.9	2,455	23.1
London, 1683–86	608	69.2	270	30.8
Middlesex, 1683–84	655	80.7	157	19.3
Liverpool, 1697–1707	1,039	72.0	404	28.0
London, 1718–59	3,013	94.5	174	5.5
London, 1773–75	3,359	90.6	350	9.4
Total	16,847	81.6	3,810	18.4

century, in which women accounted for more than 36 percent of the servants bound.

The pooled evidence of all the registrations shows that whereas in the seventeenth-century registrations women comprised 23.3 percent of the servants covered, in the eighteenth century they made up only 9.8 percent. This proportional decline of more than one-half in the importance of women in the registrations over time is striking. Our present knowledge of relevant conditions in both England and the colonies is not sufficient to provide a full explanation for this apparently considerable temporal shift in the sex composition of the servant population. On the supply side, these would include the effects on emigration of possibly changing relative opportunities for men and women in the English economy during the seventeenth and eighteenth centuries.

Yet several factors of possible importance on the demand side can be indicated. These are specific mechanisms through which the changing sex composition of the populations of the principal servant-importing colonies could have affected the demand for immigrants. For it is known that an early acute shortage of women existed in many British American colonies in the seventeenth century, whereas by the eighteenth century there was a strong tendency toward a more even balance between the sexes in most colonies.[2] Evidence to be presented later in this study from samples of servants registered in 1683–84 and 1718–59 indicates that with a number of other characteristics held constant, American colonists offered a premium for women relative to men.[3] One possible reason for this is the shortage of wives for colonists in many areas, particularly in the seventeenth century. The comments of contemporaries indicate that at least some English women who emigrated to the colonies under indenture were purchased upon arrival by men for the purpose of marriage. Thus one author wrote of Maryland in 1666 that "the Women that go over into this

24

Table 2.2. *Sex distributions of servants by decade*

Decade	N	% men	% women
1650s	2,954	75.5	24.5
1660s	4,548	76.0	24.0
1670s	2,549	78.7	21.3
1680s	2,267	76.9	23.1
1690s	873	77.5	22.5
1700s	570	63.5	36.5
1710s	179	84.9	15.1
1720s	1,237	93.9	6.1
1730s	1,506	95.9	4.1
1740s	16	93.8	6.2
1750s	249	96.8	3.2
1770s	3,709	90.6	9.4
1654–99	13,191	76.7	23.3
1700–75	7,466	90.2	9.8

Province as Servants . . . are no sooner on shoar, but they are courted into a Copulative Matrimony," and a British planter wrote in 1649, in reference to his experience in sending female servants to work on his estate in Virginia, that

if they come of an honest stock and have good repute, they may pick and chuse their Husbands out of the better sort of people. I have sent over many, but could never keepe one at my Plantation three Moneths, except a poor silly Wench, made for a Foile to set of beautie, and yet a proper young Fellow must needs have her, and being but new come out of his time and not strong enough to pay the charges I was at in cloathing and transporting her, was content to serve me a twelve Moneth for a wife.[4]

Although the frequency of this practice and the extent to which it contributed to the determination of the sex ratio of the indentured servants are not known, the decline in the early quantitative sexual imbalance in the colonies reduced the shortage of wives, and therefore might have tended to reduce the demand for female servants relative to males.[5]

The possible importance of a second factor is suggested by further analysis of the registrations of 1718–59, in which a premium appears for women only below the age of 18.[6] The relative youth of the favored group might indicate that at least in this period the principal source of the female premium did not stem from a demand for potential wives but perhaps instead for young women to perform household work. A possible parallel is the finding that in the nineteenth-century American South young female slaves were more productive economically than young males in part

25

because of the demand for young women to work in such household jobs as nursing, cooking, and cleaning.[7] If the American colonists had had a similar demand for female household labor, or for females to perform some light farm labor such as dairying and gardening, the effect of this demand on the market for indentured servants would also have declined over time as the available supply of female labor in the colonies grew.

These effects on the demand side are the most likely channels through which demographic changes in the colonies could have affected the sex composition of the indentured servant population. The quantitative importance of their role remains uncertain, as does the possibility that significant changes on the supply side could have contributed to the trends observed here.

Age distributions: levels and trends

Of the six sets of servant registrations used in this study, only one – the seventeenth-century Bristol lists – did not record the ages of any of the servants bound. The extent to which ages were recorded in the other samples varied. The proportion of the total registrants for whom ages are missing ranges from less than one-half of 1 percent in the latest of the samples and less than 5 percent in two others to 38 percent of the Liverpool registrations of 1697–1707 and 61 percent of those made in London in the 1680s. The reasons for the frequent omission of the servants' ages in the two latter sets of records are not known. However, as neither of these consisted of actual contracts of servitude – the case in two of the samples in which the recording percentage of age was high – nor had been requested by the government to gain information about the emigrants – the case in the third – it is possible that knowledge of the ages of the servants was of only secondary importance for the purposes of registration and that as a result the care taken to obtain this information in the recording process was simply less.[8]

Table 2.3 presents percentage distributions of the servants' ages by sex for each sample.[9] Although the precise shape of the distributions differs between samples, one conclusion that emerges clearly is that at the time of registration, throughout the colonial period the servants tended to be in their late teens and early twenties. At least two-thirds of both the men and women with recorded ages in each sample were aged 15 to 25, and in two of the five samples of men and four of the five of women, the share in this age group was three-quarters or more. The women were more likely to be minors, as the share of women below the age of 21 was greater than that of the men in four of the five samples. It was extremely rare for indentured servants of either sex to be below the age of 10 or above the age of 40. No more that one-fifth of the men nor 4 percent of the women with recorded

Table 2.3. Percentage distributions of recorded servants' ages

Age	London (1683–86) Men	London (1683–86) Women	Middlesex (1683–84) Men	Middlesex (1683–84) Women	Liverpool (1697–1707) Men	Liverpool (1697–1707) Women	London (1718–59) Men	London (1718–59) Women	London (1773–76) Men	London (1773–76) Women
6–10	1				2					
11–15	14	7	3	3	25	7	6	3	5	2
16–20	22	42	17	26	35	45	61	78	18	25
21–25	40	42	57	61	23	34	21	12	44	48
26–30	18	8	17	9	10	11	8	4	17	18
31–35	3		5	1	3	1	3	1	7	6
36–40	2	1	1		2	2	1		6	1
41–45									2	
46–50								1	1	
Total	100	100	100	100	100	100	100	100	100	100
N	238	107	632	153	606	287	2,871	169	3,359	338

ages in any sample were below the age of 15; no more than 16 percent of the men nor 7 percent of the women were above the age of 30.

In view of the parallel drawn in the preceding chapter between indentured servitude and English service in husbandry, it is of interest to compare these age distributions with those of life-cycle servants in England. Some information on the ages of the latter taken from available listings of the servants included in enumerations made between 1599 and 1796 of the inhabitants of five English villages is presented in Table 2.4.[10] The general outlines of these distributions are familiar from previous studies, but they serve to confirm a number of points. Thus, it was quite rare for children under the age of 10 to be in service.[11] Other information in the listings, not presented here, indicates that nearly all in this age group were living at home with their parents. This normally continued to be true of those aged 10 to 14. The age distributions, which show relatively larger numbers of men in their teens in service compared with larger proportions of women in their twenties, are consistent with the findings that boys typically went out to service younger than girls, and tended to leave service somewhat earlier.[12] Most servants of both sexes had apparently completed this stage in their life cycle by the age of 25, but some men and women did remain in service until their thirties and beyond.

Compared with the evidence of the English servant listings, it appears that the indentured servants tended to be more highly concentrated in the late teens and early twenties. This was particularly the case for females. Thus among the samples of indentured servants, the share of men aged 15 to 24 ranged from 61 to 83 percent, with a mean of 68 percent, and that of the women from 71 to 90 percent, with a mean of 81 percent. In contrast, among the English village listings the share of men 15 to 24 ranged from 50 to 84 percent, with a mean of 67 percent, and that of the women from 38 to 69 percent, with a mean of 59 percent. For both sexes, the age distributions of the English servants generally included a larger share of adults over 30 than did those of the indentured servants.

From this evidence, it would appear that some English boys and girls of the seventeenth and eighteenth centuries began to emigrate to America under indenture at ages similar to those at which others first left home to enter service in England, in the early and mid-teens, and that the peak ages for entrance into indentured servitude for both sexes were the same ones, roughly 15 to 25, at which the highest proportion of English youths were living in service. Contrary to the pattern within England, women tended to enter indentures to emigrate relatively younger than men. Another dissimilarity between the patterns is the smaller share of those above the age of 30 entering the indenture system than living in service in England.[13]

The information of the English village listings does not provide an adequate basis for analysis of possible changes in the age composition of

Table 2.4. Percentage distributions of ages of English servants

Age	Ealing, Middlesex 1599		Lichfield, Staffs. 1695		Stoke-on-Trent, Staffs. 1701		Corfe Castle, Dorset 1790		Ardleigh, Essex 1796	
	Men	Women	Men	Women	Men	Women	Men	Women	Men	Women
5–9			4		9	5	12	2	3	8
10–14	7	2	6	1	14	34	42	26	47	38
15–19	34	5	72	18	25	30	22	30	30	31
20–24	16	17	12	51	34	8	5	26	7	10
25–29	15	47	3	15	9	8	8	10	3	
30–34	10	12	1	11	3	6	3	2	2	
35–39	6	8	1	3		2	5	2		
40–44	6	5		1	3	5	3	2		
45–49									2	2
50–54	4	2							3	2
55–59									3	5
60–64		2	1		3	2				2
65–69	2									2
Total	100	100	100	100	100	100	100	100	100	100
N	68	41	102	148	35	61	40	53	66	42

Source: Files of the Cambridge Group for the History of Population and Social Structure, Cambridge.

Table 2.5. *Summary statistics of indentured servants' ages*

Sample	Mean	Median	Mode	Standard error	Number of observations
Men					
London, 1683–86	21.82	22	21	5.71	238
Middlesex, 1683–84	22.75	22	21	3.18	632
Liverpool, 1697–1707	19.70	19	20	6.74	606
London, 1718–59	20.56	19	20	4.67	2871
London, 1773–75	24.33	23	21	4.13	3359
Women					
London, 1683–86	20.79	21.0	22	3.92	107
Middlesex, 1683–84	21.44	21.0	21	3.37	153
Liverpool, 1697–1707	21.06	20.0	20	4.72	287
London, 1718–59	19.35	19.0	19	3.75	169
London, 1773–75	22.75	21.5	21	4.71	338

the life-cycle servant population over time. That contained in the indentured servant registrations, despite gaps and uneven coverage over time, does allow a consideration of possible trends.

Summary statistics of central tendency concerning the indentured servants' ages by sample are presented in Table 2.5, and the same measures are given in Table 2.6 for the men of the earlier eighteenth-century London registrations by sub-period. Two preliminary qualifications are relevant to the interpretation of this evidence. First, for reasons having to do with the terms of the legal authorization for the registration of servants given by the Privy Council in 1682, it is possible that the mean ages of the servants registered in London during 1683–86 are biased downward relative to those of the contemporary servant population as a whole, whereas those of the men and women registered in Middlesex in 1683–84 may be biased upward.[14] If this is the case, the true mean age of servants departing from the port of London during the mid-1680s would lie between the means of these two samples. Second, the apparent truncation of the age distribution of the servants registered above age 20,

Table 2.6. *Summary statistics of ages of male servants registered at London, 1718–59*

Date	Mean	Median	Mode	No. of observations
1718–19	17.45	18.0	18	152
1720–24	18.87	19.0	20	665
1725–29	20.35	20.0	20	496
1730–34	21.61	20.0	19	837
1735–40	22.28	21.0	21	599
1749–59	18.81	18.5	20	122

particularly in the early years of the records, suggests that adults were underrepresented in the London registrations of 1718–59.[15] If, as appears likely, this underregistration was greatest in the earlier part of this period, the increases over time shown by the statistics of Table 2.6 might overstate the true increase that occurred in the male servants' mean age.

Tables 2.5 and 2.6 do suggest the presence of some trends in the central tendencies of the ages of the indentured servants over time. The mean age of the men declined from approximately 22 years or slightly higher in the 1680s to just below 20 at the turn of the eighteenth century. The decline apparently continued until 1720, when the mean age may have fallen below 18 years; then a reversal of the trend raised the mean from about 19 during the early 1720s to more than 22 in the late 1730s. By the mid-1770s, the mean age of the men had risen above 24. The data on women's ages show parallel trends, although perhaps with less variation than the men's. From about 21 years in the 1680s, the mean age of the women may have remained constant through the end of the century before declining to just over 19 during the second quarter of the eighteenth century and finally rising to a peak of nearly 23 in the 1770s.[16]

The evidence of the demographic variables summarized in this chapter presents some clear outlines, suggests some less definite conclusions, and raises some puzzles. In making inferences about a population on the basis of a number of different samples surviving from it, the results which can be most confidently accepted are those that appear in all the samples. Thus it is clear that, to the extent that the samples considered are representative of the whole population of indentured servants, men predominated among this group of immigrants throughout the American colonial period, normally making up at least three-quarters of the total. It is equally clear that the age group most heavily represented among both sexes in this population, as in the contemporaneous population of life-cycle servants in pre-industrial England, was that of the late teens and early twenties.

Conclusions drawn from the analysis of trends based on the aggregation of separate samples spaced over time must normally be less certain, for this process necessarily forces a greater reliance on the representativeness of each sample, and the possible unknown systematic biases of each sample become a potentially more serious problem. Therefore a more tentative conclusion from the samples of registrations is that there appears to have been a decline in the share of women in the servant population over time, as women made up one-quarter of the servants registered in the second half of the seventeenth century but only one-tenth of those registered in the eighteenth century. Similarly, a trend appears in the age distribution of the servants over time, as a decline occurred in the servants' ages between the 1680s and about 1720, followed by a reversal and increasing mean ages from 1720 to the end of the mainland's colonial period.

The puzzles concerning these results have to do with issues of both impact and causation. Their solutions are generally beyond the scope of this study, and would require a more precise knowledge of many aspects of the social and economic history of both England and the American colonies than is currently available. However, some of the principal remaining problems can be mentioned. As noted earlier, the reasons for the apparent shift in the sex composition of the servant population at the turn of the eighteenth century await systematic investigation. Two central elements in the decline in the share of women may have been a decline in the demand for female servants to become colonists' wives and a decline in the demand for English women to perform household jobs as colonial sex ratios fell from extreme imbalance during the seventeenth century to near equality in most regions during the eighteenth. Both effects appear plausible in view both of the testimony of contemporaries and quantitative analysis of the market for servants. Yet many empirical links in these hypotheses remain untested, and the possible magnitudes of their effects are uncertain. Similarly, many questions remain concerning the impact on colonial populations of the structure and changes over time in the age composition of the servants. Some evidence on the causes of the observed trends in the servants' ages will appear in the course of later chapters, for as will be seen, these are closely related to another issue – the changing economic skills of the servant population – which is a central focus of this study.

What this examination of the demographic composition of the sample of servants has established is the existence of a considerable overall stability in the sex and age composition of the population of indentured English immigrants to colonial America. The evidence of the total sample points strongly to a population that was predominantly male and heavily concentrated in the ages from 15 to 25. Although some fluctuations in both variables occurred, and trends over time were identified, none were of a magnitude sufficient to change these basic facts. From the mid-seventeenth century to the end of the American mainland's colonial period the demographic composition of the population of indentured servants arriving as immigrants to the New World appears to have been remarkably stable.

3

The occupations of the indentured servants in the seventeenth century

The most important characteristics of the indentured servants for the concerns of this study are the skills they brought to the American colonies. A knowledge of the servants' occupations is critical to an understanding of the jobs they could perform in the colonies, and information on temporal shifts in the servants' occupational composition is central to an analysis of how the role of indentured labor in the colonial labor market changed over time. This chapter investigates the occupations of the servants from the available evidence for the seventeenth century; the following chapter does the same for the evidence of the eighteenth century and summarizes the changes in the male servants' occupational distribution that occurred over time.

The Bristol registrations of 1654–1686

The principal sources to be used for the analysis of the occupations of the seventeenth-century servants are two of the samples of English registrations.[1] The larger of these contains the registrations of more than 10,600 servants who shipped under indenture from Bristol to serve in the American colonies between 1654 and 1686.[2] Many entries not only record the names of the servant and master, the term of servitude, and the colony to which the servant was bound, but also identify the servant by status or occupation. It is on this information that this investigation concentrates.

The list contains occupational and status designations for the servants in parts of eleven years. These were divided into two periods, the first comprising the first eight years of registration, 1654–61, and the second, the final three years, 1684–6. Such descriptions disappear almost entirely from the records between July 1661 and April 1684. A tabulation of the occupational and status descriptions given for the males in the registrations appears in Table 3.1.[3]

As the table shows, many more men were registered during 1654–61 than in 1684–86. In the earlier period, 30 percent of the men bound were identified as farmers and 9 percent as laborers. One percent were given the

34

Table 3.1. *Occupations of male servants, Bristol, 1654–1660 and 1684–1686*

Category	1654–1660		1684–1686	
	No.	%	No.	%
Gentlemen	31	1		
Farmer	800	30	14	4
Laborer	232	9	45	12
Food and drink	31	1	9	2
Metal and construction	161	6	25	7
Textiles and clothing	275	10	54	15
Services	49	2	9	2
Not given	1,096	41	213	58
Total	2,675	100	369	100

Note: See Appendix G for the categorization of occupations used in this and following tables.

title of gentleman. A total of 19 percent were identified with occupations in a wide variety of skilled crafts and trades, with the largest number from clothing and textile manufacturing, followed by metal and construction crafts, service occupations, and food and drink trades. The remaining 41 percent of the men had no identifying occupational or status term recorded after their names upon registration.

The registrations from the 1680s indicate quite different proportions of these groups in the registrations. Thus the share of the farmers declined to only 4 percent of the men, that of the laborers rose slightly, to 12 percent, and the composite group of skilled tradesmen and craftsmen increased their share to a total of 26 percent. The residual of men without occupational designation rose to 58 percent, nearly three-fifths of total registrations.

A potentially serious problem exists concerning the interpretation of this summary of the evidence on the servants' occupations for the earlier of the two periods. This has to do with the periodization used in Table 3.1. The nature of the problem can be seen in Table 3.2, which presents the occupational distributions on an annual basis for 1654–61 for the same categories used in Table 3.1.

The annual distributions reveal considerable differences in the occupational composition of the male registrants over time. Table 3.2 therefore demonstrates that the percentage distribution of occupations in the Bristol records is potentially very sensitive to the period chosen for analysis. Although all the categories show some fluctuation, among the

Table 3.2. *Annual distribution of male servants' occupations, Bristol, 1654–1661 and 1684–1686*

	1654		1655		1656		1657		1658		1659	
Category	N	%	N	%	N	%	N	%	N	&	N	%
Gentlemen	2	4	10	5	5	2	3	1	2		7	1
Farmer	10	21	20	10	23	9	208	46	148	25	208	31
Laborer	1	2	71	37	108	41	34	7	9	2	8	1
Food and drink	1	2	3	2	6	2	4	1	4	1	6	1
Metal and construction	2	4	17	9	27	10	16	4	14	2	54	8
Textiles and clothing	1	2	22	11	49	19	35	8	36	6	83	12
Services			7	4	4	2	7	1	6	1	15	2
Not given	32	65	43	22	38	15	144	32	374	63	303	44
Total	49	100	193	100	260	100	451	100	593	100	684	100

	1660		1661		1684		1685		1686	
Category	N	%	N	%	N	%	N	%	N	%
Gentlemen	2				2	2				
Farmer	183	41	65	12	22	20	11	5	1	9
Laborer	2				4	4	23	9		
Food and drink	7	2	2		4	4	5	2		
Metal and construction	32	7	9	2	20	18	21	8	3	27
Textiles and clothing	48	11	26	5	3	3	31	13		
Services	9	2	1				6	2		
Not given	162	37	454	81	54	49	152	61	7	64
Total	445	100	557	100	109	100	249	100	11	100

most erratic are those of farmers and laborers. For example, if individual years were chosen as the basis for sampling, an investigation based on the entries from 1656 would find laborers to have made up more than two-fifths of all males in the sample and farmers less than one-tenth, while the data from 1660 would indicate that farmers made up more than two-fifths of all males and laborers less than one-half of 1 percent. To aggregate all years without attention to temporal variation would appear an inadequate method of dealing with data in which such sharp changes occur over time, for the source of the volatility of the shares of farmers and laborers would seem to be a matter of interest to the historian. If the fluctuations are taken to represent genuine shifts in occupational composition of the servant population, they raise questions concerning the temporal determinants of emigration; alternatively, the possibility must be considered that they raise serious problems concerning the nature of the data.

For the shifts are curious. It is odd that farmers would have been bound in Bristol as servants at the rate of fewer than 25 a year in 1655 and 1656 but at an annual rate of more than 185 during the following four years. It is similarly peculiar that 179 laborers would have been bound in the two years 1655–6, but that a total of only 53 would have been bound in the following four, despite the fact that, on the average, more than twice as many male servants left in each of these four years than in each of the preceding two. It is possible that real shifts did occur and that the registrations, at least in part, do reflect genuine changes in the composition of the servant population. Thus, for example, although the sudden increase in the share of yeomen after 1656 is difficult to explain, it could have had to do in part with a serious deterioration in English agricultural conditions beginning in 1656.[4] However the abruptness and magnitude of the changes make it appear unlikely that the observed shifts were entirely real ones. In particular, the drop in the share of laborers, together with the downward trend in the proportion of servants given occupational desig-nations, suggests a hypothesis concerning the relationship between the registration process and the recording of servants' occupations over time.

Very little is precisely known of the process by which the Bristol servants were registered. A city ordinance of September 29, 1664, stated:

Whereas many complaintes have beene oftentimes made to the Maior and Aldermen of the Inveigling, purloining, carrying and Stealing away Boyes Maides and other persons and transporting them beyond Seas and there selling or otherwise disposeing them for private gaine and proffitt and it being a crime of much villany to have children and others in such a Barbarous and wicked manner to be soe carried away stollen and sold without any knowledge or notice of the parents or others that have the care and oversight of them for the better preventing of such mischeifes for time to come: It is this day agreed ordeined and enacted by the Maior Aldermen and Comon Councell in Comon Councell assembled that all Boyes Maides and other persons which for the future shall be transported beyond the Seas as servants, shall before their going a-Ship board have their covenants or Indentures of service and apprentiship inrolled in the Tolzey booke as other Indentures of apprentiship are and have used to bee, and that noe Master or other officer wtsoever of any Ship or vessell shall (before such inrolmt be made) receive into his or their ship or vessell or therein permitt to be transported beyond the Seas such Boyes Maides or other persons as aforesaid.[5]

There is no other known description of the procedure. However, the evidence of the lists themselves suggests that, in the first years in which the records were kept, the magistrates or clerks who kept them were quite conscientious. Thus during the first three years about four-fifths of the males were given status or occupational designations. It is very possible that in this period all servants were given a status description except the young men not yet identified with a skill or occupation.[6] Over time, the registrars may have become less painstaking, or perhaps they simply became aware that not all the information they had been recording was necessary for the purpose of the registration. As they began to abbreviate the documentation, they may have continued to record skilled occupations that could serve to identify specific servants, and they may simply have begun to omit the descriptions of unskilled workers as laborers.[7] This would account both for the drop in the number of laborers recorded after 1656 and for the downward trend in the proportion of males given any designation. Finally, the registrars reduced to a minimum the information recorded. Thus, beginning in early July 1661, occupations were omitted from virtually all the servant registrations, and the entries were commonly reduced to the servants' and masters' names, often omitting specific reference even to the term of servitude and colonial destination.

This hypothesis of change in the registration process appears to be a reasonable interpretation of the evidence. If correct, it means that the most complete enumeration of the status and occupation of servants occurred during the initial years of registration, roughly 1654–7. In those years, yeomen and husbandmen made up just over a quarter (28 percent) of the men registered, unskilled laborers just under a quarter (22 percent), and tradesmen and skilled craftsmen together just under a quarter (21 percent). Two percent of the men were identified as gentlemen. The residual of slightly more than a quarter (27 percent), those without any identifying description, may have been chiefly young men, many of them below the age of twenty-one, who had not yet acquired skilled trades or worked as hired day laborers. This segment may have gone directly from servant status in England, either as apprentices or more commonly servants in husbandry, to the status of indentured servant in America.

The implications of this hypothesis for the occupations of servants in 1658–60 are clear. Farmers rose to about 31 percent of the male servants, whereas tradesmen and craftsmen declined to about 18 percent. The number of gentlemen fell below 1 percent of the total. The remaining group of half the males included both youths and unskilled adults, with only 1 percent explicitly described as laborers. It would have been possible for the share of laborers to remain constant at a quarter of the males or just under, and at the same time for the share of youths without skills or occupations to have been a quarter or slightly more.

The erratic behavior of the occupational shares shown in Table 3.2 means that generalizations about the composition of the servant population's occupational structure on the basis of the Bristol records should be drawn with caution. Nonetheless, this discussion has suggested that the records may be consistent with the statement that the male servants registered in Bristol during the later 1650s were made up, in roughly equal parts, of four groups: farmers, tradesmen and craftsmen, laborers, and youths. In addition, there was a small number of gentlemen.

The Middlesex registrations of 1683–1684

The second seventeenth-century sample that contains information on the servants' occupations is a collection of indentures recorded on individual printed forms in Middlesex County between January 1683 and September 1684.[8] Contracts survive for a total of 812 servants. A tabulation of the occupations recorded for the male servants in the sample is presented in Table 3.3.

Farmers made up 9 percent of the men in this sample, laborers 5 percent, and the composite group of skilled craftsmen and tradesmen 26 percent. A striking feature of the tabulation is its indication that no occupation was recorded on the contracts of three-fifths of the male servants registered.

Unlike in the Bristol registrations, ages were given for most of the servants registered in Middlesex, making it possible to distinguish minors from adults. Of the 632 males for whom ages were recorded, 20 percent (129) were less than 21 years old; of these, only twelve had recorded occupations. Removing the minors and those for whom ages are not given reveals that more than half the adult men in the sample had no recorded occupations.

The large numbers of men registered without occupational descriptions raise an obvious problem of interpretation, concerning the backgrounds they might have come from. A fully satisfactory answer to the question of whether the men registered without occupational or status terms actually possessed occupations and economic skills would appear to depend on answering the closely related prior question of why no occupations were recorded for these men. Several competing hypotheses can be offered in response to each of these questions, and the relatively large amount of

Table 3.3. *Occupations of male servants by category, Middlesex, 1683–1684*

Category	No.	%
Gentleman	2	
Farmer	60	9
Laborer	32	5
Food and drink	11	2
Metal and construction	42	6
Textiles and clothing	52	8
Services	64	10
Not given	392	60
Total	655	100

collateral information available about the servants from the contracts of the Middlesex sample can be used to provide information that bears on the relative plausibility of these.

One hypothesis that has been suggested by Mildred Campbell in relation to the Middlesex sample is that the omission of occupational descriptions had to do with the contracts on which some of the registrations were recorded. According to this view, the omission of occupational terms was due solely to the lack of a blank space for the servant's occupation or status. A possible implication of this hypothesis is that the omission of occupation was random, and that those servants with recorded occupations could be assumed to have been a random sample of the whole population of servants.[9]

Five different types of printed forms were used in Middlesex registrations, in addition to a number of handwritten or special forms. Following Cregoe D. P. Nicholson, the form types will be referred to by letter.[10] Of the types, only three – A, B, and D – appear more than ten times. The A form was used throughout the period of registration, from the first day from which the indentures survive to the last. The B type was also used from the beginning but was discontinued after May 12, 1684. Type D was used from May 20, 1684, to the conclusion of the surviving registrations. Examples of the three types are illustrated in Figures 3.1, 3.2 and 3.3. As can be seen, types B and D are similar in format and only slightly different in wording. The timing of the use of the two tends to indicate that form B was discontinued, for whatever reason, and replaced by D. Further, the fact that both type A and either B or D were always in use might tend to indicate that the formats served different purposes. Form A would appear to be the type referred to by the hypothesis described

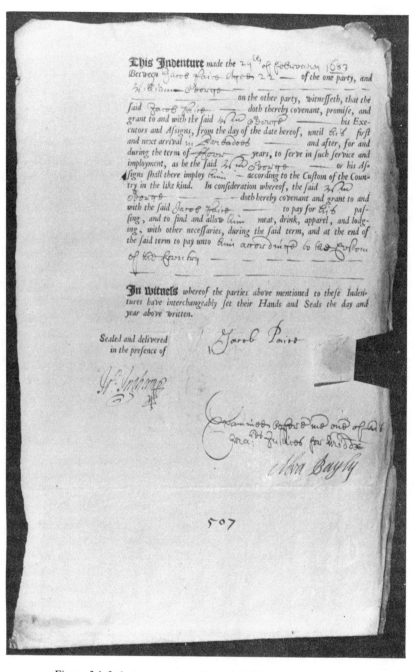

Figure 3.1 Indenture contract, Type A, Middlesex County, January 1683–September 1684

41

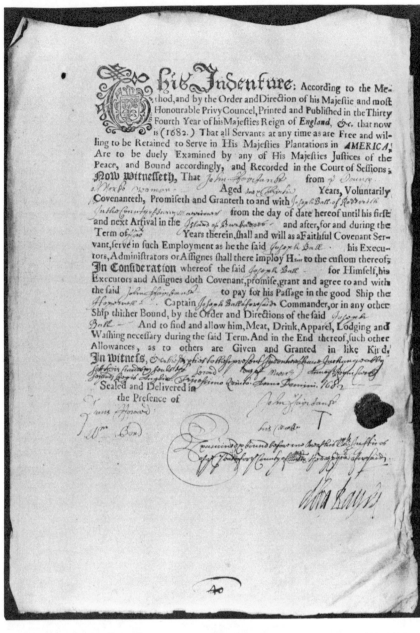

Figure 3.2 Indenture contract, Type B, Middlesex County, January 1683–May 1684

42

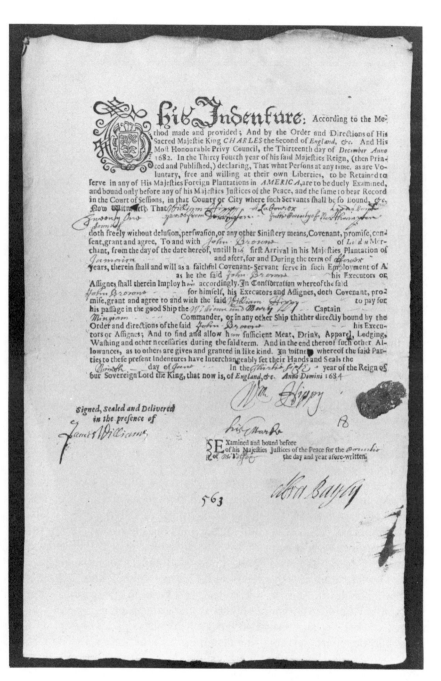

Figure 3.3 Indenture contract, Type D, Middlesex County, May 1684–
September 1684

43

Table 3.4. *Percentage distribution of male servants' occupations by type of form, Middlesex, 1683–1684*

Category	Type A (N = 179)	Type B (N = 270)	Type D (N = 186)
Gentleman			1
Farmer	2	7	20
Laborer		5	9
Food and drink	1	3	1
Metal and construction	3	10	5
Textiles and clothing		10	13
Services		8	22
Not given	94	57	29
Total	100	100	100

above that did not contain a blank for occupation, whereas B and D were apparently the ones that did.[11]

The percentage distributions of male servants by occupational category for registrations made on each of the three main types of forms are shown in Table 3.4. About 94 percent of the males registered on A forms had no occupational or status description, compared with about 57 and 29 percent, respectively, for types B and D. It is interesting to note that a combined tabulation even of the males registered on types B and D – those which, according to the above hypothesis, could be taken to represent the whole sample – shows that a majority was composed of those who had no status designation (45 percent) or were described as laborers (7 percent).

What is to be made of the differences in registration among types of form? As in the case of Bristol, we have no exact knowledge of how servants were registered. One possible assumption, stated earlier, is that the assignment of forms was random: Servants registered were arbitrarily given either form A or B before May 1684 and either A or D thereafter. If this was the case, the servants registered on B and D forms might be a random sample of all servants registered. This would imply that just under half the males in the sample would have had genuine occupations other than that of laborer. Another possibility is that forms were assigned on the basis of servant's requirements: At times when both varieties of form were in stock in the court, servants who stated professions were given B or D, whereas those who had no accepted occupation or status description were given type A. In this case, only about 35 percent of the males would have had genuine occupations other than that of laborer. The first of these assumptions, that form assignment was random, treats the assignment as independent of the servants, whereas the second, that forms were assigned according to their suitability for the servant when possible, treats the assignment as a function of the individual servant's characteristics.

The second assumption appears to be the stronger. Seventeenth-century English society was very conscious of status and rank: Men were customarily referred to by both name and occupation.[12] The status or occupational term, formally known as an "addition," was appended to a person's name for legal purposes and was usually recorded by clerks and registrars in legal proceedings of all kinds.[13] An example of its currency in legal use is afforded by a specific reference in the Privy Council act that gave rise to the servant registrations of the 1680s: The order provided that when a servant was under the age of 21, he was to be bound only with the consent of his parents or master, "and some person that knows the said servant to be of the name and addition mentioned in the Indenture is to attest his said knowledge upon the said Indenture."[14] It seems unlikely in a society so aware of rank and position that a process of legal contracting would have been so casual in the recording of status as is suggested by the first hypothesis.

But who were the servants without status or occupational entries? Were they a random sample of the whole population and therefore, on average, like the others? Three important types of collateral evidence in the Middlesex registrations indicate that they were not. Furthermore, all three are consistent with the view that those without additions were lower in occupational and economic status than those with recorded trades, and that the absence of an addition was the result of the lack of an occupation.

The first type of evidence is the ages of the servants registered. Of the 632 men whose ages were recorded, 375 (59 percent) had no addition. Of the 129 who were under 21 years old, 116 (90 percent) had no addition. Of the 41 under seventeen, 40 (98 percent) had no addition. Table 3.5 shows clearly that the age distribution of the men without additions differs considerably from that of the others. The proportion of the men without additions below the age of 21 – 31.3 percent – is more than three times the proportion of minors among those registered as laborers, more than eight times the minors' share of the tradesmen and craftsmen, and more than nine times their share of the farmers.[15] The mean ages of the men by category produce similar results, as the mean age of the men without additions (22.0 years) is one year below that of the laborers (23.0), and more than two years below those of both the farmers (24.1) and the tradesmen and craftsmen (24.1). That the age distribution of the men without additions was quite different from that of the other groups is

Table 3.5. *Percentage distributions of ages of men registered at Middlesex, 1683–84, by occupational category*

Category	Age					Total	N
	11–15	16–20	21–25	26–30	31+		
Farmers	0	3.3	61.7	30.0	5.0	100	60
Tradesmen and craftsmen[a]	0	3.7	67.0	25.6	3.7	100	164
Laborers	0	9.7	67.7	22.6	0	100	31
Not given	5.0	26.3	51.2	10.3	7.2	100	377

[a] Includes food and drink, metal and construction, textiles and clothing, and services.

evident; its low mean and disproportionately large share of young men are consistent with the presence in this group of large numbers of youths who had not yet acquired trades.

The second type of evidence is the relative ability to sign of men registered with and without additions. This ability has been used by historians as a measure of literacy, and has been found to be closely related to occupation.[16] Evidence presented in Chapter 5 shows that the low level of literacy among the male servants registered without stated occupations in Middlesex places them well below the skilled tradesmen and craftsmen in the sample, and roughly on a level with the farmers and laborers. The high level of illiteracy of the men for whom no additions were recorded suggests that they were not a random sample of the servant population, but rather that they were disproportionately drawn from the lower part of the skill or occupational distribution from which the other servants came.

Finally, the third type of evidence is the relative mean length of the indentures received by men with and without recorded occupations. This evidence, presented in Chapter 7, indicates that for minors in the Middlesex sample the effect of having a stated trade, after allowing for the servant's age, sex, colonial destination, and literacy, was to shorten the term to be served by an average of nearly nine months relative to those without skills or stated occupations. As the discussion of Chapter 7 shows, the finding that servants without occupational descriptions received considerably longer terms than those with trades, with other things equal, indicates that on average they were expected to be less productive economically, and hence less highly valued by colonial planters. The large differentials between the average terms of the indentures of those with trades and those without designation could have resulted from the fact that many of the latter were men not trained in, or accustomed to, work.

These three types of evidence therefore all indicate that men without recorded additions were not like the others. The first indicates that on average they were younger, the second that on average they were less literate, and the third that on average they were less productive economically. A simple and plausible explanation of the absence of an addition is that the individual registered had no occupation to record. The quantitative evidence summarized here supports this explanation.[17]

Some insight into the condition of some of the servants can be gained from less systematic evidence, for a number of the contracts contain notes about individual servants. Some of these, concerning young servants, were apparently recorded in compliance with the Privy Council order that authorized the registrations, quoted in part earlier. Others, apparently incidental, record information that was presumably given by the servant in the course of registration and deemed relevant by the presiding justice of the peace or recording clerk. This evidence is very incomplete, but it does afford occasional glimpses into the circumstances of a few of the servants. In the case of more than fifty individuals, it was recorded that either their father or both parents were deceased. In addition to several boys described as "poor youths," half a dozen unfortunates were described as "fatherless and friendless," while of 16-year-old Francis Haires of Staffordshire, registered without a trade in June 1684 to serve for seven years in Maryland, the clerk wrote "his father and mother and All friends dead and he a miserable wandering boy." At least three teen-aged boys came directly from the care of parish authorities, and about ten men were apparently indentured immediately after their release from houses of correction, where they had been confined for debt or vagrancy.[18] The casual nature of the recording of this evidence precludes firm assessment of its quantitative significance. Thus little direct evidence exists concerning the skills or economic status of the servants without stated occupations. Yet it is possible that more than those few specifically identified as poor orphans or vagrants came from the lowest ranks of English society, from the levels at which functional descriptions tended to run out. That the lowest groups from England's society did not make up a majority of the servant population does not necessarily mean that they were not represented in significant numbers.

That a sizable share of the seventeenth-century indentured servants were unskilled and came from the lower levels of English society should come as no surprise, for we have another variety of evidence in abundance that tells us precisely that. This is the observations of contemporaries. It is clear, as Abbot Emerson Smith has pointed out, that some of these low assessments were the attempts of writers favorable to colonization to demonstrate that England was not losing valuable members of its population to the colonies.[19] Obvious examples of this appear in the work of such authors as Josiah Child and Charles Davenant.[20] But not all writers about the colonies had this end in mind, and contemporaries with a wide range of viewpoints commented in a variety of contexts that large numbers of British indentured servants of the seventeenth century were drawn from among the poor and the unskilled. Although not all did so as flamboyantly as Henry Whistler, who wrote of Barbados in 1654 that "This Illand is the dunghill wharone England doth cast forth its rubidg: Rodgs and hors and such like peopel are thos which are gennerally Broght heare," many colonial authors agreed with William Berkeley's comment from Virginia in 1662 that "there is with us great scarcity of good men; that is, of able Workmen . . . for onely such servants as have been brought up to no Art or Trade, hunger and fear of prisons bring to us," and many English writers concurred in William Bullock's judgment of 1649 that many of those indentured were drawn from among the mother country's "idle, lazie, simple people."[21]

Both the Bristol records of 1654–60 and the Middlesex registrations of 1683–4 point to a great diversity in the economic backgrounds and occupations of the servants registered. The conclusion of this investigation is that four broad groups may have been present in the Bristol registrations of 1654–60 in roughly equal parts: farmers, laborers, those skilled in trades – both manufacturing and services – and youths without trades. The servants registered in Middlesex during 1683–4 may have included a somewhat larger share of skilled craftsmen and tradesmen, a considerably larger component of the unskilled, and smaller proportions of farmers and young men.

In comparing the evidence of these two samples, it is clear that a higher proportion of the men registered at Bristol during 1654–60 had some occupational skills and training than did those registered in Middlesex in 1683–4. Thus even using the aggregated figures from Table 3.1 for the Bristol registrations for comparison with those for Middlesex from Table 3.3, the share of the men with skilled occupations – defining skill broadly to include all those registered with occupations except the unskilled laborers – was 50 percent in Bristol, compared with only 35 percent in Middlesex. The question of whether the difference in these shares can be taken to indicate a downward trend over time in the share of the skilled among the servant population is complicated by the difference in the places of registration; seventeenth-century London was widely known to contemporaries to attract large numbers of unskilled workers, and the comparison between samples might therefore reflect only the difference between servants recruited in the vicinity of the metropolis as opposed to elsewhere.[22] However, additional evidence from the registrations suggests that the observed difference in occupational composition between the Bristol registrations of 1654–60 and those of Middlesex from 1683–4 might have resulted primarily from a decline in the proportion of the skilled among the male servant population as a whole over time. The additional evidence comes from the continuation of the Bristol registrations. As noted above, occupational descriptions disappear from the Bristol registrations between mid-1661 and 1684. Following a gap in the registrations in early 1684, a total of 449 servants were registered before the surviving registrations end in June 1686. In these final two years of the records, occupational descriptions again appear, and the occupational distribution of the 369 men registered is shown in Table 3.1. Laborers and men without recorded occupations together made up 70 percent of the total, actually five percentage points more than their total in the Middlesex registrations of 1683–4. This evidence therefore indicates that the relatively high unskilled share of the Middlesex registrants may have been very similar to that in contemporaneous registrations made in Bristol and suggests that there may have been a significant decline in the proportion of male indentured servants who possessed occupational skills between the 1650s and the 1680s.

Historiographically, the indentured servants of the seventeenth century have led a checkered career. The view prevalent among historians in the first half of the twentieth century depicted the great majority of them as unskilled workers.[23] More recently, this characterization has been rejected in favor of the judgment that the servants were predominantly drawn from the ranks of England's farmers and skilled workers.[24] This investigation has produced a result intermediate between these two positions, for the analysis of the direct information of the registrations on the occupations of the servants, together with the collateral evidence of their ages, literacy, and economic productivity, has pointed to the conclusion that the male servants of the seventeenth century represented a cross-section of a very broad segment of English society. Lawrence Stone has estimated that 90 to 95 percent of the population of seventeenth-century England was composed of the members of three groups: farmers and artisans, laborers, and servants and other dependents.[25] The evidence examined here indicates that significant proportions of the indentured servant population of the seventeenth century might have come from each of these groups. A large number of the servants were farmers, both yeomen and husbandmen. Another sizable portion was made up of men skilled in a wide variety of trades and crafts, among whom all kinds of construction and textile craftsmen were represented. A third substantial part was composed of those without such skills or fixed occupations, most of whom had probably worked for hire by the day in agriculture: These were the laborers. Finally, a significant group comprised the young men who had not yet entered independent positions in English society and who chose to complete their life-cycle service in America.

4

Occupations of the eighteenth-century indentured servants

Two of the sets of eighteenth-century registrations used in this investigation included entries for the registrants' occupation or status. These – from London for 1718–59 and from Treasury records of registrations made principally in London during 1773–75 – can be used to analyze the servants' skills in the same way as was done for the two seventeenth-century samples examined in the previous chapter. The evidence of each sample on occupations is examined in turn in the first two sections of this chapter. A final section considers the evidence of the four samples together, comparing them in order to establish the dimensions of the changes that occurred in the economic skills of the British indentured servants bound for America between the mid-seventeenth century and the end of the American colonial period.

The London registrations of 1718–1759

Frequency and percentage distributions of the men's occupations by category tabulated from the London registrations of 1718–59 are presented in Table 4.1.[1] Relatively few of these servants were described as farmers (11 percent) or laborers (6 percent). The five groups of non-agricultural trades and crafts together accounted for 46 percent of the men. Of these, textile and clothing crafts accounted for the largest share of registrants (14 percent); more than half of these were either tailors or weavers. Construction trades, with 11 percent of the men, included carpenters, the single most numerous of the skilled crafts in the registrations. The categories of services, metal and wood crafts, and food and drink followed, in order of their relative frequencies.

More than one-third of the men registered had no occupation or status recorded. As shown in Table 4.2, 96 percent of these were minors, with 15 percent below the age of 16. In contrast, the largest proportion of any other category made up of minors was the 66 percent of the laborers, and the smallest was the 37 percent of the construction workers who were less than 21 years old. No category other than that of men without recorded occupations had more than 1 percent of its total made up of men under 16.

Table 4.1. *Occupations of male servants by category, London, 1718–1759*

Category	No.	% of total
Gentlemen	2	
Farmer	328	11
Laborer	179	6
Food and drink	120	4
Metal and wood	202	7
Construction	337	11
Textiles and clothing	417	14
Services	300	10
Not given	1,128	37
Total	3,013	100

Table 4.2. *Percentage distributions of servants' ages by occupation, London, 1718–1759*

Category	Age					
	12–15	16–20	21–25	26–30	31+	Total
Farmer	0	45	30	17	8	100
Laborer	1	65	21	8	5	100
Food and drink	0	43	39	14	4	100
Metal and wood	0	38	38	17	7	100
Construction	0	37	39	15	9	100
Textiles and clothing	0	60	28	7	5	100
Services	1	49	33	8	9	100
Not given	15	81	3	1	0	100

Another measure of the relative youth of the men without stated occupations is presented in Table 4.3. The mean age of the men without recorded additions was 17.5 years, whereas the mean ages of the men in the other categories tabulated were all over 21, ranging from 3.6 to 5.3 years higher than that of the men registered without occupations. Of the other categories, the mean age of the unskilled laborers was the lowest.

The almost total absence of adult men from the group registered without additions suggests that the recording of occupations may have been quite conscientious and complete in this set of servant contracts and that the bulk of those who lacked occupational terms were young men who did not have specific skills or trades. As in the case of the seventeenth-century evidence, the circumstances in individual cases without occupational

Table 4.3. *Mean ages of men by occupation, London, 1718–1759*

Category	Mean years	No.
Farmer	22.74	306
Laborer	21.09	179
Food and drink	22.34	114
Metal and wood	22.83	196
Construction	23.69	324
Textiles and clothing	21.40	405
Services	22.29	278
Not given	17.52	1,069

descriptions cannot be established from the available information. Some in this group could have been apprentices who had not yet completed their training and taken the additions of their trades. Others might have been orphans or vagrants, attached neither to an occupation nor a household. Many may have come to the indenture system from positions as servants in husbandry.

Because of the diversity of the actual economic activities performed by those in preindustrial England without specific occupational skills or trades, it is not possible to assign those registered without additions to particular industries. However, some inferences about their levels of education and economic productivity relative to the other registrants can be drawn from collateral information contained in the registrations. As in the seventeenth-century Middlesex registrations, the servants bound in London were required either to sign or mark their contracts to indicate their agreement. Again using the ability to sign as an index of literacy, those without additions had the lowest literacy rate, significantly below that of the men in each of the other seven occupational categories.[2] Analysis of the relative length of indenture received by men in the different occupational categories also places the men without additions in this sample distinctly below the others in economic productivity. Thus in this sample multiple regression analysis indicates that, other things being equal, men without additions received terms of indenture significantly longer on average not only than farmers and men in the other skilled trades and crafts, but also than the men registered as laborers. The interpretation of this result may be that the men without additions were not only unskilled but that, perhaps because of a lack of work experience or ability, their work was less highly valued even than that of the unskilled laborers.[3]

As in the case of the seventeenth-century servants, the conclusion concerning the men registered without occupations is that although it is not possible to determine what kinds of work they might have done and what positions they held before entering the indenture system, they did have some distinctive characteristics relative to the men in other occupational categories. Specifically, on average they were younger, less literate, and less productive economically than the men who recorded trades or occupations of any kind on their contracts.

In these mid-eighteenth-century registrations, therefore, farmers made up just over one-tenth of those registered, laborers just over one-twentieth, men in a wide variety of nonagricultural trades and crafts just under one-half, and predominantly younger men not identified by occupation just over one-third. Yet these proportions are based on aggregation over an elapsed time of more than forty years, and the surviving registrations are drawn from thirty-three different years. In view of the long sampling period, it is useful to examine the data for possible trends in the servants' occupations over time.

A basis for the consideration of temporal changes of the servants' composition by occupation within the sample is provided in Table 4.4, which shows the percentage distributions of the men by occupation in six sub-periods. A number of definite trends emerge from this tabulation, particularly when only the years 1718–40 are considered. There is a lapse in the surviving contracts during almost the entire decade of the 1740s; following this break, an important change occurred in the format of the surviving registrations.[4] Although the reasons for the change cannot be determined, it is possible that it was symptomatic of some basic alteration either in the process by which servants were registered or in the diligence of the responsible officials, and therefore the evidence of the final period, 1749–59, may not be strictly comparable to that of earlier years. In the absence of any direct evidence on the registration process other than the surviving registrations, this hypothesis must remain speculative, but the possibility that the trends of 1718–40 actually were reversed during 1749–59 should be considered only with the qualification that this reversal may be an artifact of some change in the method by which the data were generated.

There was a decline in the proportion of men registered without recorded occupations between each two periods shown in Table 4.4 except the final two. That more than two-thirds of the men registered in 1718–19 was made up of those without occupational descriptions may have been due to a great extent to the initial nonregistration of adults noted earlier in this study,[5] but the levels of the share without additions of the 1720s, when adults were registered in significant and increasing numbers, were in the range of 44 to 55 percent of all men, whereas those of the 1730s fell to 14 to 29 percent of those registered. The rising share of the men with additions during 1718–40 was distributed quite evenly among

54

Table 4.4. Percentage distributions of servants' occupations by period, London, 1718–1759

Category	1718–19 (N = 152)	1720–24 (N = 665)	1725–29 (N = 496)	1730–34 (N = 839)	1735–40 (N = 607)	1749–59 (N = 254)
Farmer	3	6	9	12	15	17
Laborer	3	5	4	7	9	2
Food and drink	2	2	3	5	7	2
Metal and wood	1	3	6	8	11	6
Construction	1	9	11	14	15	7
Textiles and clothing	17	13	17	14	15	7
Services	5	7	6	11	14	15
Not given	68	55	44	29	14	44
Total	100	100	100	100	100	100

the occupational categories. There was a tendency for the proportion of men in every category except textile and clothing trades to increase over time, and this was part of a trend that made the shares of all the categories in total registrations progressively less unequal.

As noted earlier, these trends were reversed in the 1750s, as 44 percent of the men were registered without additions and the shares of five of the other seven categories in total registrations fell. However, because the change in registration procedure raises the possibility that this was not a real reversal, the trends in the servants' occupational composition before the 1740s might be considered. In the second half of the 1730s, farmers made up 15 percent of the men registered, laborers 9 percent, and men in all nonagricultural trades and crafts 63 percent. A decade earlier, farmers had accounted for 9 percent, laborers for 4 percent, and nonagricultural tradesmen and craftsmen 53 percent. So for most of the period covered, the evidence of the London registrations is of increasing proportions of men in nearly all stated occupations. The observed correlation between age and possession of an addition indicates that this trend was associated with the changing age composition of the servants over time. The overall picture presented by the records is therefore of increases over time in both the mean age and the average level of skill of the men whose agreements to serve in the colonies survive in the London registrations of the second, third, and fourth decades of the eighteenth century.

The London registrations of 1773–1775

The emigrant lists from the final years of the American colonial period were ordered by the English government to be collected by customs officers beginning in 1773 for the purpose of providing information about all passengers on ships leaving England.[6] They therefore include many people who were not indentured servants. Mildred Campbell found that servants and redemptioners together made up about 61 percent of all those registered.[7]

A tabulation of the distribution of the male indentured servants' occupations by category is presented in Table 4.5. The occupations of the indentured servants were apparently very similar to those of all the men registered. Campbell found that 16 percent of all the men in the lists were farmers of various descriptions, the same percentage found here for the servants alone, and that 68 percent were tradesmen and craftsmen, very close to the 69 percent of servants in the five categories of nonagricultural trades and crafts shown in Table 4.5.[8] One difference arises in the shares of unskilled laborers in the whole sample of all departing passengers and in the sub-sample of servants, as Campbell found laborers to make up only 11 percent of the former, compared with the 15 percent of the latter given

56

Table 4.5. *Occupations of male servants by category, London, 1773–1775*

Category	No.	% of total
Farmer	539	16
Laborer	495	15
Food and drink	225	7
Metal and wood	479	14
Construction	519	15
Textiles and clothing	625	19
Services	471	14
Not given	6	0
Total	3,359	100

in Table 4.5.[9] It would not be surprising that unskilled laborers had a larger proportional representation among the servants than among the free passengers, for that laborers tended disproportionately to emigrate as servants would be expected as a consequence of their lack of capital relative to wealthier farmers and craftsmen.

An interesting feature of the lists of 1773–5 is the virtual absence of servants registered without occupational descriptions. This may have been due to the nature of the registration process, for the purpose of the lists was to inform government officials, worried about excessive emigration and depopulation, about the emigrants, and the customs officers who made the original reports may have been instructed to give additions for all passengers. As a result, it is possible that servants without occupations or trades were simply described as unskilled laborers. The evidence on men's ages by occupation is consistent with this possibility, as Table 4.6 shows that laborers made up more than two-thirds of the men under 16, and declining shares of higher age groups, whereas every other occupational category increased its share of the male registrants until at least early adulthood. One man described as a laborer was only 11, and eighteen were less than 15 years old. It is possible that these additions were accurate, but in view both of the youth of many of the laborers and of the absence from the lists of significant numbers of servants without additions, it would appear more likely that the addition of laborer was used in these lists not only to identify those who had worked in unskilled jobs but also more generally to describe men who had no trade or skills. That the laborers and those without recorded trades together made up a total of only 15 percent of the male registrants nonetheless contrasts sharply with all the earlier samples of servant registrations considered in this study.

The high proportion of men in the servant lists of 1773–5 described as

Table 4.6. *Percentage distributions of male servants' occupations by age, London, 1773–1775*

Occupation	Age					
	11 to 15	16 to 20	21 to 25	26 to 30	31 to 40	41+
Farmer	5	13	16	20	19	18
Laborer	68	34	7	7	6	3
Food and drink	2	4	8	8	6	9
Metal and wood	2	11	16	14	17	19
Construction	3	9	17	18	21	12
Textiles and clothing	7	16	21	18	20	31
Services	12	13	15	15	11	8
Not given	1	0	0	0	0	0
Total	100	100	100	100	100	100
N	182	598	1,479	566	460	74

Table 4.7. *Mean ages of men by occupation,
London, 1773–1775*

Category	Mean Years	No.
Farmer	25.26	539
Laborer	19.54	495
Food and drink	25.18	225
Metal and wood	25.35	479
Construction	25.31	519
Textiles and clothing	25.84	625
Services	23.89	471
Not given	19.83	6

other than unskilled workers was associated with generally high ages of the registrants. As shown in Table 4.7, of the occupational groups, only the laborers had a mean age under 21; their mean of 19.5 was considerably lower than those of the other categories, which ranged from 23.9 to 25.8 years. This tends to support the validity of the occupational terms recorded in the lists. Certainly, in view of the association found in the other samples between age and the possession of an occupation, the generally high ages of the men registered are consistent with the small share made up of those who had no trade or craft.

Long-run trends in the occupational composition of the indentured servants

Taken together, the four sets of registrations from which evidence on the occupations of the indentured servants has been examined span a period of nearly a century and a quarter, reaching from Bristol in the 1650s to London on the eve of the American Revolution. As important as establishing the occupational structure of the servants in each sample individually is to consider that of all together, for it is only by comparison of the full evidence of the samples that the changes can be seen that can constitute the basis of an analysis of how the functions of the indenture system might have changed over time, and for a consideration of how changes in the English and colonial labor markets might have affected the composition of the group of British workers who chose to emigrate in bondage. This overview will be the final topic to be considered in this chapter.

A few summary comments concerning what the data can and cannot tell us about the servants are in order. The additions recorded in the registrations do not necessarily give a precise indication of the servants' economic status or productivity. This is not simply the result of the broad categorization used in this discussion, for a problem would remain even if the many occupations recorded were tabulated individually. Nor is it due to false recording; although this could have been present to some extent, for reasons considered earlier it is not likely to have been widespread. The basic problem is that a man's occupation indicates relatively little about the level of his training and experience, and therefore of his proficiency at his craft and his productivity and earning ability in that trade.

Yet the additions of the men registered do give an important indication of the economic skills the indentured servants possessed. Several important distinctions are possible on the basis of the occupational entries. Two are of particular interest. One distinction is that between those who came from agriculture and those drawn from nonagricultural occupations. This is an important difference in any preindustrial economy, even if the precision with which it can be drawn is not always fine.[10] Among the servants, the farmers – yeomen, husbandmen, ploughmen, and increasingly over time simply farmers – can be separated from the whole array of nonagricultural tradesmen and craftsmen engaged primarily in manufacturing or service occupations. The term *laborer* as used in seventeenth- and eighteenth-century England also normally referred to hired agricultural workers.[11]

Those without additions cannot easily be categorized and will be excluded in making this division. If those in this group had been typical of the English population as a whole, the great majority probably would have been former servants in husbandry and therefore agriculturalists.[12] Additionally, insofar as no addition was recorded because the servant had no skill, given the preponderance of agricultural workers in the preindustrial economy, it might be argued that the majority had been employed in agriculture. However, this would assume random sampling from the whole population, whereas the servant registrations were made in England's largest cities. Therefore the servants without additions may have been drawn disproportionately from the marginal workers engaged in service occupations in the city, such as peddlers and hawkers, as well as those disproportionately urban people who had no real occupations, such as beggars and vagrants. Because this cannot be tested in particular cases, this group will not be assigned to either the farm or nonagricultural category.

The second distinction of interest concerns skill levels. The division to be drawn here between skilled and unskilled will once again be quite crude, but should nonetheless capture a generally significant difference between workers. The only specific term used in the registrations to refer to unskilled workers was that of laborer.[13] Farmers who worked land on their own account, and even those hired agriculturalists with specific skill titles, must all generally be considered skilled to some extent. Most were entrepreneurs, if typically on a small scale, but even the husbandmen who may have worked directly under the supervision of a landlord generally possessed some significant knowledge and skills specific to agriculture. Similarly, it will be assumed that the entry of any specific nonagricultural trade on a servant's contract can be taken to represent the possession of at least some minimum level of skill. The few gentlemen in the registrations will also be considered to have been skilled. Although these skills would typically not have been craft skills, most gentlemen must have been sufficiently educated to perform as clerical workers, and most of the relatively small number bound were probably used to fill skilled administrative or supervisory positions in the colonies.

Men registered without additions pose a special problem in regard to this division by skill. However, three types of collateral evidence from two of the samples examined demonstrate that the men without additions were not simply a random sample of the whole population of registrants and, as seen in earlier discussions, all three are consistent with the view that those without additions had lower average levels of economic skills and social status than those with recorded trades, and that the lack of an addition was the result of the absence of an occupation. Thus, in both the Middlesex registrations of 1683–4 and the London sample of 1718–59, the low mean ages and large shares of young men among the group registered without additions relative to all other occupational groups are consistent with the presence in this category of large numbers of youths who had not yet acquired trades. In the same two samples, men without additions were significantly less literate on average than those with additions of any kind. Finally, in the same samples, analysis of the length of indenture received by men with different occupations indicates that on average the labor of the men registered without additions was less highly valued than that of the others. It was suggested in the preceding chapter that a plausible explanation for the absence of a recorded addition appeared to be that the man had no occupation to record. The quantitative evidence summarized here supports this explanation, and is the basis on which the men without additions will be placed in the unskilled category. Many of these were too young to have occupations, and therefore additions; many more might have been members of the lower ranks of English society in which men had no trade or steady employment of any kind.

The evidence on male servants' occupations from all the relevant samples has been aggregated in Table 4.8 according to the two divisions suggested here. The greatest temporal change in the proportion of agri-

Table 4.8. Distributions of male servants by occupational type, 1654–1775

Sample	Bristol 1654–60			Bristol 1684–86			Middlesex 1683–84			London 1718–59			London 1773–75		
	N	%ᵃ	% of sample	N	%ᵃ	% of sample	N	%ᵃ	% of sample	N	%ᵃ	% of sample	N	%ᵃ	% of sample
Agriculturalᵇ	1,032	67	39	59	38	16	92	35	14	507	27	17	1,034	31	31
Nonagriculturalᶜ	516	33	19	97	62	26	169	65	26	1,376	73	46	2,319	69	69
Total	1,548	100	58	156	100	42	261	100	40	1,883	100	63	3,353	100	100
Skilledᵈ	1,347	50	50	111	30	30	231	35	35	1,706	57	57	2,858	85	85
Unskilledᵉ	1,328	50	50	258	70	70	424	65	65	1,307	43	43	501	15	15
Total	2,675	100	100	369	100	100	655	100	100	3,013	100	100	3,359	100	100

Note: The following definitions are expressed in terms of the occupational categories described in Appendix G.

ᵃPercent of those classified.
ᵇIncludes farmer and laborer.
ᶜIncludes food and drink, metal and construction, textiles and clothing, services.
ᵈIncludes gentlemen, farmer, food and drink, metal and construction, textiles and clothing, services.
ᵉIncludes laborer and not given.

cultural workers was a considerable decline between the Bristol registrations of the 1650s and all subsequent registrations from both Bristol and London. Thus two-thirds of the men whose occupations can be classified in the Bristol registrations of 1654–60 came from agriculture, compared with 38 percent in Bristol in 1684–86, 35 percent in Middlesex in 1683–84, and 27 and 31 percent in the two eighteenth-century London samples. This decline combined with the progressive decline after the 1680s in the share of men registered without stated occupations to produce a significant upward trend in the ratio of men with nonagricultural occupations to farmers. Although there were only half as many men registered with nonagricultural occupations as there were farmers in Bristol in the 1650s, in the two sets of registrations from the 1680s there were more nonagricultural workers than farmers – 1.6 and 1.8 times as many in Bristol and Middlesex, respectively – and in each of the two eighteenth-century samples there were more than twice as many nonagricultural workers as farmers, with ratios of 2.7 to 1 in the earlier and 2.2 to 1 in the later sample.

Trends also appear in the skill composition of the servants. The Bristol registrations of 1654–60 were evenly divided between skilled and unskilled men. The proportion of skilled workers among the servants then fell to 30 and 35 percent, respectively, in the Bristol and Middlesex registrations of the 1680s, before rising in each of the succeeding periods, to 57 percent of the men registered in London during 1718–59 and finally to 85 percent of those registered during 1773–75. Within the skilled category, the group that increased its share of total registrations most between the seventeenth and eighteenth centuries was that of metal and construction craftsmen.

The principal patterns that emerge from this consideration of trends in the occupational composition of the male servants therefore appear straightforward. After an initial decline during the third quarter of the seventeenth century, the final hundred years of the colonial period were marked by rising skill levels among those servants registered in England before their departure for the colonies. A disproportionate share of this increase was made up of men in a wide variety of nonagricultural trades and crafts. From the 1680s until 1775, therefore, the male servants were becoming on average both more likely to have occupational skills and less likely to have come from agricultural occupations.

These secular changes in the skill composition of the servant population are of considerable importance to an understanding of the changes that occurred over time in the function of indentured servants in the colonial labor market. Yet toward this end the analysis of the servants' skills is not yet complete. The next chapter analyzes the evidence of the servant registrations alluded to earlier on the servants' ability to sign. This analysis both provides additional evidence on the validity of the interpretation of the occupational entries suggested here and offers one opportunity to compare the skills of the emigrating servants with those of other Englishmen of the same period. Chapter 6 will then add an important dimension to this consideration of trends in the servants' occupational distributions by examining the skill composition of the servants bound for different colonial destinations.

5

Literacy and the occupations of
the indentured servants

Two sets of servant registrations analyzed in this study are unique among sizable collections of surviving records of emigrating British servants in that they consist of actual indentures, or contracts of servitude. The earlier of these collections comes from the records of the County of Middlesex Quarter Sessions, where the contracts of 812 servants bound before justices of the peace have survived from the years 1683–4, whereas the later is a collection of contracts recorded before the Lord Mayor of London, which survive for a total of 3,187 servants registered between 1718 and 1759. Because the indenture was a bargain between master and servant, these contracts were to be signed, or marked, by the servant to indicate his agreement to the terms of the indenture. As a result, these two samples are the only ones that contain this information on the servants' ability to sign.[1]

As mentioned in the preceding two chapters, a number of quantitative investigations of literacy in preindustrial England have taken the ability to sign as an index of the presence of literacy.[2] These studies have found that literacy so measured was closely related to occupation and social status.[3] The findings of these investigations make the information of the contracts on the servants' ability to sign of interest for two distinct, though related, purposes. Both of these use the evidence on the servants' literacy as a check on the validity of the interpretations of their recorded occupations offered in Chapters 3 and 4, but both also serve to provide additional information about the skills of the servants.

Both of the primary uses of the information on the servants' literacy result from problems of interpretation raised by the analysis of the servants' occupations. The first involves the assessment of the skills of the servants who recorded trades of any kind. There is some possibility that, knowing skilled craftsmen to be more highly valued in the colonies than the unskilled, prospective servants could falsely have claimed to possess skills that would result in their receiving preferential treatment. For legal reasons discussed earlier, fraud of this sort is not likely to have been widespread. Yet a related problem of interpretation not subject to the same objections would result from the alternative possibility that the servants who did practice the trades recorded upon registration could have been drawn disproportionately from among the lowest members of their professions in skill and economic status. In either of these cases, simply counting the frequencies of occupations would tend to overstate the true economic and social status of the servants represented.

The second major problem of interpretation has to do with the large numbers of men registered in the seventeenth and early eighteenth centuries without occupational terms. As discussed in the preceding chapters, their large numbers make it important to know why no occupations were recorded for those servants: Was the omission merely random, resulting from accidents in the registration process, or was it systematic? Were these servants a random sample of the whole population of registrants, as the former hypothesis suggests, or were they systematically different, and if so, how?

The utility of the evidence of the servants' literacy for the first of these problems results from the availability of estimates of literacy by occupation of the English population for periods close to those from which the servant contracts to be analyzed here are drawn. This makes possible a test based on a comparison of the servants' literacy rates with those of their contemporary Englishmen. If the servants' literacy rates by occupation are found to have been as high as those of other Englishmen, this would provide support for the validity of the occupational terms as well as for the conclusion that the servants were not disproportionately the lowest members of their professions in status; alternatively, the finding that the servants were less literate by occupation would tend to suggest that some combination of the opposite was true – the presence of false recorded occupations in significant numbers and/or systematic overrepresentation of the lowest members of each occupational group.

The close relationship that has been found between literacy and economic and social status in preindustrial England similarly underlies the usefulness of evidence on the servants' literacy for the second problem. As a result of these correlations, the literacy rates of the servants registered without additions, or occupational terms, can provide an independent measure of their status relative to that of the other servants bound, as well as an indication of the level of the English economy from which they were drawn.

Literacy of the female servants

Table 5.1 shows the number of servants of each sex who marked and signed their contracts by age in each sample, for all servants for whom all the relevant information is available. The numbers of women in both samples are small and do not provide a basis for extensive analysis. The low proportion of women in the Middlesex sample able to sign, 11 percent, is the same as that found by David Cressy for women in seventeenth-century Norwich.[4] The proportion of women who signed is considerably higher, 35 percent, in the later London registrations. This is very similar to the estimate of female literacy obtained by Roger Schofield from a national sample for the mid-eighteenth century.[5] In the London registrations, the proportion of adult women who signed is greater than that of the minors, by 43 percent to 33 percent.[6] Further subdivision indicates increases in the proportion able to sign between each of the age groups 15 to 17 (29 percent), 18 to 20 (35 percent), and 21 and over (43 percent). Although the size and nonrandom character of the sample limits the strength of the conclusions, the proportion of adult women able to sign is nearly half again as large as the proportion of those aged 15 to 17, raising the possibility of sizable increases in the ability to sign among women in the late teens and early adulthood.

Literacy of the male servants by occupation

A first step in analyzing the evidence for the men is to divide the registrations by occupational category. This is done for both samples in Table 5.2. These group literacy rates can be compared with the results of two studies of literacy in England by occupation in roughly the same periods.

Considering first the earlier sample, the 27 percent of the husbandmen able to sign is higher than both the 11 percent obtained by David Cressy from East Anglian legal depositions of the 1680s and the 21 percent average he found for seventeenth-century Norwich.[7] The 30 percent literacy rate for laborers is twice the 15 percent for East Anglia given by Cressy.[8] And the 56 percent literacy rate found by Cressy for East Anglian tradesmen and craftsmen is virtually the same as the 55 percent obtained by pooling the five categories of skilled crafts shown in Table 5.2 – food and drink, metal and wood, construction, clothing and textiles, and services.[9] Though, as Cressy cautions, literacy figures from the diocese of Norwich do not necessarily apply to other parts of England,[10] that the servants' literacy rates by occupational type are not lower than those found for East Anglia in a comparable period provides some support for the propositions that the occupational labels the servants gave were generally accurate, and that the skilled servants who had occupations were not systematically the least educated among Englishmen of the same trades.

The rates shown in Table 5.2 for the servants covered by the eighteenth-century London registrations can be compared with Roger Schofield's estimates of illiteracy for the period 1754–84 drawn from a national

Table 5.1. *Ability to sign by age, Middlesex and London registrations*

	Middlesex, 1683–84				London, 1718–59			
Age	Men marked	Men signed	Women marked	Women signed	Men marked	Men signed	Women marked	Women signed
11	1							1
12	2				3	1		
13	3	1			2	1	1	
14	3	2	2		17	11	1	
15	7	1	3		72	64	4	3
16	17	2	5	1	103	108	9	9
17	6	4	3		98	146	17	8
18	33	7	10	3	128	244	18	13
19	4	11	8	1	159	288	26	12
20	12	8	7	2	147	315	17	3
21	98	68	42	5	31	153	3	3
22	43	37	19		20	125	5	
23	28	15	8		19	79	2	
24	23	16	8	1	13	69		
25	10	12	5		19	75	4	1
26	11	10	2	1	16	69	3	1
27	11	8	3		5	50		1
28	14	11	1		5	38		
29	3	8	2		11	24		
30	16	10	3	2	6	27	1	1
31	6	8	1		5	21		

32	7	2			3	12		1
33	1	2			1	15		1
34	1				2	10		
35		1			1	14		
36					3	13		
37					1	4		
38	1	2			1	7		
39					1	1		
40+	2	1			2	16		1
Total	363	247	132	16	894	1,970	110	59

sample of marriage registers. Schofield's rates actually come from a considerably later period than the servant registrations, for not only does his period extend twenty-five years past the date of the last surviving London registration, but more than 90 percent of the servants in the latter sample were actually registered before 1740. The comparison is therefore between samples drawn chiefly from successive quarters of the eighteenth century.[11]

Despite the difference in sampling period, the rates reported by Schofield are similar to those obtained from the London registrations. Schofield's rate of 54 percent is eight points below the 62 percent of the husbandmen in the London sample who signed.[12] Schofield's 81 percent literacy rate for food and drink is seven points below the 88 percent rate of the servants. A weighted average of the separate rates given by Schofield for metal and for wood crafts gives a rate of 82 percent, three points below the 85 percent servants' rate.[13] A pooled rate obtained from Schofield's separate rates for clothing and textiles of 71 percent is almost identical to the 70 percent reported in Table 5.2. The servants' rate of 85 percent for construction cannot be compared to Schofield's different category of construction and mining; the much lower 49 percent rate of the latter could be due to the lower literacy of miners. There is no comparable category in Schofield's tabulation to the services category of Table 5.2. The only major apparent discrepancies between the results of Schofield's investigation and the present one occur for laborers – Schofield gives the literacy of "laborers and servants" as 41 percent compared to the London sample's 62 percent for laborers – and for those with no stated occupation, for whom Schofield's 76 percent is considerably above the servants' 57 percent. The first of these discrepancies probably is due in part to the geographic composition of the groups compared, as will be seen in the following discussion. The second is more problematic; the issue of the literacy, and status, of the servants registered without stated occupations will be considered later at some length.

The important result of these comparisons is that the literacy rates shown in Table 5.2 for the London servant registrations tend to be very close to those obtained by Schofield from marriage registers. This reinforces the conclusions drawn from the comparisons made for the first sample. Although further analysis of the servants' literacy will consider some of the compositional factors that yield the literacy rates presented here, the comparisons made to this point show that, compared with a national sample of literacy for the mid-eighteenth century and a regional sample for the 1680s, the servants bound in the sample considered here were overall apparently no less literate by occupation than their counterparts elsewhere in England.[14] This provides support both for the validity of the occupational titles recorded in the servant registrations and for the

Table 5.2. *Literacy by occupational category, Middlesex and London registrations*

Occupation	Middlesex, 1683–84		London, 1718–59	
	No.	% signed	No.	% signed
Husbandman	56	27	328	62
Laborer	30	30	179	62
Food and drink	11	55	120	88
Metal and wood	20	35	201	85
Construction	21	48	336	85
Clothing and textiles	51	61	415	70
Services	60	58	299	88
Not given	382	37	1,124	57
Total	631	41	3,002	69

contention that the servants who recorded occupations were not disproportionately the least educated and skilled of those who practiced their trades.

The evidence on which this investigation is based is unusual among the types of sources used for quantitative studies of literacy in preindustrial England in that it includes large numbers of minors. In the Middlesex registrations, 29 percent of the male minors signed, compared with 43 percent of the adults.[15] Given the considerable differences in literacy that existed among occupational groups, before this is accepted as evidence of an increase in literacy with age rather than simply the result of systematic differences in the occupational composition of the two age groups, it is desirable to hold occupational category constant in making the comparison. There are too few minors with stated occupations in the Middlesex registrations to make such analysis of that sample worthwhile, but the presence of significant numbers of minors with trades in the later registrations makes possible the division shown in Table 5.3, with the literacy of the servants in each occupational category given separately for minors and adults. The result is striking: In every case the proportion of adults able to sign is above that of minors.[16]

The minor–adult literacy rate differentials fall into two groups by size. For five categories – food and drink, metal and wood, construction, clothing and textiles, and services – the differentials are small, with the proportion of minors able to sign about 90 percent or more of the adult rate. The largest differentials occur for farmers, laborers, and those without stated occupations: For each of these, the minors' rate is about 70

Table 5.3. *Literacy by occupation and age, London registrations,*
1718–59

Occupation	Minors		Adults	
	No.	% signed	No.	% signed
Husbandman	139	49	167	72
Laborer	117	55	62	76
Food and drink	49	86	65	91
Metal and wood	74	82	121	86
Construction	118	80	205	87
Clothing and textiles	241	66	162	74
Services	137	85	140	91
Not given	1,031	55	34	100
Total	1,906	62	956	83

percent of the adults' or less. Leaving aside for the moment the men registered without stated occupations, the division between these two groups would appear to be significant. The first group includes the skilled trades and crafts, whereas the second consists broadly of the agricultural and unskilled classes; it is likely that those in the former occupations typically had more formal occupational training than the latter as well as more literary skills.

The relatively small minor–adult literacy rate differentials in the skilled trades and crafts do not necessarily mean that boys did not learn to sign in the course of their professional training, but perhaps that by the time they took the addition of their trade, most who would ever be able to sign could already do so. Significant numbers of skilled occupations do not appear in the registrations for servants below the age of 17.[17] It cannot be determined to what extent the higher proportions of the skilled able to sign were due to informal education obtained in the course of professional training as opposed to the entry into skilled trades of those who were already more educated.

In the case of the farmers and laborers, there is a variety of possible explanations for the observed differences in literacy between minors and adults. One category of explanation would attribute it to some type of selection bias. An example of this class would be the possibility that the difference arose from a demand phenomenon. Thus it may be that although young servants were preferred as agricultural laborers, perhaps because they were more easily controlled,[18] older servants would have been accepted by colonial planters only if they had other economic advantages over younger men, such as higher levels of technical skills and education. If such a demand bias existed, it would mean that the minors and adults in the sample were drawn from different ranges of the men in a given occupation, with the mean skill and educational level of the servants registered increasing with age relative to all Englishmen of the same age and trade.

Alternatively, it is possible that no such selection bias is present in these data. The substantially higher proportions of adults able to sign compared with minors might then indicate that considerable numbers of men who earned their living in agriculture, as husbandmen or laborers, learned to write their names after the school-leaving age. Furthermore, the comparisons offered from this evidence can bear only on changes in literacy that occurred in the late teens and after, because the youngest servants registered in significant numbers, as shown in Table 5.1, were already in their mid-teens. Therefore the increases in the percentages of the husbandmen and laborers able to sign – from 49 percent and 55 percent of the minors to 72 percent and 76 percent of the adults, respectively – would be lower-bound estimates of the numbers who learned to sign through some type of informal education.[19]

As noted above, the lack of full knowledge of the process by which the servants registered were drawn from the English population makes it impossible to draw firm inferences about the whole population from the sample of servants. However, the servant registrations do raise interesting questions. In this instance, they suggest the possibility that informal education may have been an important source of literary skills for men in some occupations in the mid-eighteenth century. Thus far, the extent of informal education in preindustrial England has eluded quantitative investigation; this indirect suggestion of its possible importance might serve as an added incentive to the search for data sources that bear more directly on the issue.

Large regional differentials in the extent of literacy are known to have existed in preindustrial England.[20] In one particular case, inhabitants of London, and to a lesser extent Middlesex, were generally more literate than those who lived elsewhere in England.[21] The two samples examined here are in large part dominated by servants who had their place of origin recorded as either London or Middlesex. Thus although servants from a total of more than forty English counties appear in each of the sets of registrations, those from London and Middlesex together make up 45 percent of all registrants in the earlier, and 35 percent in the later sample.[22] In view of the heavy representation of London and Middlesex in both samples, it is worth considering whether the favorable comparisons with the samples of nonmetropolitan Englishmen seen above are the result of the differing geographic composition of the groups compared.

Table 5.4. *Literacy by occupation and place of origin, Middlesex registrations, 1683–84*

	London-Middlesex		Other	
Occupation	No.	% signed	No.	% signed
Husbandman	7	14	45	27
Laborer	4	25	24	29
Food and drink	4	75	5	40
Metal and wood	8	25	10	40
Construction	10	50	8	50
Clothing and textiles	12	58	38	61
Services	13	46	44	61
Not given				
Minors	21	19	43	26
Adults	50	38	84	31
Total	129	37	301	39

Tables 5.4 and 5.5 indicate that this was not the case. In the earlier sample, the nonmetropolitan servants actually tended to be more literate than those from London and Middlesex, as pooling the servants with skilled trades and crafts gives a nonmetropolitan literacy rate of 57 percent, well above their London counterparts' 49 percent, whereas the nonmetropolitan husbandmen and laborers had a 28 percent rate, compared with the London rate of 18 percent. Although neither of these differences is statistically significant, and therefore cannot reject the hypothesis that there was no difference in the literacy rates of servants from the London area and those from elsewhere, random samples of Englishmen from London and its surrounding area and from elsewhere in this period would presumably have found the metropolitan area residents to have been somewhat more literate than the others, and the absence of this expected relationship for the servants in the Middlesex registrations is of some interest. Specifically, it suggests the possibility that on average the natives of London indentured to serve in the colonies in this period were lower in economic status than their counterparts from elsewhere in England who had similar occupations.[23]

In the later sample the same geographic comparison reveals little difference in the literacy rates. Pooled estimates show the literacy rates of the skilled tradesmen and craftsmen from the capital and elsewhere to have been almost identical, at 81 percent and 80 percent, respectively. Husbandmen and laborers from the metropolitan area were more literate than those from elsewhere; 73 percent signed compared with 59 percent of the others.[24]

Table 5.5 *Literacy by occupation, age, and place of origin, London registrations, 1718–59*

Occupation and age	London-Middlesex		Other	
	No.	% signed	No.	% signed
Husbandman				
Minors	9	67	130	48
Adults	23	78	144	72
Laborer				
Minors	41	66	76	49
Adults	31	81	31	71
Food and drink				
Minors	17	82	32	88
Adults	28	93	37	89
Metal and wood				
Minors	23	87	51	80
Adults	55	91	66	82
Construction				
Minors	39	79	79	80
Adults	101	88	104	87
Clothing and textiles				
Minors	76	68	164	65
Adults	73	75	89	73
Services				
Minors	43	79	94	88
Adults	68	91	72	90
Not given				
Minors	332	66	699	50
Adults	19	100	15	100
All				
Minors	580	70	1,325	58
Adults	398	86	558	80
Total	978	76	1,883	65

Literacy of the men registered without occupations

The second problem raised at the outset of this chapter remains to be considered. What can the evidence of literacy tell us of the economic and social status of the servants who had no occupations recorded on their contracts? Table 5.6 presents the evidence for these servants from both samples. In the Middlesex sample the proportion of the servants without additions able to sign was 37 percent, compared with 55 percent of the

Characteristics of the servant population

Table 5.6. *Literacy of men with no occupational entry by age, Middlesex and London registrations*

Age	Middlesex 1683–84		London 1718–59	
	Marked	Signed	Marked	Signed
11	1	0	0	0
12	2	0	3	1
13	2	1	2	1
14	3	2	17	10
15	7	1	70	61
16	17	2	91	95
17	6	4	80	100
18	31	7	87	140
19	4	8	70	93
20	11	4	39	71
21	56	40	0	14
22	25	17	0	3
23	13	7	0	3
24	12	9	0	3
25–29	17	21	0	8
30–34	21	10	0	3
35–39	1	3		
40–46	1	1		
Total	230	137	459	606

skilled tradesmen and craftsmen and 28 percent of the husbandmen and laborers.[25] In the later London sample, 57 percent of the men not identified by trade signed, compared with 81 percent of the skilled tradesmen and craftsmen and 62 percent of the husbandmen and laborers.[26] The table also shows that in both samples the proportion of servants without additions who were able to sign rose considerably with age in the late teens.

The evidence of both samples therefore tends to place the servants without additions closer in status to the agricultural and unskilled category of husbandmen and laborers than to the skilled tradesmen and craftsmen. The generally low literacy rates of the young men indicate that most had little formal education, and the increases in literacy that occurred in the group in the late teens suggest that many of these servants might have gone through a process of informal education upon entry into adulthood that this investigation found to have been an apparent characteristic of the unskilled laborers and husbandmen of the London registrations.

The tentative nature of this conclusion hardly needs emphasis. However, the evidence on literacy can be used to provide a stronger test of a more restricted hypothesis concerning the status of the men without additions. As noted in Chapter 3, Mildred Campbell argued that the servants without occupational terms could simply be assumed to have been a random sample of the whole population of the servants registered. To test this argument with respect to the ability to sign, the servants in each sample can simply be divided into those with and without additions. In the Middlesex sample, of servants who either signed or marked the contracts, 46 percent of the 250 men with additions signed, compared with 37 percent of the 382 without the occupational terms. In the London registrations, 76 percent of the 1,881 men with additions signed, while 57 percent of the 1,124 without additions signed. These differences provide direct support for the contention that the men without additions were not a random sample of the servant population.[27] In the absence of an occupational term, the ability to sign is the most direct indicator available in the registrations of the economic and social status of the servants. Although the status terms could have been omitted for more than a single reason, and the men without additions could have been drawn to some extent from the skilled as well as the unskilled, the evidence of literacy places them clearly below the average of the other men in their samples, and on average at a level of English society distinctly closer to the unskilled groups than to the skilled.

One of our most important sources of information about the occupations of the indentured servants of the American colonial period has been two surviving collections of their contracts recorded in England before their departure. In investigating the skills the servants brought with them to the American colonies, the first use of these records was to analyze the servants' occupations recorded in them. The results of this analysis, presented in Chapters 3 and 4, raised problems of interpretation that required more information. Using the collateral evidence of the servants' ability to sign their contracts, this study found that the evidence of literacy suggests that the great majority of the occupational additions were valid, and further that the servants in the registrations who had additions were of no lower status on average than other Englishmen of the same occupational groups. The evidence of literacy also indicated that the servants without occupational terms were not a random sample of all men registered: They were significantly less literate on average than the men registered with additions. The literacy rates of the servants without occupational terms placed them closer on average to the less skilled groups in England's population than to the skilled tradesmen and craftsmen. Thus the analysis of this chapter supports the conclusion that the recorded occupational terms were generally accurate, and also suggests that many of the men registered without additions genuinely had no occupation or trade.

The result of this analysis of the literacy of the indentured servants has therefore been to reinforce the results of the earlier investigation of their economic and social origins through analysis of their recorded occupations. This chapter has strengthened the conclusion that both the earlier historians who portrayed the indentured servants as a human cargo chiefly drawn from among England's unskilled and ignorant and the more recent scholars who depicted the servants as emigrants who came primarily from among the more prosperous and skilled groups in English society overstated their cases, for colonial America's bound immigrants were apparently drawn more evenly from a wider range of English society than either of these characterizations suggests. Although the precise distribution will never be known with confidence, the evidence analyzed in this study indicates that the indentured servants probably came in significant numbers from all levels of the broad segment of English society bounded at one end by the gentry, and at the other by the paupers.

Part III

Migration and the transatlantic market for indentured servants

6

Patterns of servant migration from England to America

The previous four chapters of this study used the evidence of the servant registrations to consider the sex and age distributions, occupational composition, and literacy of the servant population as a whole. This chapter examines the colonial destinations of the servants, and then compares the characteristics of the groups of servants bound for different colonial regions. The patterns that emerge will constitute basic observations for subsequent analysis of both the colonial market for servants and the colonial labor market as a whole.

Determination of where the servants went is based on entries made on their contracts or the lists of registrations. Because these were made prior to embarkation, they constitute statements of intent rather than evidence of delivery. However, the records examined in this investigation were made by government functionaries acting upon legal authority, often with the specific intention of preventing fraud by either master or servant; consequently, systematic falsification of these entries appears unlikely. Moreover, in the samples of actual contracts of service, all entries were enforceable by law, and servants sent to a colony other than that for which they had contracted could have appealed to the courts of the colony where they were delivered. In some cases they might have preferred the actual to the negotiated destination, and therefore chosen not to contest the change in destination. It is likely, however, that widespread fraud by merchants in the delivery of servants would have left a considerable legal record of colonial litigation. The absence of such a record suggests that the colonies recorded in the registrations were generally those to which the servants were sent.

This conclusion does not mean that the registrations can invariably be taken to indicate the colony where the servant was sold. Even with good faith this degree of precision is unlikely in view of the way the colonial shipping trade operated, as ships sometimes changed their original plans or stopped in a number of different colonial ports in search of return cargoes. Hints of the resulting uncertainty appear in the registrations. For example, some entries bound servants to serve in one of several colonies: "Virginia or Maryland" is the only case in which this occurred frequently, but other combinations can be found in the registrations. As a result, in some cases the precise intended destinations of servants are not known. It is nonetheless likely that in most cases the specific colonies recorded in the registrations were the servants' actual destinations.

Colonial destinations of the servants

Tabulations of the servants' recorded colonial destinations are presented in annual series, separately by sex, in Appendix I. An overview of this information is given in Tables 6.1 and 6.2, which present percentage distributions of the destinations of servants of each sex for those decades from which registrations are available. A number of clear trends emerge from these tabulations.

Barbados was by far the most important single destination of the servants in the 1650s, the first decade the registrations cover. During that decade it received 70 percent of the men and 65 percent of the women registered. Its importance then fell sharply. The island received less than a quarter of both the men and women registered in the 1660s, and only about one-tenth of the servants of both sexes registered in the 1670s. Its share of the men recovered to about one-fifth of the total registered in the 1680s, but it ceased to be a quantitatively important destination thereafter, as from 1690 Barbados never received as much as one-tenth of the servants of either sex registered in any decade.

Jamaica first appears as a major destination for servants during the 1680s, when it received more than a quarter of the men registered and just under a quarter of the women. The registrations also indicate that it was the only important West Indian servant importer in the mid-eighteenth century, as it received about one-fifth and three-fifths of the men registered in the 1720s and 1730s, respectively, and continued to receive servants in the 1750s. The implication might be drawn that it probably remained an important destination for servants throughout the period between 1690 and 1720. Yet there is one piece of conflicting evidence from the registrations, the complete absence of Jamaica as a stated destination in the Liverpool registrations of 1697–1707. This has been cited as evidence that servants had stopped coming to Jamaica by the end of the seventeenth century.[1] The large numbers of servants bound for Jamaica in the mid-eighteenth century make it clear that the Liverpool list cannot be taken as a sign of the conclusion of Jamaica's importation of servants, but it does raise the question of whether there was a temporary halt at the turn of the century. However, analysis of the seasonality of the registrations of the nearly half of the total servants registered in Liverpool without stated destinations suggests that most of these servants may actually have been bound for the West Indies. Appendix E presents the basis for this

Table 6.1. Percentage distributions of destinations of male servants by decade

Decade	Barbados	Jamaica	Nevis	Other West Indies	Chesapeake	Pennsylvania	Other mainland	Not given	Total	No. of servants
1650s	70		2	1	27				100	2,230
1660s	22	1	18	2	55		2		100	3,456
1670s	10	4	16	2	65		3		100	2,007
1680s	19	28	2	2	43	3	3		100	1,743
1690s	3			1	56	2	5	33	100	677
1700s				4	28		4	64	100	362
1710s	7	3			87	2	1		100	152
1720s	1	22		15	47	13	2		100	1,161
1730s	1	60		4	24	8	3		100	1,444
1740s		79		7	7	7			100	15
1750s		34		11	41	6	3	5	100	241
1770s					79	19	2		100	3,359
All	17	11	6	3	52	6	2	3	100	16,847

Source: Table I.1.

83

Table 6.2. *Percentage distributions of destinations of female servants by decade*

Decade	Barbados	Jamaica	Nevis	Other West Indies	Chesapeake	Pennsylvania	Other mainland	Not given	Total	No. of servants
1650s	65		1	1	33				100	724
1660s	21		15	2	61		1		100	1,092
1670s	11	3	14	1	69		2		100	542
1680s	7	24	2	4	59	1	3		100	524
1690s					61	4	5	30	100	196
1700s					24			76	100	208
1710s				7	74	19			100	27
1720s		3		8	57	27	5		100	76
1730s		39		1	26	18	16		100	62
1750s		50		13	37	15	2	4	100	8
1770s					79		2	6	100	350
All	21	5	7	1	55	3	2	6	100	3,809

Source: Table 1.2.

conclusion, which is drawn from a comparison of the seasonality of the Liverpool registrations with those of servants in other samples bound for different colonial regions. Although for reasons discussed in the appendix this evidence cannot be considered definitive, it does imply that the apparent sharp decline in West Indian servant imports at the close of the seventeenth century may never have occurred. The evidence of the later eighteenth-century registrations indicates that Jamaica's servant imports did virtually cease sometime in the middle of the eighteenth century, as it received less than one-half of 1 percent of the men registered in the 1770s and none of the women.

Among the other islands that received servants, Nevis was the only one that received a significant share of the servants bound in any period. It received the bulk of its servants in two decades, the 1660s and 1670s, when it received 18 and 16 percent of the men, respectively, and only slightly lower shares of the women. It virtually disappeared from the registrations after the 1680s. Antigua was second to Jamaica among West Indian destinations in the mid-eighteenth-century registrations, but received relatively small numbers of servants. St. Kitts received a trickle of servants in both the late seventeenth and early eighteenth centuries.

The Chesapeake colonies were not only the most important mainland destination for servants, but also the most important destination overall in these samples: More than half the men and women in all the records considered were bound to serve in Maryland or Virginia. Together, they were the only destination to receive a significant share of the servants from each of the six samples analyzed, and in each of the decades covered by them from the 1650s through the 1770s. They are combined as a single destination in Tables 6.1 and 6.2, although the tabulations in Appendix I retain the individual colonies as given in the registrations. If the specific entries on servants' registrations are held to have been strictly accurate, Virginia was the destination of the great majority of those bound for the Chesapeake in the 1650s through the 1670s, the two colonies received roughly equal numbers of servants in the 1680s, and Maryland received the bulk of the eighteenth-century Chesapeake registrants. This may have been the case. However, in some cases the names of the two colonies might have been recorded indifferently, and in several samples a significant number of servants were described as bound for either Virginia or Maryland. As there is only a minor loss in specificity from treating the Chesapeake as a unit, and a possible gain in accuracy, the two colonies will be combined in the following discussion.[2]

Of the other mainland colonies that imported servants, Pennsylvania was quantitatively the most important. It first appeared as a recorded destination in the 1680s, but only became a major importer in the eighteenth century. It received about one-tenth of the total men registered from the 1720s through the 1740s, and about one-fifth of the women in the same period.

A number of other mainland colonies appear as destinations for small numbers of servants. New England received a small number of the servants registered in most periods. Carolina imported a few from the 1680s on, as did New Jersey and New York. Georgia accounted for a small number after the 1730s.

A significant difference in the destinations of servants by sex appears in the registrations. Throughout the period covered, there was a persistent tendency for the share of the total men bound for the West Indies to be greater than the corresponding share of the women. This difference was apparently not caused by the migration of women to any single colony. In most decades, a larger share of the females than of the males was registered for the Chesapeake, and the same tended to be true of Pennsylvania in periods when it received significant numbers of servants. Thus, in a comparison of the sexes, men tended to be bound proportionately more often for the West Indies, and women more frequently for all major mainland destinations.

A significant feature of the servant registrations for particular destinations is their distribution over the course of the year. It is likely that the registration of servants normally occurred close to the date of their departure. Merchants were responsible for all maintenance of the servants after the indenture was signed, and their costs were therefore positively related to the elapsed time between the servant's binding and the date of departure.[3] In addition, the longer the period between registration and sailing, the greater the opportunity for servants to doubt the wisdom of their decisions to emigrate, and the more numerous the chances for them to run away. It was therefore in the merchant's interest to ship his servants as soon as possible after binding them, both to minimize maintenance costs and to prevent the possible dwindling of his stock. In the large ports considered here, with a considerable volume of both ships and servants, the lag between registration and sailing was likely in most cases to have been short, and the date of registration can probably be used as a good indicator of the approximate date of departure.

When the servant registrations are divided by colonial destination, two distinct seasonal patterns emerge. One of these is for servants bound for the West Indies. Percentage distributions of registrations for the West Indies by month, for the four samples that had significant numbers recorded, are shown in Table 6.3. Although the difference between months was generally not extreme, in the seventeenth-century samples there was a persistent tendency for the number of registrations to be lowest during the months from June through September.

A more pronounced pattern of seasonal variation appears in the

Table 6.3. *Percentage distributions of month of registration of servants bound for the West Indies*

Month	Bristol, 1654–86	London, 1683–86	Middlesex, 1683–84	London, 1718–59
January	12	5	8	9
February	11	6	24	7
March	9	14	20	6
April	7	15	12	3
May	7	11	10	4
June	5	4	9	2
July	6	2	1	7
August	6	6	3	11
September	6	4	3	8
October	10	11	1	15
November	11	14	2	17
December	10	8	7	11
Total	100	100	100	100
N	5,178	428	294	1,560

Chesapeake's registrations. Evidence of their distribution over the year from all six samples is given in Table 6.4. In the seventeenth century shipments to the region apparently virtually ceased between December and June, and a high concentration of registrations occurred during the summer months. In the three earliest sets of registrations, the four months from July through October accounted for from 72 to 80 percent of the servants bound for Maryland and Virginia, and between 22 and 32 percent of all Chesapeake registrations in these samples were entered in the single peak month of August.

The final three samples suggest that a change occurred over time in the seasonal pattern of Chesapeake registrations. The peak months and season apparently became progressively later in the year. Thus, although October was the single most important month for Chesapeake registrations in the Liverpool sample with 32 percent of the total, December was the most important in the London sample of 1718–59 with 15 percent, and January was the peak in the final sample with 16 percent. The peak seasons shifted similarly, so that the summer months fell in importance, and first the fall, then the winter, gained in relative importance over time. In the Liverpool sample the peak period occurred in the four months from October through January, which together accounted for 78 percent of all Chesapeake registrations. In the London sample of 1718–59 the most important period consisted of the four months from November through February, when 54 percent of the servants were

Table 6.4. *Percentage distributions of month of registration of servants bound for the Chesapeake*

Month	Bristol, 1654–86	London, 1683–86	Middlesex, 1683–84	Liverpool, 1697–1707	London, 1718–59	London, 1773–75
January	2	4	0	18	13	16
February	2	0	0	1	13	11
March	1	3	0	0	6	14
April	0	0	1	0	7	11
May	2	1	3	0	2	7
June	5	2	13	10	2	6
July	14	25	22	7	4	9
August	22	25	32	4	8	1
September	19	15	18	32	9	4
October	17	14	8	15	8	3
November	12	7	2	13	13	6
December	4	4	1		15	12
Total	100	100	100	100	100	100
N	5,251	386	486	568	1,203	2,932

registered, and in the final sample five months, December through April, accounted for 64 percent of all Chesapeake registrations. The declining shares of the servants registered in the peak months and seasons points to another apparent tendency during the eighteenth century, namely, a shift toward a more even distribution of the Chesapeake registrations over the year.

Several factors contributed to the marked seasonal patterns of the seventeenth-century Chesapeake registrations. The first of these was the seasonality of the tobacco trade. English merchants trading for tobacco in the seventeenth century normally wanted their ships to arrive in the Chesapeake late in the fall, after the tobacco had been harvested, cured, and packed for shipment.[4] The two- or three-month voyage from England would put a late July, August, or September departure in port in Maryland or Virginia by October or November, in time to trade its cargo of servants for the first hogsheads of the tobacco trading season. The continuing high level of registrations in the following few months may have been due to another pattern described by Philip Alexander Bruce, as some merchants sent their ships to the Chesapeake somewhat later, to transport the tobacco that had not been ready for shipment earlier in the fall.[5] These merchants might have hoped to obtain tobacco at lower prices from planters still holding unsold crops after the height of the trading season.

Another reason for the seasonal pattern of seventeenth-century departures for the Chesapeake had to do with the nature of servants as an import. Edmund Morgan has pointed out that seventeenth-century Virginia planters preferred to buy servants who arrived in the fall or early winter to avoid the worst of the summer months' hazards to the health of new white immigrants, known as "seasoning," and that evidence from the 1660s makes it clear that by then English shippers had adjusted their schedules to comply with the colonists' wishes, which had been voiced as early as the 1630s.[6] Although Morgan's earliest cited evidence on the seasonality of deliveries is a letter of 1666, he speculates that the pattern of fall and winter arrivals had probably been fixed earlier, in the 1640s or 1650s. A breakdown of the monthly distribution of the Chesapeake servant registrations made in Bristol during 1655–66, shown in Table 6.5, provides strong evidence that the pattern of late-year arrivals was well established by 1655: Thus in that year all of the 113 registrations for the Chesapeake were made in the months from July through November. A similar seasonality appears in the following years.[7]

The progressive modification of the seasonal pattern of Chesapeake registrations that is apparent in the eighteenth-century samples may have been due in part to the recognition of the declining importance of seasonal mortality.[8] The change in the pattern apparently made the eighteenth-century servant trade in the Chesapeake coincide more closely

Table 6.5. *Month of registration of servants bound for the Chesapeake, Bristol, 1655–66*

Month	1655	1656	1657	1658	1659	1660	1661	1662	1663	1664	1665	1666
January					19			4				
February					6			1				
March			7									
April								9				
May						12	10	57	1	2		
June				4	3	27	54	79	9	4	3	
July	6		18	16	67	86	126	101	49	31	1	
August	13	22	43	80	62	35	106	125	54	42	57	4
September	28	46	37	69	44	28	52	56	23	18	93	22
October	31	24	9	6	20		11	48	16	9	69	74
November	35	22	5					32	8	15	20	123
December		24		23			5				1	33
Total	113	138	119	198	221	188	364	512	160	121	244	256

with the slave trading season, which was concentrated in the period from late spring to the end of summer. The seasonality of the latter may have resulted in part from concern for the Africans' health, and the belief that the cold of fall and winter could be lethal to new arrivals.[9] However, a different and perhaps more important consideration, which would have extended to servants as well, may have been that described by Governor Jenings of Virginia in a letter written to the Board of Trade in 1709. In discussing seasonal variation in the price of newly imported slaves, Jenings noted:

When Negroes come in about the begining of the Summer, the planters are abundantly more fond of them, and will give greater price for them, because they are sure of the advantage of their labour in that years Crop, whereas Negros bought at the Latter end of the year, are of little Service till the next Spring, and this is the true reason of that difference of price.[10]

Because slaves were put to work upon arrival, the peak demand for them in the Chesapeake was the season of peak effective demand for labor, the months from the planting season through the harvest. The same consideration might have caused the shift seen in the seasonality of the servant trade to the Chesapeake. Both the tendency toward equalization of the distribution of the trade over the year and the tendency, implied by the shift in the peak season, for ships to arrive at times other than those when the tobacco crop had just been prepared for shipment may have been symptoms of the increasing diversification and complexity of the Chesapeake economy in the eighteenth century.

That the seasonal variation of West Indian registrations was smaller in magnitude than that of those for the Chesapeake was probably due to the calendar of sugar production. In the British West Indies, the sugarcane was normally harvested over a relatively long period, beginning in January and running through June or July. As the cane was cut, it was milled, boiled, and then drained for about a month. The brown muscovado usually exported by English planters was then packed into hogsheads, ready for export.[11] Captains leaving England in the late fall, winter, or spring months may have hoped to receive export cargoes of sugar in return for their servants with a minimum of delay, and to complete their round trip in time to avoid the hurricane season, which began in August and continued until fall.[12]

Differences in characteristics of the servant population by colonial destination

With an outline of the changing destinations of the servants over time established, it is possible to consider the identification of more specific patterns within the flows of the servants' migration. Comparison of the ages of servants bound for different destinations indicates that men bound to serve in the West Indies tended to be consistently older on average than those bound for the mainland. Comparing the two groups of all men registered for the islands and those registered for the mainland in the three samples that had significant numbers bound for both regions, the difference in mean ages was 3.5 years in the London sample of 1683–86, 1.2 in that of Middlesex from 1683–84, and 1.8 in the London sample of 1718–59.[13] Differences in the mean ages of the servants bound for the individual colonies within each of these broad regions are generally small and not consistent between samples. The major result that appears from the examination of servant migration by age is therefore the considerable and persistent age differences that existed on average between men bound for the West Indies and the mainland.

It is of particular interest to this study of the colonial labor market to analyze the distribution of servants among the colonies by occupation. In doing this, the nine categories used in the earlier occupational analysis proved too detailed, and a broader categorization was needed.[14] The occupational categories were therefore aggregated into the two categories of skilled and unskilled in the manner suggested earlier. Table 6.6 shows the proportions of all men bound for the major destinations in each sample made up of those in skilled occupations, according to the definitions set out in Chapter 4.

Comparison of the proportions of skilled servants by colony produces a notable result. With the exception of the Bristol registrations of 1654–61, in each of the samples from which the West Indies received a significant number of servants, a higher proportion of the total men bound for West Indian destinations was made up of skilled servants than of those bound for the mainland.[15] The same result appears in comparisons of the largest individual West Indian and mainland importers by sample, as the share of the skilled among migrants to the leading West Indian destinations tended to be greater than among those bound for the principal destinations on the mainland. The differences underlying these conclusions were generally considerable. The share of the skilled among all men bound for the West Indies was 20 percent greater than the corresponding share of the mainland imports in the Bristol registrations of 1684–86, 35 percent greater for the Middlesex registrations of 1683–84, and 35 percent greater for the London registrations of 1718–59.[16]

Corresponding differences in the share of the skilled in servant imports appear in comparisons between the major individual colonial destinations in the West Indies and on the mainland. Pooling the two sets of registrations from the 1680s, those from Bristol and Middlesex, reveals that the skilled made up 24 percent and 20 percent greater shares of male

Table 6.6. *Shares of skilled men among servants bound for major colonial destinations, 1654–1775*

Place and date of registration, destination	Number of skilled men	Total men	Total servants	Skilled as proportion of: Men (%)	All servants (%)
Bristol, 1654–June 1661					
Barbados	924	1,860	2,430	49.7	38.0
Chesapeake	402	794	1,126	50.6	35.7
Nevis	90	223	267	40.4	33.7
All West Indies	1,033	2,118	2,746	48.8	37.6
All mainland	403	796	1,129	50.6	35.7
Bristol, 1684–86					
Jamaica	76	222	254	34.2	29.9
Barbados	10	48	56	20.8	17.9
Chesapeake	14	60	96	23.3	14.6
All West Indies	88	280	323	31.4	27.2
All mainland	23	88	125	26.1	18.4
Middlesex, 1683–84					
Barbados	77	184	193	41.8	39.9
Jamaica	28	63	81	44.4	34.6
Chesapeake	115	366	487	31.4	23.6
All West Indies	111	269	297	41.3	37.4
All mainland	118	385	514	30.6	23.0
London, 1718–59					
Jamaica	866	1,233	1,263	70.2	68.6
Antigua	53	109	109	48.6	48.6
Chesapeake	533	1,121	1,203	47.5	44.3
Pennsylvania	130	281	318	46.3	40.9
St. Kitts	30	82	82	36.6	36.6
All West Indies	991	1,520	1,560	65.2	63.5
All mainland	713	1,480	1,614	48.2	44.2
London, 1773–75					
Chesapeake	2,361	2,654	2,932	89.0	80.5
Pennsylvania	425	617	671	68.9	63.3
All West Indies	12	12	12	100.0	100.0
All mainland	2,846	3,347	3,685	85.0	77.2

servants bound for Barbados and Jamaica, respectively, than for the Chesapeake in the period.[17] The share of skilled registrants among men bound for Jamaica in London during 1718–59 was 48 percent greater than the skilled share of men bound for the Chesapeake.[18]

The effective skill differences between the servant populations bound for the West Indies and those migrating to the Chesapeake may have been even greater than these comparisons suggest, for two reasons. One is that there was a consistent tendency for the skilled servants bound for the West Indies to be older on average than those bound for the mainland. Thus, pooling all the skilled categories, the mean age of the skilled men bound for West Indian destinations in the Middlesex registrations of 1683–4 was 24.3 years, whereas that of those bound for the mainland was 23.7. The mean age of skilled men bound for the West Indies in the London sample of 1718–59 was 22.9, compared with 21.9 for those bound for the mainland.[19] The significance of these age differentials may have been considerable for men concentrated in the late teens and early twenties, ages at which productivity was rising rapidly for those in skilled trades.[20] The skilled servants bound for the West Indies may therefore have been significantly more productive on average than those classed as skilled who migrated to the mainland.

The second possible source of understatement in the above comparisons of the skill composition of servants by region of destination results from the neglect to this point of female servants. Women bound as servants were virtually always registered in England without occupational descriptions. Little evidence is available on the jobs female servants performed in the colonies, but it is likely that some worked in the fields, while some worked in household occupations.[21] The typical relative proportions in the two types of work are not known, nor is it clear whether most of the latter jobs would be classified as skilled or unskilled. It does seem likely that on average the women bound for a given destination at any time would have been less skilled than the men. If this was the case, the fact noted earlier in this chapter that, in comparison with men, women were always disproportionately bound for mainland rather than West Indian destinations would imply that the comparisons presented above based on an analysis of the skill differentials of male servants bound for the two regions would understate the true skill differentials that existed in total servant flows. Although incomplete evidence concerning the possible skills of the women makes firm estimates impossible, upper-bound estimates of the effect of including women are presented in Table 6.6; the final column of the table shows the share of skilled men in total servants bound for each destination under the assumption that all female servants were unskilled. In some cases the possible effects resulting from the inclusion of women are considerable. In the Bristol registrations of 1654–61, the share of the skilled among all registrants for Barbados now becomes 6 percent greater than the share of the skilled among those bound for the Chesapeake. In the pooled registrations of the 1680s, the share of Jamaica's registrants made up of skilled servants is now 40 percent greater than that of the Chesapeake's, and the share of Barbados' registrants who had skills is fully 58 percent greater than that of the Chesapeake's. In the

London registrations of 1718–59, Jamaica's skilled share rises to 55 percent greater than that of the Chesapeake's.[22] It must of course be kept in mind that these are upper-bound estimates of the skill differences of servant flows to the two regions that could result from the inclusion of women in the analysis, and therefore may overstate the true effect. Yet it does appear likely that the disproportionate numbers of women bound for the mainland throughout the colonial period would have tended to lower the skilled share of all servants bound for the mainland in comparison with the West Indies.[23]

The number and distribution over time of the indentured servant registrations on which this investigation is based make them useful both in describing the changing distribution of the servant population among the colonies between the middle of the seventeenth century and the third quarter of the eighteenth and in indicating the typical differences between the servants bound for different destinations. The registrations suggest that over time the principal destinations of servants in the West Indies changed, as first Barbados, then Nevis, and finally Jamaica left the market for servants, so that by the 1770s the region had virtually ceased to import English servants. In contrast, on the mainland a single area, the Chesapeake colonies of Maryland and Virginia, remained the most important destination for servants throughout the whole period covered by the registrations, with Pennsylvania also becoming an importer on a significant scale in the early eighteenth century.

The characteristics of the servant populations bound for West Indian and mainland destinations differed considerably. Throughout the period covered by the registrations, servants migrating to the West Indies were disproportionately made up of males, whereas females tended to be bound for the mainland. From at least the 1680s through the middle of the eighteenth century, the men who went to the West Indies were older on average than those bound for the mainland. In the same period, men who migrated to the West Indies were also more likely to have some occupational skills than men who went to the mainland.

The principal remaining task of this study is to explain these patterns. This will be done through an exploration of the labor markets that produced them. The analysis will be carried out in two parts. The first, which examines the market for indentured servants that linked Britain and the American colonies, involves the isolation and investigation of some of the principal factors influencing the demand for, and supply of, servants. The second part will then consider the colonial labor market as a whole, in order to place the role of the indenture system in perspective. The central issue will be the interaction of indentured labor with free and slave labor. Analysis of this will focus on the similarities and differences between the three types, including a consideration of both the conditions under which substitution was possible between them and the degree to which the factors identified as important influences in the market for servants had similar or differential effects in the markets for the other types of labor available to the colonial economy.

7

The market for indentured servants

Indentured servitude and the market evaluation of human capital

Indentured servitude was a credit system under which human labor was leased. It functioned through two markets linked by a recruiting agent. In England, in the first market, a prospective servant signed a contract, or "indenture," with a merchant, promising to serve the latter or his assigns in a particular colony for a given period under stated conditions. The servant was then transported to the specified colonial destination, where the merchant or his representative sold his contract to a colonial planter or farmer in the second market. In return for the commitment of his labor, the servant received passage to the designated colony, maintenance during the term of the contract, and certain freedom dues at its conclusion. Once signed, the indenture was negotiable property, and at any time before its conclusion the servant could be sold to a new master for the balance of his term. When the contract expired, the servant became free. The conditions of servitude were regulated by colonial statutes as well as by specific agreements written into the contracts. The terms of the contract were binding upon both master and servant.

The indenture system normally operated within a context of competitive markets in both England and the colonies. In the colonies, the sale of servants was usually done on shipboard shortly after arrival in port. The sales were open to all comers, as servants were generally sold individually to colonial merchants or more often directly to the planters who needed workers to grow their crops or to do the skilled work of their plantations.[1]

The presence of large numbers of recruiting entrepreneurs in the major ports made the British market for indentures highly competitive as well. At least 2,871 different recruiters are listed in the servant registrations made in Bristol during 1654–86; the names of 208 and 399 different individuals appear in the lists made in Middlesex and London, respectively, during the 1680s; and 170 recruiters appear in the contracts registered in London during 1718–59. The trade in servants was a natural one for merchants who imported sugar, tobacco, rice, and other agricultural products from the colonies to engage in, for servants could be exchanged directly for colonial produce. The servant trade was basically a return haul operation, yet it was apparently a relatively lucrative one to English shippers involved in the colonial trade.[2] As a result, merchants competed actively for recruits. There were no legal barriers to entry into the trade, and for merchants or captains already engaged in the colonial trade, economic barriers to entry were small, for the additional investment required to indenture and transport servants was not great.[3]

The colonial planter's demand for indentured servants was based on his calculation of the discounted value of their net future earnings, after deducting the expected costs of the servant to him. The present value of the servant to the planter therefore depended upon the expected value of the servant's output in each year of the contract, the expected costs of maintenance, supervision, and training for the servant during each year of the term, the discount rate, and the value of the freedom dues to be paid to the servant. The expected value of the servant's output depended not only on the planter's estimate of the servant's productivity and expectations of the future prices of the goods he produced, but also on the probability of the servant's surviving and remaining in the master's service in each year of the term. The determinants of the value of a servant to a master are the same basic considerations that enter into the derivation of a free worker's age–wealth profile.[4] Yet the difference in institutions meant that whereas for free workers evidence on flows of income and costs is used to calculate the implied values of capital stocks, in the case of servants these calculations were performed by planters, who based their demand for stocks of bound labor for fixed terms on their calculations involving the relevant flows of earnings and costs. Therefore, like the slave market, the market for indentured labor produced explicit capital values, and the flows underlying these must be inferred.

The institutional arrangements that provided for the ownership of human capital for discrete periods also produced potential differences between the patterns of human capital values under indentured servitude and those implicit in the operation of free labor markets. An advantage of the indenture system to the planter relative to the hiring of free workers was the greater degree of control it gave him over the servant's time and effort once the bargain was made. Because the servant would have been compensated for his loss of freedom, in the absence of uncertainty the price of indentured human capital would have been higher than that of free workers.[5] In practice, however, uncertainty makes the direction of the inequality between these prices unpredictable without additional information, for it cannot be determined a priori whether the insurance value of the contracts was normally greater to the planter or the servant.[6]

There were a number of potentially variable dimensions to the contracts. These included the length of the term for which the servant was bound and the amount of freedom dues he was to receive. Provisions could be inserted into the contracts for cash payments to be made to the servant, either as an initial lump sum or as a salary during the course of the contract. Restrictions might also be placed on the kind of work the servant could be required to perform. The determination of these variables should have depended on the servant's expected net productivity in the colonies: the higher the individual's productivity, ceteris paribus, potentially the shorter the term, the higher the freedom dues, the higher the probability of cash payments – and the larger their amount – and the more favorable the working conditions.

The indenture was the outcome of a process of bargaining between the prospective servant and a recruiter competing with other merchants for the servant's business. There is evidence that many potential servants were sufficiently well informed about currently available offers that they refused to accept inferior bargains.[7] All servants who migrated to America incurred debts of similar value. Contemporary fare quotations indicate that the charges for passage from England to America were uniform at a given time for all individuals and did not vary by specific colonial destination, and maintenance costs and freedom dues varied little across individuals.[8] As a result, every servant contract was a promise to repay approximately the same sum of money. Therefore the present discounted value of every servant's contract should have been approximately the same at the time of binding. Because the productivity of servants varied, the conditions of their indentures had to vary. The higher the servant's marginal value product above the cost of his maintenance, the faster he could repay the loan made to him, and the shorter the term of the contract. The length of indenture across servants should therefore have been negatively correlated with individual productivity, or equivalently, with the market valuation of the current flow of income generated by the individual's stock of human capital.

Strictly, if costs had been precisely the same for all servants, all should have been bound on conditions that would yield the same expected price on arrival in the colonies. This of course does not imply that no variation should have occurred in the realized auction prices of servants in the colonies, for random disturbances between the time of binding and auction – such as illnesses of servants during the voyage, or changes in the prices of colonial outputs – could have produced differences between actual and expected prices. What the analysis does imply, however, is that if the market for contracts of servitude was efficient, variation in servants' auction prices should have been uncorrelated with all the characteristics of the servants that were known at the time of making the indenture bargain in England.[9]

Very little evidence of the prices of newly arrived servants at colonial auctions has survived: From the entire colonial period the only known complete records of auctions of English servants come from the accounts of two ships, the *Tristam and Jeane,* which sold 68 servants in Virginia in late 1636 or early 1637, and the *Abraham,* which sold 56 servants in Barbados in January 1637.[10] Although there was a substantial range in the prices paid for individual servants from both ships, the listings of the amounts paid for the servant show that both the median and modal prices of both men and women were identical – 500 pounds of tobacco – in both auctions.[11] Thus, although as will be seen both sex and colonial destination had a significant effect on the length of servants' indentures, the available evidence, although limited, suggests that neither may have affected the initial colonial auction prices of the servants. This is consistent with the hypothesis that the variable dimensions of the contract were adjusted in view of the servants' characteristics so as to make the expected auction prices of all servants the same.

A comparison of the auction prices of servants with the simple cost of passage reveals relatively little difference between them. The modal price of 500 pounds of tobacco observed in the auctions was 11 percent greater than the fare two free passengers each paid for passage to Virginia on the *Tristam and Jeane* on the same voyage as the servants, and 4 percent above the fare quoted elsewhere for passage from England to Maryland in 1638.[12] That in these cases the typical auction prices tended to be higher than the fare alone may have been due to the cost of recruiting servants, or to the existence of a premium received by merchants for bearing the risk of servant mortality on the ocean voyage.

Related evidence on the nature of the labor-market equilibrium in the colonies that induced flows of labor from England is available from surviving valuations of indentured servants recorded in Maryland for probate courts. The mean price of twenty-eight male servants with four remaining years of servitude recorded on Maryland's lower western shore during 1704–57 was £8.95, with a median of £9 and a mode of £10, and the mean price of nineteen females with four years remaining was £7.75, with a median of £8 and a mode of £10.[13] The typical marginal cost to an English merchant of delivering servants to the colonies cannot be estimated precisely, but probably fell within a range bounded at the lower end by £5, the usual cost of passage, and at the upper end by the £10 estimated by Abbot Emerson Smith as the maximum expense of delivery.[14] The evidence of the probate valuations, although again limited in quantity, suggests that the central tendency of the colonial price of servants did fall within this range, and therefore offers additional support for the hypothesis that the price of a servant's indenture in the colonies was equal to the marginal cost of delivering labor there from England.

A number of other considerations relating to the adjustment of the bargain deserve mention. One is the role of mortality. The smaller the probability of a servant's surviving a given year of his term, the lower his expected net earnings and, ceteris paribus, the less favorable the terms of the contract he would be able to sign. This is true whether the mortality in question is that during the Atlantic crossing, when the merchant bore the risk, or that after arrival in the colonies, when the planter had purchased the contract and assumed the risk.[15]

A second factor with a similar effect was the possibility of a servant failing to serve out his term for a reason other than death, principally running away. All the colonies enacted legislation intended to discourage servants from running away; of these, some were preventive measures, others punitive. Although some colonies provided for corporal – and even capital – punishment for runaways, the most common penalty was extension of the servant's contract by some multiple of the time he was absent.[16] A standard provision of the contract, the servant's freedom dues, constituted a nonvested pension and therefore also acted to discourage servants from running away. Although the form and worth of the dues varied across colonies and over time, they were often of substantial value, and could have constituted a significant deterrent to servants who considered escaping from their masters.[17]

Servants were not allowed to marry during their terms. Because, by English practice, the expense of raising the illegitimate children of servants fell on the county, colonial legislation provided that the father should be discovered by the oath of the mother, and that he should reimburse the county for the expense of rearing the child until it could be bound out to work. As servants could not normally pay this sum, either the master would pay it and the servant's term would be extended, or the servant would be bound over to the county for an additional period after the conclusion of his normal term, to be sold for the necessary amount. The mother's term was also extended to reimburse the master for her lost working time.

An element nearly always negotiated by the servant and the merchant, the servant's destination, also had a bearing on the other terms of the indenture. Mortality rates were considerably higher in the island colonies, and work conditions harsher, and many servants were willing to accept longer terms in the mainland colonies.[18] It is also possible that "deficiency" legislation, enacted by West Indian colonies to increase the proportion of whites in the population, might have been effective to some extent. The laws took a number of forms. One type attempted to provide cost incentives to merchants to ship servants to the islands. An example is a Jamaican act of 1681 freeing any ship bringing fifty servants from port dues. Another type of act, first used in 1679 in Antigua, attempted to stimulate local demand for servants, either by assessing fines on planters who failed to maintain a minimum ratio of white to black laborers, or by forcing planters to accept servants from the island government at a fixed price.[19] Although the degree of the laws' success was limited, apparently because the size of the incentives they typically provided was not great, both the reduction in merchants' costs and the increase in planters' demand for servants would have had the same tendency in a competitive market, specifically to reduce the terms of servants sent to the islands. The first effect, by lowering costs, would have meant that merchants would indenture servants for a shorter term at a given colonial price, and the second, by raising local prices, that servants would be bound for a shorter term at a given level of costs. Thus the result of both types of act would have been to reduce the terms of servants sent to the West Indies.

Analysis of the length of indenture: empirical results

The principal sources of quantitative evidence bearing on the market for English servants in the American colonies are the servant contracts recorded and held in English courts. The two largest surviving collections, from Middlesex during 1683–4 and London during 1718–59, will be analyzed here.

The principal variable analyzed is the length of the indenture. Furthermore, this analysis is concerned only with the minors in both samples, who comprise 22 percent of the servants with known ages in the earlier, and 67 percent in the later, sample. The selection of the variable to be analyzed and of the sub-sample of the minors follows from consideration of the evidence of the contracts. It is clear that four years was the normal duration of an adult's indenture in both samples, yet for a combination of legal and clerical reasons a full account of all the conditions of adults' servitude does not appear to have been recorded in either set of indentures.[20] For the minors in both samples, however, the full conditions do appear to have been recorded, and the duration of the contract appears to have been the chief variable dimension of the agreements. Provisions for extraordinary freedom dues and restrictions on the servants' occupations in the colonies rarely appear in either collection of contracts. Although it is uncertain whether payments were recorded in all cases in which they were made, less than 7 percent of the contracts in the earlier sample record cash payments for either minors or adults. Cash payments made to adults do not generally appear to have been recorded in the later sample, but the contracts of the minors, in which they appear to have been recorded conscientiously, show that fewer than 6 percent received cash payments. A notable feature of the payments recorded in both samples is that virtually all – 95 percent in the earlier, and 97 percent in the later, sample – were made to servants bound for four years. Insofar as payments

were made (or strictly, promised) and recorded, analysis of the characteristics of the servants who received them reinforces the results obtained
from the analysis of the length of indenture.[21] The evidence of both
samples therefore suggests that for minors the greatest variation in the
conditions of indenture occurred in the duration of the term of servitude,
whereas for adults this was not the case, as four years was both the
standard term for adults and normally the minimum assigned.[22] For
adults, cash payments were apparently substituted for reductions in the
term of servitude below four years.

The analysis presented earlier in this chapter suggested that a servant's
term of indenture would be inversely related to the market valuation of his
stock of human capital. According to the analysis, the length of the term
would therefore constitute an index of the value of the servant's human
capital. This index can be specified as a function of a number of
observable characteristics, provided by the contracts, of the individual
servants and their bargains, which are all potentially relevant to the
determination of the present value of the servant's stock of human capital;
these include the servant's age, sex, literacy, occupation, and colonial
destination. When this relationship is estimated by multiple regression
analysis, the estimating equation differs from the common hedonic method
of price analysis only in the use of an index for price.[23] The estimated
coefficients of the independent variables age, sex, literacy, and occupation
can be interpreted as the marginal prices paid for servants' characteristics
in units of the index, whereas those of destinations represent compensating
differentials between regions.[24]

Table 7.1 presents a number of the basic relationships underlying the
market valuation of human capital in the market for servants. In both
samples the length of indenture was negatively related to both age and
skill; with other things equal, servants with skilled occupations and those
able to sign received shorter terms. Women received shorter terms than
men, ceteris paribus, and servants bound for the West Indies received
shorter terms than those bound for the North American mainland.

A comparison of the estimated coefficients of the sex variable across
samples indicates that on average women received considerably larger
reductions in their terms in the 1680s than in the eighteenth century. The
implied decline in the premium for females is not surprising in view of the
generally declining colonial sex ratios during this period, for while women
may have been preferred for some kinds of household work and light
farming, their increasing relative availability in most colonies would be
expected to lower the size of the implicit wage differentials they
received.[25]

Table 7.2 provides a more detailed analysis of the length of indenture
for the later sample, allowing separate age profiles of the length of

Table 7.1. *Estimated regression coefficients, Middlesex and London samples*

Independent variable	Middlesex, 1683–84		London, 1718–59	
	Estimated coefficient	Standard error	Estimated coefficient	Standard error
Age (years)[a]				
Less than 15	2.655	0.385	2.749	0.134
15	2.201	0.400	2.147	0.080
16	1.457	0.304	1.304	0.068
17	0.893	0.367	0.728	0.062
18	0.174	0.270	0.331	0.055
19	0.738	0.306	0.169	0.050
Sex[b]	−1.484	0.207	−0.195	0.073
Literacy[c]	−0.575	0.217	−0.082	0.037
Date[d]			−0.0060	0.0023
Trade[e]	−0.727	0.445		
Farmer[f]			−0.313	0.074
Laborer			−0.146	0.079
Services			−0.348	0.066
Metal and construction[g]			−0.320	0.067
Clothing and textiles			−0.313	0.060
Antigua[h]	−0.227	0.812	−0.403	0.110
Barbados	−0.553	0.274	−0.176	0.154
Jamaica	−0.398	0.462	−0.233	0.060
Other West Indies[i]	−0.401	1.094	−0.479	0.088
Maryland	0.203	0.209	0.306	0.059
Virginia			0.127	0.073
Other mainland[j]	−0.389	0.673	0.050	0.116
Constant	5.227		4.665	
R^2	0.555		0.539	
F	12.87		112.82	
N	171		2,049	

Note: Dependent variable: number of years indentured; method of estimation: ordinary least squares.
[a]For age variable, indicated age = 1; zero class = age 20. [b]Male =0, female = 1. [c]Marked = 0, signed =1. [d]Date entered as final two digits of year of registration. [e]Trade = 0 for laborers and no recorded occupations; trade = 1 for all other men's occupations. [f]For all occupational variables, indicated occupation(s) = 1; zero class = no recorded occupation. [g]Includes metal and wood and building and construction. [h]For all destination variables, for Middlesex sample, zero class = Virginia; for London sample, zero class = Pennsylvania. [i]Includes Nevis, St. Christopher, etc. [j]Includes Carolina, New York, etc.
Source: Data used are all records of minors (age less than 21). For full references to the Middlesex and London samples, see Appendix A.

Table 7.2. *Estimated regression coefficients,*
London sample, 1718–59

Independent variable	Estimated coefficient	Standard error
Age (years)		
Less than 15	2.976	0.144
15	2.378	0.092
16	1.542	0.084
17	0.959	0.084
18	0.473	0.079
19	0.260	0.083
Women, age[a]		
Less than 15	−1.034	0.460
15	−0.472	0.390
16	−0.969	0.228
17	−0.302	0.161
18	0.041	0.159
19	0.090	0.135
20	0.198	0.156
Trade, age[b]		
15	−1.496	0.392
16	−0.884	0.206
17	−0.502	0.117
18	−0.275	0.085
19	−0.224	0.073
20	−0.103	0.076
Literacy	−0.076	0.036
Date	−0.0093	0.0024
Antigua[c]	−0.260	0.235
Barbados	−0.005	0.268
Jamaica	−0.084	0.209
Other West Indies	−0.363	0.221
Maryland	0.194	0.063
Other mainland	−0.039	0.072
February[d]	−0.100	0.092
March	0.171	0.113
April	0.156	0.119
May	−0.095	0.164
June	−0.431	0.132
July	−0.196	0.113
August	−0.486	0.098
September	−0.223	0.096
October	−0.400	0.101
November	−0.225	0.100
December	0.014	0.097

Table 7.2. *(cont.)*

Independent variable	Estimated coefficient	Standard error
West Indies, month[e]		
January	0.095	0.160
February	0.089	0.165
March	−0.328	0.180
April	−0.073	0.218
May	0.069	0.233
June	0.383	0.225
July	0.196	0.175
August	0.500	0.154
September	0.003	0.161
October	0.376	0.151
November	0.293	0.148
Sugar[f]	−0.0162	0.0074
Constant	4.830	
R^2	0.566	
F	52.06	
N	2,044	

Note: Dependent variable: number of years indentured; method of estimation: ordinary least squares.
[a]Female-age interactions: indicated variable = 1 for women of given age.
[b]Trade-age interactions: indicated variable = 1 for men of given age who recorded a trade (as defined in Table 7.1).
[c]For destinations, zero class = Virginia.
[d]For months, zero class = January.
[e]West Indies–month interactions: indicated variable = 1 for servants bound for West Indies in given month. The coefficient of the interaction term between West Indies and December could not be estimated because of colinearity with the other independent variables.
[f]Sugar = average annual price of muscovado sugar in London, in shillings per hundredweight, lagged one year, for servants bound for West Indies.
Source: Richard B. Sheridan, *Sugar and Slavery: An Economic History of the British West Indies, 1623–1775* (Barbados, 1974), pp. 496–7, with linear interpolation of 1717–20 and 1727.
All other variables defined as in Table 7.1.

indenture by sex and skill. It reveals that whereas there was a tendency for women to receive indentures from 5 to 15 percent shorter than those of men through the age of 17, for servants aged 18 to 20 there was no statistically significant difference in the length of term by sex. In a suggestive parallel result, Robert Fogel and Stanley Engerman have found that, excluding the value of childbearing, the net earnings of female slaves in the nineteenth-century South were greater than those of men under the age of 18, apparently as a result of the more rapid physical maturation of women.[26] The sex differentials in the terms of young indentured servants might have resulted from the same source.

The results of Table 7.1 indicate that premiums for skills were reflected in the length of servants' indentures: In both samples, with other things equal, servants identified as possessing skilled trades and those able to sign their contracts received reductions in their terms. The more detailed specification of the occupations presented in Table 7.1 for the London sample[27] indicates that the marginal premium paid for servants in each of four occupational categories – farmers, service occupations, metal and construction crafts, and clothing and textile trades – was virtually the same.[28] That skilled artisans were more highly valued than other servants is not surprising in view of the abundance of contemporary testimony to this effect. An example appears in a letter sent in 1676 by Christopher Jeaffreson of St. Kitts to his cousin in London: "If you can procure me a carpenter or two, and one or two masons, they will bee very serviceable . . . I pray you hearken out for such, and for a joyner, Such servants are as golde in these partes."[29] Agricultural skills could equally be prized, as in 1761 Samuel Martin wrote from Antigua to his English merchants that "I am in great want of English servts who are bred to husbandry for they make ye best planters."[30] Unskilled laborers received terms longer than servants with skilled occupations, but shorter than those with no recorded occupations;[31] the latter result may indicate that some premium was paid for the laborers' work experience.

Economists have devoted considerable attention to the analysis of the relationship between productivity and age, and have accumulated much evidence on the association between age and wages in recent periods. Less is known of the nature of this relation in past times. It is therefore of some interest to consider in more detail the implications of the estimated relationships between age and length of indenture for the age/earnings profiles of servants.[32] Table 7.3 presents estimates of the relative annual net earnings of servants by age for unskilled and skilled men in the London registrations of 1718–59. The calculations are based on the assumption that the expected colonial sale price of each individual's contract was equal to the constant marginal cost of delivering servants to the colonies.[33] The relationship between age and net earnings is assumed to have been

Table 7.3. *Estimated relative net annual earnings of servants by age, 1718–59*

	Unskilled			Skilled	
Age	Mean net annual earnings	Relative net earnings (age 22.9 = 1.00)	Age	Mean net annual earnings	Relative net earnings (age 22.9 = 1.00)
19.1	£2.01	.742	18.4	£2.39	.413
19.7	2.20	.812	19.2	2.86	.495
20.4	2.36	.871	20.1	3.32	.574
21.2	2.52	.930	21.0	4.08	.706
22.0	2.60	.959	21.9	4.22	.730
22.9	2.71	1.000	22.9	5.78	1.000

Source: Calculated from Table 7.2 and note 34, chapter 7. See text for procedure. The unskilled profile is calculated from the basic age profile of Table 7.2, that of the skilled from the basic age profile combined with the skilled ("trade") coefficients.

linear, making average net productivity during the term equal to net productivity at the term's midpoint. The estimates of average net productivity are derived from the following formulation of the mean present value of the contracts of servants of age a at the beginning of the term:

$$PV_a = \sum_{j=1}^{n_a} \frac{NP_j - w_j}{(1 + r)^j}$$

where NP = expected mean annual net productivity during the term; n_a = mean length of term for servants entering indentures at age a; w = mean annual wage payments made to servants during the term; and r = discount rate. To solve for the value of NP for each entering cohort, the mean present value of the contracts was set equal to £10, an estimate of the marginal cost of delivering servants to the colonies. The mean age of each group at the time of binding was taken as the recorded age plus one-half year to allow for the rounding of age upon registration. The mean length of term by age was derived from the coefficients of Table 7.2, and the mean annual wage payments for skilled servants were taken directly from the indenture contracts.[34] The estimates were made with a discount rate of 10 percent.

The estimates of Table 7.3, which indicate that the net-earnings profile of skilled servants was steeper than that of the unskilled, are consistent with the normal positive relationship between the steepness of age/earnings profiles and investment in training.[35] The ages at which the servants considered here were bound, between 15 and 20, were prime

108

ones for training in a wide variety of skilled crafts in preindustrial England, through either apprenticeship or less formal arrangements. It is therefore not surprising that the net productivity of those in skilled trades rose rapidly during this period of the life cycle.

Skilled servants received a considerable premium at every age: Even at 15, a skilled servant received a term 21 percent shorter on average than his unskilled counterpart. The existence of a sizable premium at such an early age could have been due in part to differences in the relative average work experience of the skilled and unskilled. Thus possession of a skilled trade at any age implied prior work experience. The age of entry into the labor force for those men registered without occupations cannot be determined, but it is possible that the typical age of entry for the unskilled into employment was that at which English boys normally left home to live in service, roughly 15. If this were the case, work experience and acquired on-the-job training might have accounted for a significant portion of the premium for skilled workers. This would particularly be true for the younger servants, as the relative level of work experience of a skilled to an unskilled worker would be greatest at the lower ages observed here, and would decline with age thereafter. That the ratio of skilled to unskilled net earnings increased with age would appear to be strong evidence of the presence of formal training for those in the skilled group.

An interesting feature of the relative age/net-earnings profile of the unskilled shown in Table 7.3 is its close resemblance to those obtained by Fogel and Engerman for unskilled male slaves in the southern United States during 1790–1860.[36] In view of the considerable differences between these samples with respect to such variables as the location of the workers and the crops they cultivated, the similarity of the shapes of the profiles might suggest the importance of physiological factors, particularly the rate of physical maturation, in determining the change in the productivity of unskilled workers with age under conditions of plantation agriculture in the eighteenth and nineteenth centuries.

The relatively small premium paid for the ability to sign in the later sample may have been due to both the abundance of literate servants and high literacy rates in the colonies. Christopher Jeaffreson had written from St. Kitts as early as 1681 that he would give wages to servants who were skilled craftsmen, then added: "For one that can handle his pen, – he may deserve as much, but wee seldome give it, because such men are more plenty."[37] The decline in the size of the reduction of the term deriving from the ability to sign between the dates of the two samples, from about seven months on average to only one month, may have resulted in part from a considerable increase in literacy among the servants, as only 35 percent signed their contracts in the earlier sample compared with 67 percent in the later one.[38]

In both samples, with individual characteristics constant, servants bound for the West Indies tended to receive shorter terms than those bound for mainland colonies. The differences could be considerable. In the 1680s the estimated marginal difference in the term of a servant bound for Barbados rather than Maryland was nine months, and the difference between Antigua and Maryland in the eighteenth century, with the price of sugar at its mean for the period, was more than eight months. That servants who emigrated to the West Indies received shorter terms to compensate them for their choice is consistent with the fact that both working conditions for servants and economic opportunities for freedmen were known to be poor in the islands after the introduction of large-scale sugar cultivation in the second half of the seventeenth century, with its attendant gang labor and consolidation of small farms into large estates, whereas the mainland long continued to be thought of as a land of opportunity for poor immigrants, where freed servants could hope to own land and become prosperous members of society. Thus, for example, in 1683 Christopher Jeaffreson wrote in regard to the chronic difficulty of obtaining servants for the West Indies that "Carolina and Pennsylvania are the refuge of the sectaries, and are in such repute, that men are more easily induced to be transported thither than to the Islands."[39] A persistent theme of West Indian complaints appeared in a 1675 petition sent to the King of England by the Council and Assembly of Barbados: "In former tymes Wee were plentifully furnished with Christian [i.e., white] servants from England . . . but now Wee can gett few English, haveing noe Lands to give them at the end of their tyme, which formerly was theire main allurement."[40] The higher mortality rates of the West Indian colonies decreased their servants' expected productivity and made servants reluctant to go to the region, but in conjunction with the high productivity of labor in sugar production acted to raise the demand for new flows of replacement immigrant labor. That servants bound for the West Indies received terms shorter than those bound for the mainland in spite of the higher mortality rates in the islands implies that in both the periods covered by these samples the marginal productivity of labor was higher in the West Indies than in the mainland colonies. With the servant's choice of destination capable of accounting for such large differences in the length of indenture, there can be little surprise at Abbot Emerson Smith's finding, concerning prospective English emigrants' knowledge of available bargains, that "most striking of all evidences is that which shows servants preferring one colony over another."[41] These were not casual preferences, for their cost to many servants was high.

Both the decline in the intercept between samples and the estimated negative time trend of the later sample indicate a secular decline in the length of indenture. The direction of change is consistent with a number of long-term trends, including rising reservation wages of servants resulting from rising real wages in England between the mid-1680s and the middle of the eighteenth century, falling real shipping costs, and declining colonial mortality rates, which could have produced a secular increase in the colonial demand for labor.[42] The negative estimated trend in the length of indenture further indicates the presence of a secular increase in real wages in the colonies during the period spanned by these two samples.

Some seasonal patterns in the length of indenture appear in the results of Table 7.2. For the West Indies, the results suggest that, other things being equal, servants bound in March received considerably shorter terms than those bound in the later summer and fall. Servants bound for the mainland – most of whom were destined for Maryland or Virginia – whose indentures were signed between June and November received sizable reductions in their terms relative to servants bound in winter and spring. In both cases the observed seasonal effects on the length of indenture may have been related to the sugar and tobacco regions' respective calendars of staple crop production. The seasonality of production could have affected not only the colonial demand for labor, but also the costs involved in supplying servant labor in the colonies. The shipping patterns resulting from the timing of the harvests dictated that the greatest amount of backhaul space was available for servants bound for the West Indies in the winter and spring, and for those bound for the Chesapeake colonies in the summer and early fall. As servants were provided with food and lodging from the time they signed their contracts, the costs of delivering a servant to the colonies may have declined in peak shipping seasons because the more frequent departures of ships reduced the average waiting time in port between binding and sailing. The lower costs of the peak seasons could therefore have resulted in shorter indentures for servants bound in peak seasons than for those bound in slack shipping months.[43]

Another potential source of variation in the length of indenture was annual changes in the colonial demand for labor. The results presented in Table 7.2 indicate that the lagged annual average price of muscovado sugar in London had a significant and negative effect on the length of indentures of servants bound for the West Indies during 1718–59; the estimated effect of a change in the price of sugar from its minimum to its maximum in the period with other things equal was a reduction of about five months in the term of indenture. The sign of this effect would be the one predicted if, as appears to have been the case, high sugar prices normally resulted from high levels of demand for sugar rather than reductions in supply, for high sugar prices would then have tended to produce high demand for labor and, ceteris paribus, to shorten terms.[44]

Migration and the transatlantic market for servants

The price paid for human capital in the colonial American market for indentured servants varied systematically with respect to factors that influenced the productivity of the servants. All servants incurred debts of similar value in emigrating to the colonies and sold claims on their future labor, in the form of indentures, to repay these debts. Characteristics that raised the expected productivity of servants in the American colonies raised the market valuation of their human capital, and therefore shortened the term for which the servant was bound. Thus servants with skilled trades and those able to sign received shorter terms than the unskilled and illiterate of similar age and sex. Women were found to have received shorter terms than men until the age of 18, perhaps because of their earlier physical maturation. The results also indicated that servants bound for the West Indies received shorter terms in compensation for their undesirable destinations. Servants bound during peak shipping seasons were found to have received reduced terms, perhaps as a result of shorter average waiting time prior to departure in those months when return-haul cargo space was most abundant. Finally, the length of the indentures of servants bound for the West Indies was found to have varied inversely with the price of sugar, suggesting that increases in the colonial demand for labor shortened the term of servitude.

The estimates presented in this chapter provide concrete evidence about the nature of the choices prospective servants faced when considering whether to leave England as bound emigrants. The estimated coefficients of the independent variables are in this sense the prices servants paid, in years and months of servitude, for their decisions to travel to America, as well as for such related choices as when to go and where to serve.

The present research has also indicated that the outcomes produced by the market for indentured servants are consistent with the implications derived from the analysis of identifiable economic forces operating within the context of a competitive market for servants. The success achieved both by the regression analysis of the length of indenture presented in this chapter and by the parallel analysis of cash payments made to servants presented in Appendix F provides considerable support for the contention that servants in these samples typically entered indenture contracts voluntarily, by bargaining individually with merchants. The results indicate that merchants adjusted the term of service for minors, and the size of cash payments for adults, in view of the cost of transportation to America and the price the servant was expected to bring in the colonies. If coercion had played an important part in the recruiting process, merchants would have had no need to give more valuable servants preferable bargains in the form of wages or shorter terms; that they did so indicates that they lacked the ability to force all servants into uniformly long terms.

112

One reason for this inability was clearly the competition among large numbers of English merchants for recruits.

The results of this investigation therefore indicate that many indentured servants were among the earliest of the stream of immigrants who came voluntarily from the Old World to the New. Although the institutional arrangements of the indenture system were different than those surrounding the immigration of free Europeans to colonial America, the same is not necessarily true of the servants' motives. Though some of the hardships they faced may have been different, the potential rewards were much the same for servants as for other European immigrants. The samples analyzed here represent only a small part of the total servant migration, but the results obtained from them nonetheless suggest that the indenture system may have played such an important role in the economic history of colonial British America because many English men and women were content, in the prophetic words of Sir George Peckham in 1583, to hazard their lives and serve for a term without wages "in hope thereby to amend theyr estates."[45]

Part IV

White servitude in the colonial labor market

8

The role of the indenture system
in the colonial labor market

The problem

The principal remaining task of this study is to place the indenture system in perspective as a source of labor to the colonial economy. This will be done in two stages. The first, contained in this chapter, delineates the role of the indenture system in the labor market of the British American colonies and indicates the changes that occurred in its function over time. This investigation will show that the indenture system began as a supplier of unskilled labor, but that in most colonies it did not retain this function throughout the colonial period. In areas in which slavery came into use on a significant scale the role of the indenture system changed, as slaves were initially used in unskilled field work and servants were increasingly purchased primarily to provide skilled and supervisory labor. As the slave economies of the plantation colonies continued to grow, slaves were trained to fill many of these skilled and managerial positions, and the indenture system tended to decline further in importance. This evolution did not begin at the same time in all the colonies where it occurred, nor did it proceed everywhere at the same pace, and one of the purposes of this chapter is to provide evidence on the differences between colonies with respect to the timing of the growth and decline of the indenture system.

The second stage of this overview, presented in the following chapter, explores the forces that shaped the role of the indenture system in the colonial economy. This will include a consideration not only of the causes of the change just mentioned in the functions of the indenture system in certain colonies, but also of the more general issue of why the indenture system became important in some colonies and not in others. The analysis of Chapter 9 attempts to isolate the principal factors responsible for the observed patterns of labor use in the colonial economy, considering both differences across colonies and changes over time in particular colonies, by providing an explanatory framework with which to analyze the evidence produced by this and other investigations.

White servitude in the colonial labor market

Quantitative aspects of the composition of colonial labor forces

Because of the central importance of the growth of slavery to the evolution of the indenture system, a useful first step in describing the basic patterns of colonial labor-force composition[1] is to indicate when and where slavery developed in British America. The composition of colonial populations by race can be used both to gauge the extent of each colony's reliance on slavery at a particular time and to indicate the timing of changes in that extent over time.[2] There is a uniform set of population estimates for the British mainland colonies by decade from 1610, which contains separate decennial series for total and Negro population by colony.[3] There is a separate but similar set of estimates for the British West Indian colonies from 1650.[4] Based on these two collections Tables 8.1 and 8.2 show, for major British colonies or regions, estimates of the composition of population by race, expressed as the proportion of blacks in the total population.

The patterns shown for the mainland colonies are distinct and familiar. New England consistently had the lowest share of blacks, never above 3 percent of total population, with little tendency for the proportion to change over time. The Middle Colonies had higher proportions of blacks: New York–New Jersey had roughly 10 percent after the mid-seventeenth century, and Pennsylvania–Delaware had a somewhat lower, and declining share. The Chesapeake colonies of Maryland and Virginia experienced a rapid increase in black population in the late seventeenth century, rising to about a quarter of total population by 1710 and nearly two-fifths by 1750. South Carolina had the highest share of blacks of any of the mainland colonies for most of its history, as more than half its population was made up of blacks after the early eighteenth century.

A strong and again familiar common pattern also appears in the West Indian population figures. The estimates do not begin in every case in the earliest stages of the growth of the black population, but for Barbados and St. Kitts start at a point when slavery was well established and the share of the black population was rising rapidly. Most of the islands are seen to rise from black shares of about one-quarter or less in the mid-seventeenth century to levels of roughly two-thirds or more by the turn of the eighteenth century, with continuing growth producing black shares of around 90 percent in nearly every colony by the middle of the century.

These population figures show the basic differences that existed between colonies and the changes that occurred over time in particular colonies in the relative importance of stocks of white and black population, and by implication labor;[5] but the indenture system must also be considered in relation to the flows of immigrants to the colonies. Information on these flows can be derived from the stock population figures:

118

Table 8.1. *Proportion of blacks in total population, major colonies or regions: mainland (in percent)*

Years	New England[a]	New York and New Jersey	Pennsylvania and Delaware	Maryland and Virginia	North Carolina	South Carolina	Georgia
1630	0	3		2			
1640	1	12		2			
1650	2	12	8	3			
1660	2	12	6	5			
1670	1	11	6	7	2	15	
1680	1	11	5	7	4	17	
1690	1	10	3	15	4	38	
1700	2	9	3	22	4	43	
1710	2	10	7	26	6	38	
1720	2	12	7	25	14	70	
1730	3	12	3	23	20	67	
1740	3	12	3	28	21	67	0
1750	3	11	3	39	27	61	19
1760	3	11	3	38	30	61	37
1770	3	10	3	39	35	61	45

[a]Includes Maine, New Hampshire, Vermont, Plymouth, Massachusetts, Rhode Island, and Connecticut.
Source: U.S. Bureau of Census, *Historical Statistics of the United States, Colonial Times to 1970* (Washington, D.C., 1975), Series Z1-19, Part 2, p. 1168.

Table 8.2. *Proportion of blacks in total population, major colonies or regions: West Indies (in percent)*

Year	Antigua	Barbados	Jamaica	Montserrat	Nevis	St. Kitts
1650	0	30		3	9	28
1660	20	51	13	9	24	35
1670	28	64	47	24	20	35
1680	56	69	67	51	55	58
1690	72	73	79	58	66	57
1700	79	76	85	65	77	60
1710	82	80	89	70	77	82
1720	84	77	92	69	81	73
1730	87	78	93	83	84	81
1740	88	80	95	83	88	86
1750	90	82	95	86	90	89
1760	92	83	95	87	88	90
1770	93	84	94	88	85	92

Source: John J. McCusker, "The Rum Trade and the Balance of Payments of the Thirteen Continental Colonies, 1650–1775" (Ph.D. diss., University of Pittsburgh, 1970), Tables B-84, B-86, B-87, B-88, B-89, B-91; pp. 692, 694, 695, 696, 697, 699.

Net migration is estimated as a residual when natural increase is subtracted from the change of population between two dates. Decennial estimates of net white and black migration by colony between 1650 and 1780 are presented in Appendix H together with a more detailed description of the estimation process and the evidence on which it is based. Although the resulting estimates are rough, and are intended as no more than preliminary suggestions of the volume of black and white immigration to colonial America, they do provide indications of the major patterns and trends in migration. The estimates are generally consistent with our current knowledge of the magnitudes of both black and white migration to the colonies of British America, and constitute a useful quantitative basis for the purposes of this discussion.

An indication of the quantitative importance of the immigrant flows is given by Tables 8.3 and 8.4, which present the estimates of total white and black net migration for each colony by decade, expressed as a proportion of the colony's population at the beginning of the relevant decade. Although the figures fluctuate somewhat, they do provide a basis for some generalizations. The most striking of these is the persistently greater importance of immigration relative to existing population for the West Indies than for the mainland colonies throughout the colonial period after 1650. Within the mainland colonies, throughout the colonial period there was also a persistent tendency for immigration to be greatest relative to existing stocks of population in the southern colonies, with the magnitudes for New England consistently lower than for the Middle Colonies.

Table 8.3. *Total net migration by decade, as proportion of colony's total population at beginning of decade: mainland (in percent)*

Years	New England	New York and New Jersey	Pennsylvania and Delaware	Maryland and Virginia	North Carolina	South Carolina	Georgia
1650–60	14	−8	143	81			
1660–70	24	7	1	52	327		
1670–80	3	58	98	34	50	546	
1680–90	−2	32	558	27	42	237	
1690–1700	−20	19	25	10	37	42	
1700–10	−3	−2	8	33	37	88	
1710–20	18	29	1	23	37	53	
1720–30	−1	1	43	29	37	73	
1730–40	5	5	40	29	56	34	
1740–50	−3	1	11	10	25	27	139
1750–60	−3	13	16	6	22	18	52
1760–70	−1	4	−1	1	47	4	107
1770–80	−5	−3	6	−7	8	16	103

Source: See Appendix H.

Table 8.4. *Total net migration by decade, as proportion of colony's total population at beginning of decade: West Indies (in percent)*

Decade	Antigua	Barbados	Jamaica	Montserrat	Nevis	St. Kitts
1650–60	281	113		37	142	177
1660–70	129	64	427	5	−11	−22
1670–80	184	46	143	323	106	49
1680–90	138	41	108	38	40	30
1690– 1700	140	68	108	76	76	53
1700–10	77	39	85	42	3	358
1710–20	92	62	79	44	81	−18
1720–30	61	51	72	113	45	158
1730–40	33	34	43	5	25	40
1740–50	46	33	53	47	47	34
1750–60	41	35	48	54	40	35
1760–70	21	17	32	19	20	15
1770–80	8	1	38	5	18	17

Source: See Appendix H.

Information about the composition of these flows of immigration is given by Tables 8.5 and 8.6, which show the share of black net migration as a proportion of total net decennial migration by colony. Very similar patterns appear between these shares and those just examined for the relative importance of total net migration. Blacks consistently made up a larger share of net migration to the West Indies than to the mainland colonies, and within the mainland group the share of blacks in total migration tended to be greatest for the southern colonies.

What the immigration estimates therefore suggest is that it was the colonies that had the largest flows of new immigrants relative to their existing population that relied most heavily on black immigration. The most extreme cases of high levels of immigration and large shares of slaves among the immigrants occurred in the British West Indies, with clear evidence of a similar dependence on blacks in the southern colonies that had the largest relative flows of immigrants on the mainland. In contrast, the northern and middle mainland colonies generally had both relatively low rates of net immigration relative to their existing populations after the mid-seventeenth century and low proportions of this immigration made up of blacks. The strong positive association across colonial regions between the quantitative importance of immigration and the share of blacks in these flows is one of the most basic and important facts about the colonial labor market. This pattern constitutes the quantitative background against which the evolution of the indenture system can be approached.

The quantitative description of servant flows, based on the information

Table 8.5. *Proportion of blacks in total net migration, by colony: mainland (in percent)*

Years	New England	New York and New Jersey	Pennsylvania and Delaware	Maryland and Virginia	North Carolina	South Carolina	Georgia
1650–60	2	12	4	7			
1660–70	−4	−6	33	10	4		
1670–80	−1	10	4	10	4	17	
1680–90	−25	6	2	44	4	48	
1690–1700	−2	7	3	104	4	54	
1700–10	−12	−20	69	37	12	31	
1710–20	3	21	12	24	38	137	
1720–30	−76	−64	10	14	37	61	
1730–40	6	13	3	49	24	67	
1740–50	0	−88	3	155	53	37	35
1750–60	12	9	2	16	48	61	79
1760–70	−17	−19	12	124	48	47	54
1770–80	17	40	16	43	11	4	28

Source: See Appendix H.

Table 8.6. *Proportion of blacks in total net migration by colony: West Indies (in percent)*

Decade	Antigua	Barbados	Jamaica	Montserrat	Nevis	St. Kitts
1650–60	35	65		20	32	38
1660–70	34	84	55	288	52	32
1670–80	70	78	80	59	85	100
1680–90	83	82	89	74	91	57
1690–1700	83	78	90	73	88	63
1700–10	87	89	93	80	95	87
1710–20	86	72	95	68	86	−115
1720–30	91	81	94	93	88	85
1730–40	90	86	98	100	104	98
1740–50	94	88	95	91	93	98
1750–60	96	85	94	88	83	92
1760–70	101	92	94	98	69	108
1770–80	107	−39	90	85	66	94

Source: See Appendix H.

of the English legal registrations, was carried out in Chapter 6. The basic outline can be summarized by the decennial percentage distributions of the destinations of servants who appear in the registrations, which are presented in Table 8.7. As seen earlier in the investigation of servants' destinations from the English registrations, there are some gaps in time resulting from lack of records in some periods and a failure to record destinations systematically in some samples, but large numbers of registrations survive from a sufficient number of decades to make it likely that these distributions do represent accurately the general trends in the relative importance of different colonies as servant importers. Thus Barbados, after dominating the market for servants during the 1650s, virtually ceased to import servants after the 1680s. Nevis received a significant share of the total indentured migrants only during the 1660s and 1670s. Jamaica first appeared as a major importer during the 1680s, probably remained a major destination for servants during the following decades through the 1750s, and then virtually left the market. Only the Chesapeake colonies of Maryland and Virginia remained an important destination for English servants throughout the entire period from the 1650s to the 1770s. Pennsylvania first began to import servants in the late seventeenth century, and increased its share after the 1720s. By the time of the American Revolution, no West Indian colony was receiving significant numbers of indentured servants, and on the mainland only the Chesapeake colonies and Pennsylvania were importing English servants on a significant scale.

Table 8.7. *Percentage distributions of indentured servants bound for major colonial destinations, by decade*

Decade	Barbados	Jamaica	Nevis	Other West Indies	Chesapeake	Pennsylvania	Other mainland	Total	N
1650–59	69		2	1	28			100	2,954
1660–69	22	1	17	2	56		2	100	4,548
1670–79	10	4	15	2	66		3	100	2,549
1680–89	16	27	2	3	47	2	3	100	2,260
1690–99	3			1	85	3	8	100	586
1700–09				8	84		8	100	180
1710–19	6	2		1	85	5	1	100	179
1720–29	1	21		14	47	14	3	100	1,237
1730–39	1	60		4	24	8	3	100	1,506
1750–59		37		12	42	6	3	100	230
1770–79		1			79	18	2	100	3,697

Note: Decades with less than 100 registrations excluded. Servants without known destinations excluded.
Source: Appendix I.

White servitude in the colonial labor market

There was considerable variation in the share of blacks in a colony's total population at the time the colony first became an important servant importer, but with the exception of Pennsylvania, blacks came to make up a large share of each colony's population – 40 percent or more – during the period the colony remained a major destination for English servants. The three colonies that had been major servant importers and left the market before 1770 – Barbados, Nevis, and Jamaica – did so when blacks made up from 55 to 95 percent of their total population. Pennsylvania was the single case in which a colony that received a significant share of the servants registered did not have a large and growing share of blacks in its population.

The evolution of colonial labor forces

Considerable evidence indicates that the labor forces of the British colonies that became agricultural staple producers and exporters went through a series of identifiable periods as a result of systematic changes in the relative cost of servant and slave labor. The role of the indenture system went through basic changes in the course of this process. Although the duration of the periods varied across colonies, as did the time at which each occurred, the difference in the timing of the evolution of the indenture system in different places need not obscure the similarity of the basic process.

Initially, before introduction of the staple, the demand for labor was quite low. This was a period of mixed farming on a small scale, usually that of the family farm. In some British colonies, chiefly in New England and parts of the Middle Colonies, this regime persisted throughout the colonial period. Demand was chiefly for unskilled agricultural labor, and was met by free hired labor and small numbers of indentured servants. What demand for skilled labor existed in this period could normally be met by the available supply of free white tradesmen and craftsmen.

The introduction of a profitable staple crop raised the demand for labor, and therefore tended to raise the level of immigration to a colony. The primary demand was for workers to grow the staple, and initially planters continued to rely on indentured workers. In addition, as output increased, there was a growing demand for skilled labor to build houses and farm sheds, to make the hogsheads to pack and ship the sugar, tobacco, or rice, and to perform a variety of other crafts, many of them associated with the processing and transportation of the staple. At some point, relatively early in the colonial period in the West Indies and relatively late in the southern mainland colonies, when the demand for labor grew sufficiently large, the rising cost of white labor tended to make slaves a less expensive source of unskilled labor than additional servants, and the majority of the bound

126

labor force changed from white to black. By this time, the supply of free white skilled labor available for hire tended to be small, and skilled wages high; in some regions skilled craftsmen typically emigrated after obtaining their freedom, whereas in others, the availability of land and the profitability of staple cultivation combined to produce a situation in which, as one planter wrote of eighteenth-century Virginia, "we have no merchants, tradesmen, or artificers of any sort here but what become planters in a short time."[6] Although some skilled workers were usually available for hire, particularly recent freedmen, in many places the operation of these forces meant that in this period white servants were a principal source of skilled labor.

Where the size of productive units grew, and transformed an economy of small farms into one increasingly dominated by large plantations, skilled labor assumed an additional function. In both the West Indies and to a lesser extent the southern mainland colonies a demand arose for white workers not only to perform the plantations' skilled artisanal jobs, but also to work as estate managers and supervisors of slaves. This demand was increased in the West Indies by both the large size of plantations and the high rate of absentee ownership.

Therefore, as the demand for labor grew in the staple-producing colonies of the late seventeenth and eighteenth centuries, their unskilled labor forces tended increasingly to be made up of black slaves, while white servants performed skilled trades, crafts, and services, and in many cases acted as managers and overseers. Although large plantations ultimately developed in all the regions where slavery was adopted on a large scale, they were not necessary to the growing racial division of labor by skill described here. With the exception only of the tendency for white servants to act as managers in regions of large plantations, the basic changes in the role of servants would tend to occur regardless of the size of the typical unit of cultivation. The result was more readily apparent where large numbers of skilled servants and unskilled slaves worked on a single plantation, but the shift in skill composition of the servant population could take place even where many farms were too small to use the full-time labor of a worker skilled in a particular craft. In such regions, as in many parts of the Chesapeake, the time of skilled servants could be shared among a number of farms, as a skilled servant would be owned by one planter and rented out to others.[7]

But this was not the final phase of development. As the level of production increased further, the demand for labor, both unskilled and skilled, continued to rise. The price of skilled white servants tended to rise sharply. The result was the investment in the training of slaves to take over the skilled jobs of the plantation. Although the dates at which labor supply conditions and the level of demand for skilled labor combined to produce

127

White servitude in the colonial labor market

this result differed across colonies, and particularly sharply between the island and mainland colonies, the tendency was present in all the staple colonies, as the relative price of skilled white servants apparently rose significantly over the course of the late seventeenth and eighteenth centuries. The final result of this process was clearly visible by the end of the colonial period, as in many colonies significant numbers of large plantations were based almost exclusively on slave labor, with considerable numbers of skilled slaves as well as unskilled field hands.

The organization of plantation labor forces

Evidence for this scheme of development is incomplete, for much remains unknown of the specific processes of change over time in the colonial labor force. Some studies offer important insights into this development through their attention to the organization of colonial plantations. Richard Sheridan has given a description of the great colonial West Indian sugar plantations at the height of their development. Although based on large work forces of unskilled slaves, these plantations had a consistent hierarchical structure of Europeans at the highest levels. The individual highest in rank was the attorney, who directed the business of the plantation in the absence of the proprietor. Immediately below him was the overseer or manager, who acted as superintendent of the planting, directed the field workers, and looked after the welfare of the slaves. White bookkeepers were next in rank. Then came a series of white artisans – carpenters, millwrights, masons, rope makers, distillers – "who were assisted and not infrequently supplanted by their mulatto and black apprentices."[8]

Comments by contemporaries give support to the view that plantation labor forces were commonly based on a racial division of labor by skill. In calculating the costs of making a new plantation in Jamaica in 1672, Sir Thomas Lynch allowed for twenty-four white servants and one hundred slaves.[9] More modestly, a group of Barbados planters wrote in 1688 in relation to a plantation of one hundred acres that "to manage this Land well it will require seven white servants and fifty good negroes"; among the whites would be included an overseer, a doctor, a farrier, a carter, and a smith.[10]

Similar comments refer to the training of slaves to take over the plantations' skilled positions. In Virginia, Hugh Jones wrote "of the Negroes" in 1724 that "their Work is to take Care of the *Stock*, plant *Corn, Tobacco, Fruits*, & c.," but added that "several of them are taught to be *Sawyers, Carpenters, Smiths, Coopers*, & c. and though for the most Part they be none of the aptest or nicest; yet they . . . will perform tolerably well."[11] In 1776, reporting on the state of the metal trades in

Virginia, Francis Fauquier noted that "gentlemen of much property in Land and Negroes, have some of their own Negroes bred up in the Trade of blacksmiths, and make axes, Hoes, plough shares, and such kind of coarse work for the use of their Plantations."[12] Three years earlier, a Scottish visitor to the Chesapeake had remarked: "There are negroes here of all trades; they are very true and come to be very good tradesmen."[13]

Occasional detailed occupational listings of the labor forces of individual colonial plantations survive among probate records and collections of family papers. Although such listings are not available in sufficient numbers to provide a systematic test of the scheme suggested above, they do appear to provide illustrations of its operation. Some of the listings show the extent to which slaves were ultimately trained to do the many skilled jobs of the large plantations. An occupational listing of the male slaves on a Jamaica plantation in 1764, included in an inventory of the estate, is shown in Table 8.8. The twenty-six different job descriptions for the 188 men illustrate the wide range of jobs blacks performed by the second half of the eighteenth century. Slaves appear in a variety of skilled crafts, including such important positions as carpenter, cooper, sawyer, mason, smith, and even doctor. Five are also listed as drivers; these men supervised individual gangs of workers in the fields.

Samuel Martin's listing of the slaves on his Antigua estate in 1768 is shown in Table 8.9. Making the list in anticipation of a possible sale of the plantation, Martin included estimated prices, and the list therefore indicates not only the range of skills present among the slaves, but also the variation in their prices according to skill. Sixteen of the carpenters, coopers, and masons are valued at £100 apiece, more than double the estimated prices of the field hands. One of the craftsmen, a smith, was listed together with his apprentice.

Other plantation labor-force listings illustrate the racial division of labor by skill that existed in an earlier phase of the scheme of development suggested here. Table 8.10 presents an occupational listing of the male labor force of Parham Hill Plantation in Antigua in 1768. The eight white indentured servants on the estate included a manager, a clerk, a chief overseer for each of the two sub-plantations, and a total of four assistant overseers. In separate listings of 1767 and 1769, one indentured blacksmith was present in addition to these managerial servants,[14] but as Table 8.10 shows, all other skilled jobs on the plantation were performed by slaves, again including drivers, carpenters, masons, coopers, and doctors.

A similar listing, made upon the death of Robert "King" Carter in 1733, is presented in Table 8.11. This enumeration shows the labor force of a Virginia plantation at both an earlier date and, according to the scheme suggested here, an earlier stage of evolution. This inventory was taken at a time when the number of slaves in skilled and supervisory jobs

Table 8.8. *Male Negro labor force of Dukenfield Hall Plantation, Jamaica, 1764*

Occupation	No.
Driver	5
Carpenter	6
Cooper	9
Sawyer	4
Mason	2
Doctor	2
Smith	1
Taylor	1
Sailor	4
Pantry man	2
Wain man	6
Wain boy	6
Head mule man	1
Mule boy	15
Head cattle man	2
Cattle boy	8
Hog driver	1
Fowl keeper	1
House keeper	1
Cook	1
In the house	3
Shepherd boy	1
Field	67
Fence cutter	2
Watchman	22
Grass carrier	15
Total	188

Source: "Appraisement of Negroes and Stock upon Dukenfield-hall Plantation taken 28th April 1764"; Greater London Records Office (Middlesex Section), Acc 775/931.

on Chesapeake tobacco plantations was increasing rapidly, and the number of servants on the plantations was falling.[15] Yet while Carter used slaves both in a number of skilled jobs and as the majority of the foremen or drivers on the plantation's many scattered "quarters," there were still thirteen skilled white servants, who made up more than half of the total skilled workers at the home plantation.[16] Similarly, although on a smaller scale, when Daniel Dulany of Annapolis died in 1754, the inventory of his estate showed that while he had owned forty able-bodied tithable male slaves and only five male servants, two of the total of seven men described as having skilled occupations were indentured servants.[17]

An elusive aspect of the scheme described here is the relation between

Table 8.9. *Samuel Martin's valuation of the slaves on his estate in Antigua, 1768*

Martin's description	No.
"Working Negroes including 5 good boylers, many Coopers, Distillers & Firemen belonging to the Field, house, & Garden at £45 st. per head . . ."	217
"Young Negroes from 5 to 12 years old . . . at 20 Str. per head . . ."	28
"Children from 5 years to one month old at 5£ st. per head . . ."	37
"Carpenters one of which is a boy, but is recon'd at the same rate with the others because Philip is able to build a windmill from top to bottom is also a good house carpenter Joiner & wheelwright worth at least £200 ster. yet one with the other are only sold at £100 ster."	5
"Coopers. Light Cooper able to make light casks one with the other [£100 each]"	7
"Mason Exclusive of Cambridge who is distempered, but Jack being as good a Mason as any in this Country for hanging Coppers and all other masonry worthy at least £200 ster. but is rated on with the other at £100 str."	4
"Shaddock a Smith able to shoe well and to do other plant. Business with his apprentice Fisher [together £150]"	2
"Elderly women about the stock at 20£ st. each"	4
"NB Spencer & Cambridge are left out of the list"	304

Source: "A fair estimate of Samuel Martin's Plantation in New Division in Antigua according to the General rule of Appraisement," June 24, 1768; Martin Papers, Vol. V, British Museum, Add MS 41,350, ff. 68v–69v.

skilled servants and slaves. It seems likely, as Sheridan suggests, that slaves were often trained by white servants, but little direct evidence of this process survives. Samuel Martin had a series of white servants as overseers and craftsmen on his Antigua plantation, and devoted considerable attention both to their training and to their oversight of his slaves. Thus in his published *Essay Upon Plantership,* Martin reflected: "White servants as well as negroes are the planter's dependents: and if according to the principles of humanity, the latter ought to be treated with great kindness, how much more is due the former, who are directors of the others labors, and stand in a nearer relation to us?"[18] In a letter to his son in 1751, Martin provided a description of how he had his slaves perform what was normally one of the most highly labor-intensive jobs on the West Indian plantations, the fertilization of the fields to prevent the exhaustion of the soil by the sugarcane, and in the process described the use of an English servant to train black field workers:

Of this I thought fit to give you a precise description, that . . . you may direct yr. future managers how to render this soil as fruitfule as any in ye Island; and that too with infinitely less expence of negroes labr. than is used here in ye common way of dunging: for I use, spades, shovels, & Carts, to load and Carry out all my Soil & require not above 10 negro men for ye purpose, who are as dexterous in the use of

Table 8.10. *Male labor force of Parham Hill Plantation, Antigua, 1768*

Servants: Old plantation		Servants: New plantation	
Occupation	No.	Occupation	No.
Manager	1	Chief overseer	1
Clerk	1	Under overseers	2
Chief overseer	1		
Under overseers	2		
Total	5	Total	3

Slaves: Oldwork		Slaves: Newwork	
Occupation	No.	Occupation	No.
Drivers	4	Drivers	3
Doctors	2	Boiler	1
Carpenters	4	Cooper	1
Masons	5	No occupation listed	60
Coopers	8		
Blacksmiths	2		
Boatmen	5		
No occupation listed	128		
Total	158	Total	65

Total servants: 8 (3.5%); total slaves: 223 (96.5%); total male labor force: 231 (100%).
Source: "List of Negroes on Parham Plantation Oldwork, July 21, 1768"; "List of Newwork Negroes, July 21st, 1768"; "List of Servants upon Parham Plantation, July 21, 1768"; Tudway of Wells MSS, Somerset Record Office, DD/TD, Box 14.
Note: Ages are not given for slaves in the listings. This tabulation includes all males.

those husbandry tools as other people: I thank an excellent Plowman whom I sent out of England for all that dexterity: his name is Fiffet, and admirable fellow in skill, fidelity, diligence & husbandry: and is actually the briskest and best field overseer I ever had in my life.[19]

Another description of the training of slaves by whites was given by the friend of a Palatine weaver in 1747. When the latter proposed to move from Pennsylvania to South Carolina to earn a better living, his friend warned that "his service in Carolina will last probably no longer than until two negro slaves shall have learned the weaver's trade from him and can weave themselves." More generally, the friend noted: "So it goes through all Carolina; the negroes are made to learn all the trades and are used for all kinds of business."[20]

J. Harry Bennett has traced the development of one of the first Jamaica sugar plantations, and the evolution of its labor force provides an additional illustration of both the early racial division of labor and the

Table 8.11. *Male labor force on plantation of Robert "King" Carter, 1733*

Home plantation: servants		Home plantation: slaves	
Occupation	No.	Occupation	No.
Carpenter	2	Butcher	1
Ship Carpenter	1	Tailor	1
Glasier	1	Carpenter	1
Tailor	2	Slooper	4
Gardener	1	Carter	1
Blacksmith	1	Smith	1
Sailor	2	Not given	2
Bricklayer	2		
Cook	1		
Not given	2		
Total	15	Total	11
Other quarters: servants		Other quarters: slaves	
Occupation	No.	Occupation	No.
Foreman	2	Foreman	42
Not given	6	Carpenter	9
		Cooper	5
		Sawyer	9
		Not given	190
Total	8	Total	255

Total servants: 23 (8.0%); total slaves: 266 (92.0%); total male labor force 283 (100%).
Source: "An Inventory of all the . . . personal Estate of the Honble. Robert Carter, County of Lancaster Esqr. Deceased, taken as directed in his last will," Virginia Historical Society, Richmond.
Note: Slaves are included in the labor force in this tabulation if tithable (aged sixteen or over) and able-bodied.

subsequent use of servants to train slaves.[21] Cary Helyar established a small estate on the island in 1669, and began production of cacao with a labor force of one indentured servant and four slaves. Three years later, in the process of converting to sugar production, Helyar had increased his landholdings considerably, and was using a total of fourteen white servants and fifty-five slaves. In the course of the conversion to sugar, he wrote to his brother in England asking him to recruit indentured servants for the estate, at the same time cautioning that "I would not have you take care for many white servants unles tradesmen." He included specific requests for a potter, sawyer, smith, carpenter, and mason. After Helyar's death in 1672, William Whaley became manager of the estate and continued Helyar's efforts to build a great sugar plantation, relying, as

White servitude in the colonial labor market

Helyar had, on white servants to do the plantation's skilled work of sugar refining, constructing the buildings needed to process the sugar, and caring for the plantation's livestock. Whaley continued to expand the estate, and at the time of his death in 1676 its labor force, with more than one hundred slaves, was the largest in the colony. A series of urgent appeals by Whaley for skilled white servants from England had gone largely unanswered, and the high cost of hired white labor in Jamaica, together with the difficulty of obtaining skilled servants, finally led his successor to begin the substitution of slaves for servants in the plantation's skilled jobs. Thus in 1677 the estate's new manager reported to its owner in England that he had indentured a white potter who would train slaves to refine sugar: "I have agreed with Thomas fforde Potter to serve you Three yeares . . . teaching two of your negroes to make potts and dripps and burne and Sett as well as himselfe." This appears to have been typical of a process that was repeated many times throughout the West Indies, and by the eighteenth century it was common to find slaves performing all the work of refining and construction on the great sugar plantations.[22]

The demand for skilled servants

In the intermediate stages of the process described here, filling the upper ranks of this plantation hierarchy meant recruiting white managers and artisans for the colonies as indentured servants. This recruitment left considerable evidence, chiefly in the form of planters' and merchants' correspondence. Examples of appeals for skilled servants survive from as early as 1645, when a Barbados planter wrote to a relative in Scotland:

Want of servants is my greatest bane and will hinder my designe. The bilding of my house and setting Upp of my Ingenue [i.e., mill] will cost above 50000 lib of Tobacco because I have not work men of my owen. In January next god willing I shall begin to make sugar. So pray if you come neare to any port where shipping comes hither indenture procure and send me [servants] . . . agree for theire passages to be payed here in Tob. att 600 li per head if you can not agree under. lett them be of any sort men women or boys of 14 years of age what I shall not make use off and are not serviceable for mee I can exchange with others especially any sort of tradesmen . . . [23]

Many later appeals for skilled servants followed this pattern. The most prominent mention was usually given to builders, but other skills were often mentioned as well, and in the seventeenth century the point was frequently made that servants of any kind would be useful. In 1677 Christopher Jeaffreson wrote from St. Kitts to his London merchant that "I confess all servants are very acceptable here; and if any laborious and industrious men woulde transporte themselves, I should gladly receive them." He wrote again in 1681:

It is long since my request to you to sende me some white servants especially a mason, carpenter, taylor, smith, cooper, or any handy craftsman; and now I am necessitated to reiterate my sayd request to you, not only for a clerke or tradesman, but for any sort of men, and one or two women, if they can be found. They are generally wanted in this island; and all my bond-servants are gone free.[24]

William Fitzhugh of Virginia wrote to his London merchant in 1681 that "if you could possibly procure me a Bricklayer or Carpenter or both, it would do me a great kindness, & save me a great deal of money in my present building." Six years later, Fitzhugh wrote to advise a friend about "building & settling plantations" in Virginia:

If you design this land to settle, a child of your own or near kinsman, for whom it is supposed that you would build a very good house, not only for their comfortable but creditable accomodations, the best methods to be pursued therein is, to get a Carpenter & Bricklayer Servants, & send them in here to serve 4 or five years, in which time of their Service, they might reasonably build a substantial good house, at least, if not brick walls and well plaister'd, & earn money enough besides in their said time, at spare times from your work, having so long a time to do it in, as will purchase plank, nails & other materials, & supply them with necessarys during their servitude.[25]

The appeals for builders and other craftsmen continued in the eighteenth century. Thus in 1732 a Glasgow merchant involved in the servant trade wrote to a correspondent in Inverness:

This is Earnestly beging you'l doe me and Company the favour as to Cause Engage a parcell of Servants as Soon as possible Vizt House and Ship Carpenters, Coopers, Black Smiths, Millwrights, and Masons or Bricklayers for Jamaica.[26]

However, unlike the requests of the seventeenth century, which tended to ask for any servants with a preference for skilled, in the eighteenth century exclusive requests for skilled servants appear. Thus, for example, the same merchant advised his correspondent:

Minde to Send none but tradesmen for they are not worth Sending any other . . .
I must beg you'l Take the further Trouble to Indent for us any Wrights, Masons, Coopers, Smiths, Carpenters, or Millwrights . . . we doe not want any other than Tradesmen at this time . . . be sure that none but good Tradesmen be Indented.[27]

The requests for skilled servants may also have tended to become more specific during the eighteenth century. The London merchants Lascelles and Maxwell wrote in 1744 to a Barbados planter that "we have frequently seen Mr. Hannay's Coachman, . . . and he bids us acquaint you he had been very solicitous to procure a good farrier for you."[28] Samuel Martin wrote to a Bristol merchant in 1757 to ask for a number of skilled men, including:

A jobbing Country Blacksmith who shoes horses very well.

A very good wheelwright who understands ye business of making Casks & Waggons well.

A good Mason who understands the common rough work of masonry; . . . and can do brick worke also particularly that of making water Cisterns & having furnaces or stills.

A good jobbing Sadler & Collar maker who understands tanning & dressing leather for his own use.

A sober Jockey who is a good rider & breaker of young horses. Of this man you must insist upon a good Character for Sobriety & skill in his profession; because generally speaking they are a drunken profligate breed of people.[29]

Requests for female servants appear to have been rare, but women were occasionally recruited for specific jobs. Thus, for example, Samuel Martin noted:

I have desired my daughter Irish & Martin to look out for a Housekeeper for me . . . part of her office is to direct the care of the Sick Negroes, to keep the keys of my provision Hous & to do all offices relating to Housekeeping, as well as to inspect my linnen the raising of Poultry & the Management of the Dairy.[30]

Skilled Scottish servants were among the most highly valued for their skills and discipline, and many planters requested them specifically. Thus in the 1730s Walter Tullideph wrote repeatedly from Antigua to his son and agent in Britain:

I wish you could bring Scotch Servants with you they are the only thing wanted here . . .

Scotts Servants and Tradesmen would answer exceedingly . . .

Wrote him . . . to send . . . a Blacksmith that can shoe well and understands Farriery . . . a Scotch man if possible.[31]

Later, having returned to his home in Scotland, Tullideph wrote to his attorney in Antigua concerning a servant he was sending to the West Indies to act as the accountant for his plantation:

This will be dd [delivered] to you by James Corss who hath bound himself to serve me . . . agreeable to the Laws of Antigua . . . he is very Capable of keeping the Plantation Accotts use him therefore kindly, take good care of his lodgeing and Dyet, and instruct him in every Branch of Plantation affairs, he will easily fall into it, as he hath been these 3 or 4 years past in My Lord Gray's Service, who is undoubtedly the best ffarmer in these parts.[32]

Similarly, Tullideph wrote from Scotland to a fellow planter in Antigua telling him of "a Young man in this neighbourhood named Farquarson that understands his pen well & is desireous to goe out to our Island . . . if you think he would answear well for you."[33]

Planters might take care to ascertain that their servants possessed the skills they claimed. Thus Landon Carter of Virginia wrote in his diary in March 1758: "I had brought from on board the *Union* a Servant pretending to be a gardiner named, Joseph Brown, a Yarmouth man. Says he was an apprentis to Kitchen Gardiner." Six days later, Carter recorded: "Sent home the fellow sent here for a gardiner. He knows nothing of the matter. Plowman . . . I keep. He seems a workman and willing fellow."[34]

The role of servants as the most readily available source of skilled labor to many regions made them a critical part of the colonial economy. Following a great fire in Charleston, South Carolina, in 1740, indentured servants were one of the first supplies requested by a merchant to repair the damage, as he wrote to his brother in London:

We must Endeavour to look forward & not Backward & if it pleases God to spare me a few Years doubt not of recovering both for you & myself, & am a good deal better off than a great many here, and as there will be a great deal of Building here, Nails of all sorts will be much in demand & Iron Ware of all sorts for Houses & Stores & if you can Indent Two House Carpenters as Servants for four years may be of good Service here.[35]

Many colonial planters and officials were dismayed by the economic forces that caused the shift from unskilled servants to slaves, and later from skilled servants to slaves, and the change in relative prices due to the rising price of white labor formed the basis of a complaint already common in the West Indies by the second half of the seventeenth century. An example appears in a petition of 1675 from the Council and Assembly of Barbados to the king:

In former tymes Wee were plentifully furnished with Christian servants from England . . . but now Wee can gett few English, having noe Lands to give them at the end of their tyme, which formerly was theire main allurement. Nor have Wee many Scotch Servants in regard our intercourse with that Kingdome is almost wholly cutt off by the Act of Navigacon, for men will not bring Servants thence, when they may bring noe other Commodityes nor carry our Commodities thither, And for Irish servants Wee finde them of small value, our whole dependence therefore is upon Negroes.[36]

A West Indian author complained in 1689 that "we cannot now be at the Charge to procure and keep White Servants, or to entertain Freemen as we used to do. Nor will they now go upon any terms to a Land of Misery and Beggary."[37]

The same process was perceived on the mainland, as one colonist remarked of Carolina in 1747 that "the negroes are made to learn all the trades and are used for all kinds of business. For this reason white people have difficulty in earning their bread there, unless they become overseers or provide themselves with slaves."[38] However, the problem was cause for louder and more frequent complaint in the West Indies, for reasons detailed by one commentator as follows:

Heretofore the Colonyes were plentifully supplied with Negro and Christian servants which are the nerves and sinews of a plantacon the most of which the latter they had from Scotland who being excellent planters and good souldiers considerable numbers of them comeing yearly to the plantacons kept the Colonies in soe formidable a posture that they neither feared ye insurreccons of theire Slaves nor a forreine invasion of forreine enimies.[39]

The governor of Barbados, in complaining to the Lords of Trade and Plantations in 1680 that lack of opportunity for new immigrants to own land made servants avoid the island and made freedmen emigrate from it, deplored the growing racial imbalance in the colony that resulted from the consequent high relative cost of white labor:

There hath certainly been great changes in six yeares time. First my Lords by reason of the greater numbers of people gon off from this place to Carolina Jamaica Antega and the rest of the Leeward Islands where they hope to gett land which this Island having none to give; Supplies will not come at us and those that doe come wch are not many are bound to serve only for foure or att most five yeares; their time expired they are ready for to seeke a new future as they hope to obteyne else where besides my Lords. Since they [the planters] have found the conveniency by the Labor & cheape keeping of Slaves they have neglected the keeping of white men with whom they formerly carried out their Plantations neither for the former reasons and for the strict acts in England for Trade can they have any white servants to come to the place though for their own safety they would willingly embrace him thus farr for some of ye reasons of the Diminution of the Militia.[40]

Similarly, a group of planters petitioned the king in 1682, complaining that a lack of servants in the West Indies would soon leave them without control over their slaves:

There is in a manner a totall stop of sending any more Servants into yor. Maties said Plantations, which will in a short time disable the Inhabitants of them from carrying on their Trade by leaving them without any persons to governe and direct their Negros and utterly disable them from furnishing the proportion of men to the Militia, which yor. Maties Laws there require.[41]

Even in the mainland colonies, the relative shortage of white servants long remained a source of concern to some planters. On July 6, 1776, Landon Carter of Virginia wrote in his diary: "Much is said of the slavery of negroes, but how will servants be provided in these times? Those few servants that we have don't do as much as the poorest slaves we have."[42]

Whereas at the beginning of the eighteenth century nearly all slaves in the Chesapeake worked as unskilled laborers, by the time of the Revolution many native-born slaves had moved into a wide variety of skilled trades, chiefly on the largest plantations: Visitors' reports and estate inventories show slaves to have performed virtually the whole range of crafts required on the plantations.[43] There is evidence that the same result had been achieved in the West Indies by the second quarter of the eighteenth century. Richard Sheridan notes that by this time, "Planters who had formerly depended on white tradesmen found that it was less costly to train their intelligent slaves as skilled craftsmen."[44]

Because little can be known about the representativeness of the surviving appeals surveyed in this discussion of the overall colonial demand for servants, this evidence can be no more than suggestive of the changes that occurred in the use of indentured labor over time. Yet two generalizations about the appeals can be made. One is that over time planters increasingly requested servants with specific skills. Construction and metal and wood craftsmen were virtually always mentioned, but orders for men with a wide variety of other skills also appear. The second is that later in the colonial period these requests for skilled servants tended to become exclusive of the unskilled. Thus, whereas appeals of the seventeenth century suggest that although skilled servants were preferred, any servants would be of use, in the eighteenth century merchants and planters began to mention that it was simply not worthwhile to transport unskilled servants, and that recruiting should be limited to individuals with skills, and often specific trades. The recruiting evidence therefore points to an increasing relative interest of planters in skilled servants over time, a shift consistent with both a rising colonial demand for skilled labor and the changing relative cost conditions that caused the substitution of slaves for servants in the unskilled field work of the colonies.

The indenture system was most important quantitatively in the early history of two of the regions of colonial British America where slavery took its strongest hold, the Chesapeake colonies of Maryland and Virginia and the islands of the West Indies. There was no necessary connection between the two forms of bound labor: Servitude was an important source of labor in colonial Pennsylvania, and slavery was not, whereas slavery was basic to the economy of South Carolina, but servitude was quantitatively of minor importance. Yet white servitude and black slavery do appear to have been closely connected historically, and certain patterns of interaction between them are suggested by an examination of quantitative evidence concerning the size and composition of flows of immigration to the colonies of British America. Those regions that had the highest levels of sustained immigration, in many cases in absolute terms, but in all cases relative to their existing populations in any period, were also those in which slavery grew, and it was in these regions that indentured servitude was quantitatively most important in the seventeenth century. Furthermore, although the regions where slavery developed on a large scale ultimately tended to cease importing servants, a variety of evidence suggests that this occurred only after a prolonged period in which a racial division of labor by skill existed, with slaves performing the bulk of the field work, and servants filling the skilled, and often the managerial, positions of the plantations.

A number of historians have perceived these patterns in particular parts of British America. The temporal sequence that occurred in the labor forces of the West Indian colonies led Eric Williams to describe white servitude as the historical foundation upon which black slavery was constructed in that region.[45] Lewis Gray and Richard Pares recognized the evolution of the indenture system from a supplier of unskilled labor to a source of skilled specialists in the southern mainland and the West Indian colonies, respectively.[46] Yet it is of intense interest to the history of colonial America to ask what the basis of these common patterns was, and why these changes occurred. Although the degree to which convincing answers can be given for the case of any particular region necessarily depends on the extent of our knowledge of the specific historical circumstances of its experience, what can be done is to devise an explanatory framework, capable of isolating specific causal factors, within which the available information for a region can be placed. Some steps toward satisfactory answers can then be taken by using the framework to aid in a critical evaluation of the available evidence. This is the task of the next chapter.

9

The indenture system and the colonial
labor market: an overview

The supply of labor to British America

Two of the three important types of labor in the economy of British
America, free and indentured labor, were composed primarily of whites.
The third, slave labor, was made up of blacks. In virtually every colony
free labor was used from the earliest years of settlement. In most colonies
indentured servitude was also introduced very early, surviving to the late
eighteenth century in some, dying out earlier in others. Slavery was
generally the last of the three types to appear, and in many colonies it
remained important throughout the colonial period.

The growth of slavery has been a central concern of many studies in
colonial history. Some historians have posed the problem of the causes of
the rise of black labor in the plantation colonies in terms of a transition
from one labor type to a substitute, from white servants to black slaves.
This formulation has tended to focus attention on a particular period in the
history of a single colony or region, normally that in which the number of
slaves first exceeded the number of servants in the colony's labor force, as
the period of transition. Although this approach has produced some
important studies of the interaction between white and black labor in the
colonial market, in order to treat the growth of slavery over longer periods
and to gain comparative perspective across colonies it is desirable to
formulate the problem of the mix of labor types in the colonial economy
more generally.

A more general formulation of the causes of the growth of slavery is
suggested by the approach used in economic studies of the diffusion of
innovations. This has concentrated on three key parameters: the date of
the innovation's introduction into a market, the rate of spread of its use,
and its eventual equilibrium market share. All three parameters have been
found to be consistently related to profitability, so that the more profitable
an innovation relative to existing techniques, the earlier it is introduced,
the faster it spreads, and the higher its final market share.[1] The growth of
slavery can be considered as analogous to the spread of an innovation that
substitutes for an existing technique. This approach has the advantage of

focusing attention not on a single point, but on the entire growth path of slavery in a colony, with the profitability of slavery relative to servitude and free labor the presumed explanation of the date of introduction, rate of spread, and final share of slaves in the colony's labor force.

The first stage of the analysis of this chapter outlines a model of labor supply to a colony or region. The implications for the colonial labor market of differential supply elasticities of the available types of labor will be considered,[2] and these will point to some important determinants of the composition of a colony's labor force. This framework will serve as the basis of a consideration of the composition of the labor forces of each of the major regions of British America. Then a further step will be taken, as the model will be extended to recognize the heterogeneity of labor in the plantation economies. The labor force will be divided into the skilled and unskilled, and some evidence will be adduced to examine the implications and determine the validity of this modification of the model.

The problem of labor choice in the British colonies can be seen as one involving a series of closely related labor markets. Differences in the price of labor across colonies could not only produce flows of workers from one colony to another, but could also serve to direct the flows from Europe between colonies in such a way as to tend to reduce the cost differentials. In the case of slaves, these flows could be directed by purely commercial means, for it was necessary only to contract for shipments with those engaged in the transatlantic slave trade. Servants and free workers, insofar as they had greater freedom in choosing their destinations, could respond to nonpecuniary conditions of work as well as wage offers, but both groups could be attracted to a colony with the proper economic incentives. The related parts of the colonial labor market will here be taken to include only the British colonies.[3]

The recognition of the interrelatedness of the colonies' labor markets provides a background against which variation in the composition of different colonies' labor forces can be considered. The principal question to be analyzed concerns the determinants of the division of the colonies' labor forces among the three types of labor. Attention is first given to determinants of the labor supply facing a British colony.

A general model of labor supply to a colony can be developed to serve as a framework for analyzing the relative importance of immigrant and domestic labor supply in a colony. It can further decompose the predicted volume of immigration into proportions of servants and slaves. The model can therefore not only serve as a framework for understanding the important differences that existed across colonial regions in the type of labor they imported, but can also provide a systematic basis for determining why continuing immigration over long periods was so critical to the economies of some regions but unimportant to others. The model focuses

142

on the short-run analysis of labor supply to a colony; long-run changes can be incorporated as shifts in particular parameters.

After initial settlement, the stock of labor in a colony changed over time as a result of two factors. The first was the natural increase or decrease of the original settlers. The second was net migration, which equally could have the effect of either increasing or decreasing the colony's population. Accordingly, the total labor supply facing a colony's planters in any year can be disaggregated into separate domestic and immigrant supply curves. When the colony's annual level of wages and employment are found by setting the demand for labor equal to total labor supply, the resulting employment figure can then be divided into domestic labor – workers present in the colony at the beginning of the year – and immigrant labor – those newly arrived in the colony during the year.

The original settlers in a colony constituted an initial domestic supply of labor. The elasticity of the supply of this labor available for hire depended on the decisions of individuals, either in relation to their own supply or in regard to that of the workers bound to them as servants or slaves. In view of the very high labor-force participation rates of both free and bound workers, this elasticity must have been extremely low; in the short run, the colony's domestic supply of labor available for hire can be represented by a perfectly inelastic supply curve. The original position of this supply curve was determined by the size of the initial stock of settlers, and was subsequently shifted by the natural increase or decrease of that population and the effects of new flows of migrants into or out of the colony.

In analyzing the characteristics of the supply of immigrant labor, distinctions must be drawn between the variables that influenced the supply of each of the available types. For slaves, all the colonies of British America must have been price takers, and would therefore have faced a perfectly elastic supply. The total share of the British colonies in the Atlantic slave trade has been estimated at 19.7 percent during the seventeenth century and 29.0 percent in the eighteenth; the largest individual British colonial importers were Barbados in the seventeenth century, with 10.0 percent of the total trade, and Jamaica in the eighteenth, with 10.9 percent.[4] In view of this relatively small share of the total trade controlled by any one of the British importers, it is unlikely that the demand of any single colony would generally have affected the price facing it: Enormous flows of slaves were exported from Africa to the Americas annually, and all a colony had to do to produce a large percentage increase in its imports was to divert a small proportion of these flows.

In contrast to this perfectly elastic supply of slaves, the supply of Englishmen, free and indentured, was less than perfectly elastic even for specific colonies and regions. Because migration to New World colonies

143

in much of the colonial period tended to occur on a strictly national basis, the colonies of British America were by far the most common destinations for English emigrants; in this period the American colonies had little competition from other parts of the British empire. The supply of white labor to a British colony was positively related to two variables controlled by colonial planters, each of which affected both the total size of the pool of immigrants to America and its distribution among the colonies. One was the quality of the bargains that planters in a particular colony were currently offering. A number of colonies competed in several economic dimensions to gain a larger number of white immigrants.[5] Principal among these was the wage rate they offered, as higher wages for free workers and correspondingly shorter indentures for servants were used to attract Englishmen to a colony, but other variables, including larger freedom dues, could be used as well. The other reason for the rising marginal cost of white labor was that increases in the number of immigrants to a colony were often achieved by active recruiting, not only in English ports, but also in the English countryside and in foreign countries. This recruiting was typically done by professional agents employed either by individual colonial planters or by English merchants.[6] The use of recruiters resulted in upward sloping labor supply curves both because they were used only when the supply of voluntary emigrants available at the ports was considered inadequate by colonists, and because it is likely that the marginal cost of recruiting servants was positively related to the number desired. The latter effect resulted from the characteristics of recruiting, including the increasing costs of transportation and maintenance involved in sending servants from their homes to ports for shipment to the colonies as agents traveled farther afield to find more recruits.[7]

The supply curve for white immigrants could be shifted by a number of variables. One was the English wage rate. An increase in English wages, by raising the opportunity cost to free workers or prospective servants of emigrating, tended to increase their reservation wages, thus shifting the supply curve for their labor upward. A second factor which shifted the supply curve for white immigrants was the availability of land in a colony. Landownership in preindustrial England was a source of status as well as income. Many servants and free English emigrants went to the New World not only to improve their economic condition in general, but specifically in the hope of becoming landowners. There is evidence that the availability of open land in a colony was positively related to the willingness of Englishmen to migrate to the colony.[8] A third variable affecting labor supply was the mortality rate of a colony. Mortality rates were considerably higher in the West Indies during most of the colonial period than in other British colonies, and the southern mainland colonies had significantly higher mortality rates than New England. To the extent that Englishmen were aware of these differentials, they tended to reduce the supply of white labor to the colonies with high mortality.

A fourth determinant of white labor supply was the nonpecuniary conditions of work in a colony. These were determined in large part by the types of crops the colony produced and the technology and forms of work organization it employed. The most important distinction between colonies in this regard was between those which produced crops on large plantations by the use of gang labor and those which were characterized by small productive units, typically family farms with a few hired workers. English workers of the colonial period, like free workers of all periods, were apparently reluctant to work in gangs, and colonies in which the gang system was important faced a smaller supply of white labor than they would have otherwise.[9] A fifth important variable was probably the racial composition of the labor force. Because gangs predominated in many colonies in which blacks were present in large numbers, this variable was correlated to some extent with the last one mentioned. Yet the correlation was not perfect, as, for example, in the Chesapeake colonies in the second half of the seventeenth century, where large numbers of slaves worked on farms that typically had only a few bound workers.[10] In addition to their dislike of gang labor, the aversion of seventeenth-century Englishmen to blacks might have produced some further reluctance to emigrate to colonies in which blacks made up a sizable proportion of the population.[11]

In the model of labor supply to be analyzed here, no formal distinction will be made between the types of white immigrants. Although the supply of both servants and free workers probably depended on the common variables listed above, there may have been some systematic differences between the two categories with respect to labor supply, and these might be briefly noted. Under the existing imperfect capital market conditions to which the indenture system was a response, the high cost of the voyage across the Atlantic could be raised by a much wider range of Englishmen by indenturing themselves than that of those who could afford to pay the passage out of savings, or by borrowing from other sources. The difference in the sizes of the potential pools from which the two groups were drawn could have tended to make the supply of indentured servants more elastic than that of free workers. Another difference might have had an offsetting effect, however, as a higher reservation wage for servants could have resulted from the preference of Englishmen of the seventeenth and eighteenth centuries to be free rather than bound workers, and from their reluctance to enter long-term contracts.[12] Therefore, the economic terms required to induce an English man or woman to bind themselves for four or more years in order to emigrate might normally have been of higher total value than of those which would lead them to emigrate as free workers, and this would imply a higher reservation price for indentured than for free labor.

The difficulties involved in measuring the net outcome of these and other possible differences between these two types of worker with respect to labor supply makes formal analysis based on a distinction between free and indentured labor supply dubious. However, in practice this is not a serious problem, for at most times and for most colonies indentured immigration was considerably more important than free immigration. The aggregate supply curve for white immigrant labor can therefore be understood in most cases to represent primarily the supply of indentured servants.

Before presenting schematic supply curves for domestic and immigrant labor, common units of measurement are necessary for each of the types of labor. Free labor can be measured in annual units of price (wages) and quantity (years). Quantities of bound labor can be measured in the same way as free labor, but for both servants and slaves corresponding prices for flows of labor services must be derived from the stocks in which transactions occurred. Implicit hire rates for both servants and slaves can be derived from a general formula relating the price of a stock of labor to the implied average annual wage:

$$C = \sum_{j=1}^{n} \frac{NP_j}{(1 + r)^j}$$

where C = purchase price of a servant or slave; n = expected years of labor to be obtained from the worker; NP = expected annual productivity net of maintenance costs; and r = discount rate. The annual cost of the labor of a slave or servant to a planter would then be equal to the sum of the annual net earnings calculated from this expression and all maintenance costs for the worker.[13] To allow aggregation of the physical units of each type of labor, adjustments would need to be made by age and sex to convert the supply of each category of labor into standardized units of equal productivity.

In this stage of analysis, the only labor market considered will be that for unskilled agricultural workers. This restriction will be removed in later analysis. The restriction is not necessarily meant to imply even at this stage, however, that the demand for labor was undifferentiated with respect to type of labor when skill is held constant. One source of differential demand could have been productivity differences between categories. Rental prices could also have differed because of discrimination by planters: Planters could have behaved as if slaves' implicit rental prices were higher than they actually were, and this would have raised the

146

prices of servants and free workers relative to slaves. Discrimination against slaves could have been caused either by planters' racial prejudice or by the initial ignorance of planters before the large-scale use of slaves in a colony, which could have led them to underestimate slaves' productivity. Because the demand for labor may have been differentiated by race, the markets for white and black labor are properly treated separately. The subsequent analysis therefore considers the implications of the existence of separate supply and demand curves for white and black labor, even with skill held constant.

Before considering applications, a brief review of the short-run model of labor supply developed here can be done in two steps. Initially, the qualification concerning possible differential demand for labor by type will be ignored. In this case, assuming that there was no differentiation of the demand for labor by type due to discrimination, and with any necessary adjustments in the measurements of quantities of labor to allow for differences in productivity across categories, the market for unskilled labor can be analyzed as one involving homogeneous units of labor with undifferentiated demand. The supply curves for domestic and immigrant labor can then be drawn schematically as shown in Figure 9.1. Here the price axis measures the annual rental price of labor – the explicit hire rate for free workers, and the sum of the implicit hire rate and maintenance costs for servants and slaves – and the quantity axis measures employment in work years of constant productivity labor.

The two parts of Figure 9.1 illustrate the two basic cases. In both, the domestic supply curve (S_d) is perfectly inelastic. In the top half, the immigrant labor supply curve (S_i) is the sum of the supply curves for white (S_w) and slave (S_s) immigrants, and total labor supply (S_t) is the sum of S_d and S_i. With the supply curves shown, no immigration to the colony will occur if the demand for labor is such that the annual market hire rate is below w_1. If the wage rises above w_1, immigration will occur; it will be composed entirely of whites if the wage remains below w_2, and will include both whites and blacks if the wage rises to w_2. The domestic labor supply is fully employed at any positive wage. The maximum quantity of servants imported will be the number that will provide $(q_2 - q_1)$ work years of labor; all increases in employment beyond the level corresponding to q_2 will consist of slaves.

In the curves shown in the bottom half of Figure 9.1, the reservation wage of white immigrant labor is above the supply price of slaves. As a result, no white immigration will occur. If the wage rises to w_2, slave immigration will occur, and all increases in employment above q_1 will be made up of slaves.

When the possibility of differentiated demand for labor by type is reintroduced, both the aggregate domestic and immigrant supply curves of

White servitude in the colonial labor market

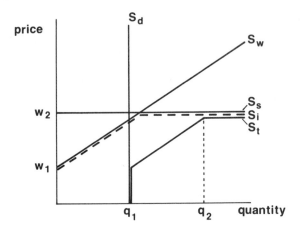

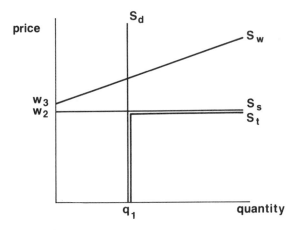

Figure 9.1 Colonial labor supply

Figure 9.1 become invalid. Each of the component supply curves for white and black labor retains its original shape, and domestic and immigrant supply curves can be aggregated for white or for black labor, but the markets for white and black labor must be treated separately. A colony therefore could have more than a single hire rate for labor, with different equilibrium rates for whites and blacks. The predictions of the model concerning the precise composition of both the labor force and immigration will depend on levels and elasticities of demand for each of the types of labor as well as the supply elasticities. However, the basic

148

qualitative predictions of the model concerning labor-force composition remain the same, as with other factors constant, increases in a colony's wage rate will tend to cause immigration, with the lower elasticity of white than of black labor producing a tendency for the share of whites in the immigrant population to decline as the volume of immigration rises.

The composition of unskilled colonial labor forces

The model of labor supply developed in the previous section is intended to illuminate several basic questions concerning the labor markets of colonial America. In this section the model will be used as a framework within which to consider why large-scale slavery developed in some colonies but not in others, and even more generally to analyze why persistent immigration of any kind of labor was characteristic of some regions and not of others. The labor markets of some major regions of British America will be examined, asking in each case what underlying variables were responsible for the composition of the labor force, and what caused any changes in that composition that occurred over time. The present discussion focuses on the unskilled labor force of each colony; the following section of this chapter considers the composition of the colonies' skilled labor forces.

The first cases considered will be those colonies in which slavery became quantitatively important. The description of the evolution of colonial labor forces offered in the previous chapter indicated that the first stage in the growth of slavery to a quantitatively dominant position in the work forces of some colonies involved a large-scale substitution of blacks for whites in the unskilled agricultural labor force. To distinguish this from the later stage in which blacks were trained to perform skilled jobs, this change in the composition of the unskilled labor force will be referred to as the initial transition from servants to slaves.

Investigation of the West Indies is hampered by the scarcity of quantitative evidence available for the region from the seventeenth century. Yet most accounts of the history of Barbados, the Leeward Islands, and Jamaica in the seventeenth century suggest that while in some places initial settlements were based on free and indentured labor, with only minor use of slaves, in all the islands the introduction of sugar as the staple crop was quickly followed by the large-scale use of slaves and a decline in the relative, and eventually absolute, importance of both servants and free workers.[14] Furthermore, it appears that many of the features of the islands' transitions, when placed within the analytical framework suggested in the previous section, point toward a consistent explanation of the causes of this change.

In each of the British West Indian colonies the introduction of sugar set in motion a process that, although it occurred with varying speeds in different places, eventually produced an agricultural system close to monoculture, as sugar replaced the islands' formerly diversified production of cacao, cotton, indigo, tobacco, and other crops. Sugar production raised the marginal productivity of labor sharply in the West Indies, and produced a sudden increase in the demand for labor. There is evidence that in Barbados the early stages of sugar cultivation witnessed both an increase in the quantity of indentured servants imported and a sharp increase in their price relative to slaves.[15] Thus an effort to recruit large numbers of servants for Barbados in order to base the new sugar economy on bound white labor failed in the face of sharply rising labor costs. These movements in the market for servants, together with the considerably greater increase in the numbers of slaves imported to grow sugar, would be the outcomes produced in the short run by an increase in the demand for labor with a less elastic supply of white than of black labor.

Yet the large-scale importation of slaves of Barbados and the other islands continued well beyond the initial period of sugar production. Although most of the islands experienced some sustained growth in total population, their domestic labor supply failed to grow rapidly enough to eliminate the demand for immigrants because of high mortality among all groups in the population, as well as high rates of emigration among former servants and other free whites. Over time, the absolute numbers of servants imported annually by each of the West Indian colonies also declined. This was due to upward shifts in the supply curves for indentured servants that faced West Indian planters, as servants increasingly avoided the islands. This resulted in part from the same consideration that drove so many former servants away from the islands, namely the decreasing economic opportunities for freedmen in the islands as plantations took up the available land, as well as to fear of the islands' high mortality rates and to distaste among English workers for an economy based on slave labor.[16] Another factor in the Englishman's reluctance to emigrate to the West Indies may have had to do with the technology of sugar production and the form of work organization it produced. The technology of sugar production, with high fixed capital requirements for the mill, the boiling and curing houses, and the distillery, resulted in considerable economies of scale, with declining average cost over a greater range than perhaps any other industry of the seventeenth century. West Indian planters soon realized that "the business of sugar planting is a sort of adventure in which the man that engages, must engage deeply," and throughout the islands the consolidation of small farms into large plantations followed the adoption of sugar as the staple crop.[17] Richard Pares has described the great West Indian sugar plantations as factories set in the fields, and their basic unit of labor organization, the gang, produced what may have been as great a change in the organization of agricultural work as factories would later in that of manufacturing. That gang labor became synonymous with slavery was due to the unwillingness of white servants to labor in the large gangs of regimented workers that hoed the ground, planted the sugar, weeded the fields, and cut the cane of the great plantations.[18]

The West Indies' initial transition to slavery in the unskilled labor force therefore appears understandable as the result of a series of changes set in motion by the sudden introduction of large-scale sugar production. In the short run, the resulting increase in the demand for labor drove up the price of indentured labor sharply, and large-scale slave imports began. Over time, as high levels of demand for labor continued, emigration of free workers and high mortality rates among the islands' free populations prevented the domestic labor supply from growing sufficiently to eliminate the demand for immigrants, and all the island colonies continued to import large numbers of workers throughout the colonial period. That these immigrants were overwhelmingly slaves can probably be attributed to the dwindling of economic opportunity for poor freedmen in the islands and the unwillingness of servants to work in gangs, as the rising cost of white labor in the island colonies virtually eliminated whites from field work in the West Indies.

In the Chesapeake, the economic choice between the available types of labor was less clear, and the balance between them more nearly even for an extended period. Tobacco, the Chesapeake's staple from the second decade of Virginia's settlement, required much less fixed capital for its processing than did sugar, and as a result apparently offered no substantial economies of scale. Unlike sugar, throughout the colonial period tobacco was grown on many small farms in addition to some larger plantations. The absence of significant economies of scale retarded the growth of large plantations; although they ultimately developed, they lacked the centralization of the West Indian plantations, as production was carried out on many small "quarters," and their growth occurred much more slowly than in the West Indies. A related characteristic of tobacco, even more important for the question of labor choice, was that many of the operations involved in its production did not lend themselves to gang labor. Tobacco plants are more delicate than sugarcane, and the quality of the product depends in part on the care with which the individual plants are transplanted and trimmed. The form of work organization resulting from the available technology therefore did not make tobacco a crop produced only by slave gangs at any time in the colonial period; consequently, the source of the rise of slavery in Virginia and Maryland must be found elsewhere.

Because of the slower emergence of an economy based significantly on slavery in the Chesapeake, the issue of labor choice there has received considerable attention from historians. Their work has concentrated on the question of why, in the decades around 1700, Chesapeake planters transformed their labor force from one dominated by white servants to one composed predominantly of black slaves.

One answer that has been suggested attributes primary responsibility for the switch from servants to slaves to an increase in relative demand for slaves due to a dramatic reduction in mortality rates that occurred in the Chesapeake in the middle of the seventeenth century.[19] This explanation appears unsatisfactory. In large part, the decline in the Chesapeake's mortality rates was due to a decline in "seasoning" mortality, those deaths that occurred during the first year after an immigrant's arrival in the colonies. If seasoning mortality fell equally on both whites and blacks, it can be shown that the effect of a change in the rate of seasoning mortality would be to change the value of both a servant and a slave to a planter in the same proportion; consequently, changes in seasoning mortality should not have produced any change in the relative demand for the two types of labor.[20]

However, to the extent that the decline in the Chesapeake's mortality rates took the form of declining general mortality which extended the life expectancy of immigrants who survived the seasoning period, this could have affected the relative value of servants and slaves to planters: Clearly, the owner of a worker bound for life stood to gain disproportionately relative to the owner of a worker bound only for a fixed term if the life expectancy of both workers increased. However the timing of the decline in mortality makes it appear unlikely that this effect played a significant role in the change in the composition of the Chesapeake's labor force, for the changes in mortality were apparently largely complete by about 1660,[21] whereas the major changes in the relative shares of white and black labor occurred considerably later, in the years after 1680. It will be argued below that Chesapeake planters had access to slaves throughout this period, and their failure to buy them in large numbers until the 1680s suggests that declining mortality was not a proximate cause of the change in the composition of the region's labor force.

A more convincing explanation of the Chesapeake's initial transition from servants to slaves stresses the central importance of changing conditions of labor supply to the region. A number of recent studies have found that a combination of a large absolute decline in the number of servants on Chesapeake estates and an increase in the number of slaves during the 1680s and 1690s produced a sharply increasing ratio of slaves to servants in the region.[22] The authors of these studies have argued that a decline in the supply of servants to the Chesapeake forced planters to switch to slaves. The available quantitative evidence from the labor market is consistent with this explanation, as both the decline in the number of servants imported into the Chesapeake in the 1680s and the dramatic increase in the price of servants could have resulted from an upward shift in the servant supply curve. Estimates of the elasticity of demand for servants in Maryland and Virginia between 1675 and 1705 provide additional support for the view that Chesapeake planters abandoned the use of white servants only reluctantly, as both the low absolute value of the estimates and their failure to increase in magnitude over time suggest that planters were strongly committed to the use of servants in the late seventeenth century.[23]

Although these historians have correctly emphasized the major impact of changing conditions of servant supply on the Chesapeake's labor force in the late seventeenth century, to some extent they have neglected the importance of contemporaneous changes in the supply of slaves which also contributed to the observed shift in the composition of the labor force. Historians have long believed that it was only with the end of the Royal African Company monopoly of the British slave trade in 1698 that the Chesapeake began to receive significant numbers of slaves. Recent studies have overturned this belief, but have retained the modified view that although direct shipments of slaves from Africa to the Chesapeake had begun by the mid-1670s, until the end of the monopoly the supply of slaves to the Chesapeake was nevertheless small and unreliable.[24] Yet even this does not appear valid. As early as 1664 the governor of Maryland complained that he was unable to find enough planters to cooperate in contracting for shipments of one or two hundred slaves a year from the Company of Royal Adventurers at a fixed rate. The implication is clear that the company would offer a large number of slaves at a guaranteed contract price but, Calvert wrote, "I find wee are nott men of estates good enough to undertake such a businesse, but could wish wee were for wee are naturally inclin'd to love neigros if our purses would endure it."[25] This suggests that a steady supply of slaves was available very early, and that the deficiency that held down the size of Chesapeake slave holdings during most of the seventeenth century was rather in the effective demand of the region's planters.[26]

This situation changed during the 1680s, for at the same time the supply of servants was declining, and their price rising, the price of slaves was at a long-time low. The low price of slaves was the product of an economic depression in the West Indies and other American sugar-producing regions, as a long decline in sugar prices reached the bottom of a trough in the mid-1680s.[27] The failure of the price of slaves in the British West Indies to rise between the mid-1670s and 1690 may have prompted slave traders to look elsewhere for markets, thus producing a downward shift in the supply price of slaves to the Chesapeake. This shift may have been critical in bringing large-scale slavery to the Chesapeake, for it was during the 1670s that total slave holdings in the region began to increase steadily, with an acceleration around 1690.[28] West Indian slave prices began to rise during the early 1690s, and in the following decades no further downward shifts in slave supply prices occurred.

The Chesapeake's initial transition therefore appears to have been caused by changes in the supply conditions of both servants and slaves. A sharp decline in the supply of servants to the region in the 1680s against an inelastic demand curve, in conjunction with a downward shift in the supply curve for slaves in the same decade, produced a dramatic increase of 57 percent in the price of servants relative to that of slaves between 1675 and 1690. This triggered a massive shift in the relative holdings of the two types of unfree labor on Chesapeake farms, as a ratio of 3.88 servants to 1 slave on Maryland estates during 1674-9 was almost completely reversed in a decade, and during 1690-4 Maryland planters held 3.57 slaves for each servant.

The decline in servant supply to the Chesapeake was probably caused by a combination of declining economic opportunities for freed servants in the region in the late seventeenth century and improving opportunities in England. Although evidence on the course of these variables is incomplete, real wages appear to have been rising in England in the final decades of the century, whereas the probability that a former servant in the Chesapeake could remain in the region and acquire land was diminishing. In addition, more recently settled colonies on the mainland, including North and South Carolina and Pennsylvania, were competing for servants on increasingly favorable terms, holding out the prospect of open land and greater economic opportunity than in the increasingly stratified Chesapeake.[29]

The mainland colony perhaps closest to the pattern of the West Indies in both its continuing reliance on imported labor over an extended period and the quantitative importance of slaves in its labor force was South Carolina. Also like the islands, the increase in the black share of the population to a majority in South Carolina coincided with the rise of a single crop to dominance of the colony's economy. However, South Carolina differed from the sugar colonies in that both transitions, to large-scale slavery and rice production, occurred relatively late and relatively gradually: It may have taken five decades or more after the colony's first settlement before rice cultivation occupied more than half the labor force, and during these decades the colony's planters imported significant numbers of servants as well as slaves to grow their crops.

It has been suggested that the delays involved in adopting rice as a staple crop resulted from extended experimentation before the white settlers, who were unfamiliar with rice, were able to grow and process the crop profitably for export, and further that it was the familiarity of West African slaves with rice cultivation that made them particularly attractive to South Carolina planters, as "literally hundreds of black immigrants were more familiar with the planting, hoeing, processing, and cooking of rice than were the Europeans who purchased them."[30] This argument raises the possibility that blacks were considerably more productive than whites in South Carolina after the introduction of rice cultivation. Because rice was initially not grown elsewhere on a large scale, the difference in productivity would have been specific to the colony, and would not have been reflected in the market prices of servants and slaves that faced South Carolina planters. The ratio of marginal productivity to price could therefore have been considerably higher for slaves than for servants, giving a decisive cost advantage to slavery in South Carolina. The high eventual level of blacks in the colony's labor force would also be consistent with the high relative profitability of slaves that would have been the result of this advantage.

A different factor related to South Carolina's agriculture that con- tributed to the rise of slavery was the nature of the work involved in rice production. Like sugar, rice is a crop well suited to cultivation by gang labor, and the gang system was introduced early. The hard work involved in growing rice in gangs in the heat of the colony's summers may have been an important deterrent to servants considering migrating to the colony after rice was adopted as the colony's main product.[31] The increase in the economic importance of rice may therefore have shifted the supply curve of servants facing South Carolina upward, and speeded the colony's initial transition to black labor.

South Carolina's unhealthiness had a significant effect on both its domestic and immigrant labor supply. In 1684 the colony's proprietors complained from London that so many emigrants to Carolina had become ill that the colony had fallen into disrepute, and for many decades thereafter the colony was widely known to Europeans for its unhealthi- ness. Both high mortality rates and the emigration of free workers from the colony diminished its domestic labor supply, as free workers and servants who had gone to Carolina hoping to gain wealth became discouraged by illness and left for other colonies; attempts by colonial leaders to reduce emigration from the colony by prohibiting departures without special licenses failed, and in some decades the colony's white population actually declined.[32]

An important force underlying South Carolina's initial transitition to slavery appears to have been the nature of rice production, once that crop came to dominate the colony's economy. As in the case of sugar in the West Indies, the unwillingness of whites to do the routinized and arduous gang labor in the rice fields of South Carolina shrank the colony's alternative sources of labor, and pushed it toward slavery. The experience and skills of some West Africans in rice cultivation may have increased planters' demand for slaves and speeded the transition, as did the colony's unhealthiness for settlers, which increasingly kept out potential immigrants and drove away free workers after the colony's initial decade of settlement.

New England's labor force offers a sharp contrast to those of the other regions considered to this point. Immigration to the region was unimportant quantitatively after the middle of the seventeenth century, and New England probably had net emigration in many decades. Slaves never made up more than 3 percent of the region's population, and New England imported few European servants. Thus an anonymous commentator complained in about 1660 that although "Virginia thrives by keeping many Servants . . . New England conceit they and their Children can doe enough, and soe have rarely above one Servant."[33]

Yet it appears that New England's relative lack of need for either servants or slaves was not a conceit, but was due to its high rate of population growth and the relatively low annual marginal productivity of labor in its agricultural economy. In most areas family farms produced a variety of crops on a small scale for subsistence or local markets.[34] This agricultural system was combined in most places with high rates of natural increase among the domestic population of white settlers.[35] Together, the low demand for labor and the steady expansion of the domestic supply apparently produced expanding employment at an equilibrium cost of labor that remained below the supply prices of either servants or slaves.[36]

Some parts of New England did depart from this pattern, producing food on a larger scale either for consumption in the cities or for export to other colonies.[37] In these areas the resulting specialization raised the marginal productivity of labor, and therefore the demand for labor. In some of these places the domestic supply of labor was great enough to prevent labor costs from rising to the point at which bound labor would be profitable.[38] However, in others the demand for labor relative to domestic supply resulted in labor costs sufficiently high to produce significant flows of servants and slaves to particular localities. Examples of such areas include the Massachusetts counties around Boston, which produced agricultural crops and did limited manufacturing for both the city and export, Narragansett County in Rhode Island, which produced dairy goods and cattle on large estates for export to the southern colonies and the West Indies, and parts of eastern Connecticut.[39]

The labor force of the Middle Colonies presents a complicated case. Little detailed quantitative evidence on the region is available, but several basic features do seem clear: No colony in the region relied heavily on slave labor, and sizable flows of free and indentured immigrants came to the region over long periods. A larger proportion of these immigrants came from countries other than Great Britain, principally Germany, than was the case for any other region of colonial British America.[40]

Diversified agriculture on a relatively small scale characterized most of the production of the Middle Colonies. Yet considerable variation may have existed, across counties or even smaller areas, in the relative proportions of output farmers produced for their own consumption and for sale in the market. Pennsylvania's agriculture appears to have been quite prosperous and relatively specialized compared with that of New England; it has been estimated that by the middle of the eighteenth century between one-third and one-half of a typical farm's annual output was sold in the market. Such farms produced a variety of grains, vegetables, and livestock, with wheat, Pennsylvania's principal export, the most important market crop.[41]

Although more evidence is necessary before firm conclusions can be drawn, some suggestions concerning the labor market outcomes of the Middle Colonies can be offered. Although small areas existed in parts of the region where slaves were used in significant numbers, the low share of slaves in the region's labor force probably resulted from the combination of relatively high rates of natural increase among the domestic white population and high continuing levels of immigration to the region from Europe. These two sources of increase of the labor supply apparently held the region's hire rates below the level at which slavery would have been profitable. Yet the sustained white immigration which prevented the growth of slavery resulted from the fact that the Middle Colonies' agricultural sector offered a combination of wages and economic opportunities that gave the region, particularly Pennsylvania, a reputation as "the best poor man's country in the world."[42]

The indenture system and the colonial market for skilled labor

To this point, the only part of the labor market considered has been that for unskilled labor. The process referred to above as the initial transition, in which planters in the West Indies, the Chesapeake, and South Carolina switched from servants to slaves as their principal source of agricultural labor, did not bring an end to the use of indentured labor in any of the three regions. In part this was due to the continuing use of some indentured servants as field workers. Planters in each of these regions made frequent attempts to increase the available servant supply, and the search for cheap white labor after 1700 centered chiefly on finding sources of supply other than free Englishmen. Thus, for example, Maryland planters imported considerable numbers of English convicts, particularly after 1718.[43]

But there was a more fundamental reason for the continuing demand for

English indentured servants in the West Indies, the Chesapeake, and South Carolina. It can be understood by extending the model of the labor market presented above. In the earlier discussion the choice between different types of labor was treated as one between alternative forms of unskilled agricultural labor. It is difficult to determine whether the productivity of servants and slaves was equal for the bulk of agricultural workers: Various contemporary statements can be found claiming either that white or black field workers were more productive, and the output data for convincing quantitative tests are lacking. For most places and times in the colonial period, Lewis Gray and other historians are probably correct in their judgments that for unskilled agricultural labor the choice between servants and slaves was one between workers of approximately equal productivity.[44]

Yet the same was not initially true in all parts of the colonial labor market. In all colonies there was some demand for skilled labor. Most of the skills required were traditional European skills which slaves newly imported from Africa normally did not have. The demand for skilled labor could therefore be met either through the hire of free skilled workers, the purchase of skilled indentured servants, or the training of slaves.

The required modification to the model outlined earlier is to divide the labor market. For present purposes, it can simply be divided into two parts, the skilled and the unskilled. Some of the available free labor supply was made up of skilled workers; in the short-run this supply was fixed, and can be represented by a perfectly inelastic supply curve. Some of the potential white immigrants to each region were skilled, and their supply curve had a positive slope, as a result of the same costs of recruitment discussed earlier. Slaves could be trained to perform skilled trades; this involved costs that had to be borne by the planter, including both the direct costs of instruction and the indirect cost of output foregone during the training period. If these costs are assumed to have been approximately constant across individuals, the supply of skilled slaves would be perfectly elastic at a level above that of unskilled slaves, with the difference equal to the full costs of training a slave in a skilled trade.

Throughout most of the period during which a colony converted to slavery on a large scale there was apparently a tendency for the relative cost of skilled black labor to fall. This was due to the fact, widely accepted among colonial planters, that it was easier to train slaves born in America to skilled trades than native Africans. In large part this probably resulted from the greater ability of the American-born slaves to speak English, but the comments of planters suggest that there was also a variety of other reasons why the assimilation of American-born blacks made them easier to train.[45] Whatever the relative importance of these specific factors as causes, John Oldmixon declared in 1708:

There's a great deal of Difference between the Negroes; those that are born in *Barbadoes* are much more useful Men, than those that are brought from *Guinea* . . . the *Creolian* Negroes are every way preferable to the new Comers, (which they call Salt-Water Negroes) . . . The Children that come over young from *Africa* are also better Servants, when they are grown up, than those that come thence Men or Women.[46]

In the Chesapeake, nearly all Africans worked in the fields; it was only the American-born slaves who were trained in skilled crafts in significant numbers.[47] The difference apparently resulted from the lower training costs for those born in America, and this effect produced a tendency for the supply price of skilled black labor to fall as the share of American-born slaves in a colony's population increased. The high training costs for African-born slaves meant that in the early stages of the growth of slavery in a colony's labor force white skilled labor remained cheaper than black. Over time, the growth of the American-born share of the colony's slave population tended to shift the supply curve for skilled slaves downward.[48]

The general case was therefore one in which, following the initial transition from servants to slaves in the unskilled labor force, the implicit annual hire rate of skilled slaves was greater than that of skilled servants. A number of factors subsequently tended to reverse the direction of this relationship, and to produce a shift from white to black in the skilled labor force. One of these was the increase in the demand for skilled labor over time. Because of the more inelastic supply of skilled servants than of slaves, this tended to raise the relative price of skilled servants and lower the share of whites in the skilled labor force.

Other variables contributed to the reversal by shifting the supply curves of skilled white and black labor. One was the downward shift in the supply price of skilled slaves as training costs fell due to the increase in the share of the American-born members of the colony's black labor force. Another was the tendency for the supply price of skilled servants to rise over time owing to rising wages for skilled workers in England.[49]

In most colonies where slavery grew, these three elements – increasing demand for skilled labor with an inelastic supply of skilled white servants, increasing cost of skilled servants resulting from rising wages in England, and falling training costs for slaves resulting from the increasing American-born share of the slave population – combined to produce a substitution of slaves for servants in virtually all skilled work and a consequent halt in the importation of servants at some time following the initial transition from white to black unskilled labor. Thus throughout the West Indian colonies, servant imports tended to cease altogether once a significant American-born slave population grew up in a colony. South Carolina's experience appears to have been similar. Yet this did not occur as distinctly in the Chesapeake. Slaves replaced servants in the bulk of the region's field work during the late seventeenth century, but servants, although increasingly skilled over time, continued to arrive in the region throughout the first three quarters of the eighteenth century. The importance of servants in the region's labor force does appear to have declined rather steadily in the course of this period, both absolutely and relative to slaves, but the question arises of why Chesapeake planters did not convert sooner to a complete reliance on slaves. The answer may lie in the effect of a fourth consideration, for the available evidence suggests that during most of the early eighteenth century the price of slaves was increasing quite rapidly. Thus the price of a prime-aged male slave in Maryland may have increased by as much as 50 percent during the first half of the eighteenth century, while in comparison real wages in most parts of England probably rose by no more than 20 percent in the same period.[50] That this increase in the price of slave labor did not result in a conversion back to the use of servants for field work was probably a result of the fact that unskilled Europeans no longer found the Chesapeake an attractive destination in the eighteenth century, due to its declining economic opportunities for freedmen and perhaps also the increasingly regimented work of the plantations. However the rising price of slaves may have been sufficient to prevent the region's planters from giving up completely on white servants as a source of the skilled labor they needed.[51]

The evolution of colonial labor forces: interregional comparisons

The model of labor supply developed earlier in this chapter is designed for the analysis of the labor markets of individual regions of colonial America. Thus the parameters of each of the three component supply curves in the model – of domestic, white immigrant, and black immigrant labor – are specific to particular colonies at given times. The primary manner in which the model is intended to be applied is illustrated by the series of case studies presented earlier in this chapter, in which the model is used as a framework for the analysis of the composition of a single colony's labor market, and its evolution over time. The extension of the model to the market for skilled labor similarly applies to a single region, and the changes that occurred in it over time.

Yet the extended model does have some significant implications for interregional differences in the composition of immigration, and therefore for the structure of colonial labor forces across regions. One of these implications, of importance to both the analysis of the evolution of the indenture system and the growth of slavery, follows from the model as described above, and offers the possibility of a quantitative test. What the extended model suggests is that in those colonies in which slavery ultimately became quantitatively important, the transition from a principal reliance on bound white labor to one on bound black labor occurred in a sequence of two stages. The first involved a shift from unskilled white field workers to unskilled blacks. This could, but need not necessarily, produce a complete cessation of immigration of unskilled white servants to the colony. Yet what the model suggests is that the initial transition to slaves would tend to produce a relative increase in the quantitative importance of skilled workers among total white immigrants to the colony. Therefore if the sequence implied by the extended model of labor supply was a general phenomenon among colonies where slavery grew, and the transition from servants to the use of unskilled slaves preceded that from servants to the use of skilled slaves, then as long as the demand for skilled relative to unskilled labor was similar across colonies, the extent to which a colony relied on imports of slaves to increase the size of its unskilled labor force should have been positively related to the proportion of its white immigration made up of skilled workers.

The basis of the cross-colony prediction can be seen by reference to the top half of Figure 9.1, which is assumed to represent the relevant general case. Furthermore, the extension of the model of labor supply suggests that a similar diagram can be used to represent the supply of skilled labor to a colony, with a perfectly inelastic supply of domestic skilled labor, a more elastic supply of skilled indentured labor, and a perfectly elastic supply of skilled slave labor. Consider a comparison of two colonies, one of which typically receives larger flows of immigrants relative to its current population than the other. Initially assume that demand is undifferentiated by type of labor. Also assume initially that the colonies under comparison have labor forces of the same size, with similar shares of skilled and unskilled workers, and face the same immigrant supply curves. If both colonies annually import some slaves, annual unskilled employment in both will be greater that q_2, and both will import $(q_2 - q_1)$ unskilled servants. Clearly, the colony with greater annual immigration will import more slaves annually. If the demand for skilled relative to unskilled labor is similar across colonies, the colony with greater annual immigration will also import more skilled labor. Because the use of unskilled slaves will occur before the use of skilled slaves in a colony, increases in the skilled labor force will initially be made up entirely of servants. As a result, the colony with the larger volume of immigration will import more skilled servants than that with lower immigration, and because both colonies import the same number of unskilled servants, the colony with greater immigration will also have a larger share of its immigrant servants made up of skilled workers. This will continue to be true until both colonies have reached the point at which it is cheaper to train slaves to do skilled jobs than to import additional servants (i.e., employment in the skilled labor markets of both colonies is above q_2).

This prediction of the model will generalize to colonies of different absolute sizes as long as the ratios between q_1 and q_2 are similar in the skilled and unskilled labor markets both within each of the two colonies and across colonies. If the assumption of undifferentiated demand by type of labor is dropped, the predictions become only statements of tendencies, for the relative numbers of servants and slaves imported will not be predicted precisely without additional information about demand elasticities. However, it is likely that these two sets of assumptions are sufficiently close to actual conditions not to pose problems for an empirical application of the model. An additional influence on an empirical test derives from the probable importance of differential supply conditions across colonies. It was suggested above that for a number of reasons there was typically a greater tendency for differential conditions of white immigrant supply across colonies to reduce unskilled servant imports to areas with larger shares of slaves in the labor force than to regions with fewer slaves, and this tendency may have had a less than proportional effect on the volume of skilled servant imports. The disproportionate reduction in unskilled white imports would tend to reinforce the prediction of a positive correlation between the share of slaves in total immigration and the share of the skilled among the indentured immigrants.

Before examining the empirical evidence, the basis of the prediction might briefly be summarized. The price of slave relative to indentured labor fell as a colony's demand for labor increased because the supply of slaves was more elastic than that of servants. Slaves were initially substituted for servants only in unskilled jobs because slaves newly imported from Africa did not possess the skills needed to replace most skilled whites; furthermore, the lag involved in training slaves after the introduction of slave labor into a colony was lengthened by the fact that it was less costly to train slaves born in America than Africans. Therefore for some time after a colony had switched to a primary reliance on slaves for its unskilled labor, it continued to use servants to perform its skilled work. The prediction made here is based on this fact and the assumptions that the relationship between the supply of skilled and unskilled immigrants was similar across regions and that the relative quantities of skilled and unskilled workers needed were also similar across regions. Under these conditions, it would be the colonies which imported the largest number of slaves relative to servants that would import the greatest number of skilled relative to unskilled servants.

The evidence of the servant registrations on the skill composition of servants emigrating from England by colony of destination, in conjunction with the estimates of decennial net migration to each colony by race, can be used to test the prediction. The relevant evidence on flows of servants was presented in Table 6.6. The registrations indicated that there was no significant difference between the proportions of skilled workers among servants bound in Bristol for Barbados and the Chesapeake during 1654–61. This result does not support the prediction suggested here, for the migration estimates summarized in Chapter 8 show that the share of blacks in net labor imports to Barbados during the 1650s was nearly two-thirds, compared with less than 10 percent in the case of the Chesapeake. The explanation of the absence of the predicted relationship may have to do with the fact that in the 1650s Barbados was just undergoing its initial transition to black field workers. During the decade, some Barbados plantations continued to hold large numbers of indentured servants, and the colony's planters made considerable efforts to increase the unskilled white labor supply facing the colony.[52] The absence of the predicted relationship may be evidence of their success in shifting the white immigrant labor supply outward during the 1650s, combined with a lag in the demand for skilled labor as planters concentrated on expanding the unskilled labor force to capture the initial high returns from their newly introduced staple crop.

The Barbados planters' success in recruiting unskilled servants was short-lived, however, for as seen earlier the number of servants registered in Bristol who were bound for the colony dropped sharply after 1660, and the share of blacks in the colony's net immigration increased further. By the 1680s, both Barbados and Jamaica had converted almost entirely to black field labor, whereas the Chesapeake was just undergoing its less complete initial transition to slave labor. Blacks accounted for less than one-half of the Chesapeake's net immigration in the decade, but they made up more than four-fifths of total net migration to both Barbados and Jamaica. Pooling the two sets of servant registrations from the decade of the 1680s, those from Bristol for 1684–6 and Middlesex for 1683–4, indicates that skilled servants made up larger shares of the total servants bound for both Barbados (37.5 percent) and Jamaica (36.5 percent) than of those bound for the Chesapeake (30.3 percent).[53] By this time the difference in the composition of the labor imports of Barbados and Jamaica and of the Chesapeake had therefore been clearly established, as the island colonies had both higher shares of blacks among their total immigration and higher shares of skilled men among the indentured servants they imported.

The difference that had been established by the 1680s grew over time. A number of West Indian colonies imported small numbers of servants in the eighteenth century, but the major servant importer in the region was

Jamaica. By the time of the London servant registrations of 1718–59, the share of blacks in Jamaica's net migration was consistently more than 90 percent, whereas the share of blacks in the Chesapeake's net immigration, although erratic, was generally considerably lower. The share of the skilled among servants bound for Jamaica was over 70 percent, more than 22 percentage points higher than the share of the skilled among the Chesapeake's registrants. Thus whereas the dominance of black field labor in Jamaica produced a very high proportion of skilled servants among white immigrants, the less complete conversion to slave labor in the Chesapeake left a considerably larger unskilled share among the region's white immigrants.[54]

That the principal colonial regions that imported servants were becoming increasingly reliant on slave labor after the middle of the seventeenth century might further be taken to imply that the share of the skilled among English immigrants to the colonies would have risen over time. In the long run this did occur, as in the earliest servant registrations, from 1654–60, the share of skilled workers among all the men registered was 50.4 percent, compared with 56.6 percent skilled among the men registered in 1718–59, and 85.1 percent among those registered in 1773–5.[55] Yet this secular trend is not a necessary implication of the model presented earlier, for it would assume that changes in servant supply did not occur to offset the effects of colonial demand in producing this result. A major change in supply conditions appears to have occurred in the third quarter of the seventeenth century, as the share of the skilled servants among all men covered by the two samples from the 1680s was only 33.4 percent, considerably below the skilled share of registrants from Bristol in the 1650s.[56] As discussed earlier, rising real wages in England in this period, presumably accompanied by rising rates of employment, may have tended to reduce the supply of servants to the colonies. Russell Menard has argued that this produced a decline in the quality of servants bound for the Chesapeake in the late seventeenth century, and the evidence of the servant registrations supports this contention, as well as raising the possibility that this decline in the share of the skilled among indentured immigrants was a phenomenon common to all the major servant-importing colonies in the period.[57]

The test carried out in this section offers strong support for the validity of the extended model of labor supply developed earlier in this chapter and for the scheme of development it implies for the evolution of the labor forces of the colonies of British America. What the evidence analyzed here has indicated is that between the last quarter of the seventeenth century and the middle of the eighteenth, those West Indian colonies that had a higher ratio of slaves to servants in their total labor imports than the Chesapeake also had a higher ratio of skilled to unskilled workers among the servants they imported than did the Chesapeake. This is the result implied by the action of two central mechanisms in the suggested model of labor supply, the greater elasticity of black than of white labor supply and the lag between the use of slaves as field hands and the training of slaves to perform skilled occupations. Although the evidence of the servant registrations is not continuous over time, and therefore does not allow precise datings of the transitions described here for each colony, the spacing of the available samples does make it possible to bracket the timing of the significant changes in the evolution of the labor forces of some major regions.

During the 1650s, the demand for labor in Barbados relative to the available supply of white immigrants had not produced a complete transition to unskilled black labor; the colony's planters actively continued to recruit unskilled whites, and the skill composition of its servant imports had not become differentiated from that of the Chesapeake. By the 1680s, however, both Barbados and Jamaica had converted to a primary reliance on unskilled black labor, and the greater substitution by West Indian than Chesapeake planters of unskilled slaves for servants was reflected in the fact that a larger proportion of the indentured servants the West Indian planters imported in the decade possessed craft skills.

Barbados had been the first British colony to import slaves on a large scale, and during the late seventeenth century the colony's planters ceased to import significant numbers of indentured servants. Thus by the close of the century it had become cheaper to use blacks in Barbados' skilled occupations than white servants. This timing is consistent with the implication of the observation of Oldmixon and others, concerning the effects of the greater acculturation of American-born blacks, that it was less expensive to train American-born slaves than Africans to do skilled work, for by the end of the seventeenth century Barbados had a sizable population of slaves who had been born in the colony. Jamaica's later development of a large black population meant that it had a smaller population of American-born blacks relative to Africans than did Barbados, and Jamaica's planters continued to import skilled white servants well into the first half of the eighteenth century.

By the early eighteenth century, the extent of the Chesapeake's reliance on unskilled slave labor had also increased, but it remained below that of Jamaica's. Because Chesapeake planters continued to use some servants in field work, the share of the skilled among Jamaica's indentured immigrants was considerably higher than among the Chesapeake's during the first half of the century. By the 1770s, Jamaica's planters had ceased to import indentured servants, for the colony had come to rely on slaves for its skilled as well as its unskilled labor. Among the regions that had begun with a reliance on indentured labor and later converted to a predominant use of slaves, only the Chesapeake remained in the market for servants. By the 1770s nearly all the field work of the region's plantations was done by slaves; therefore by the close of the colonial period most indentured immigrants to Maryland and Virginia possessed skilled occupations.

The analysis presented here indicates that the process by which a number of regions of colonial America changed from a heavy reliance on white indentured servants for their labor needs to the use of black slaves can be understood through the use of an explanatory framework that focuses on differences in the conditions of supply of the two types of labor and changes in these supply conditions over time. The more elastic supply of blacks than of whites produced an increase in the relative price of white labor in regions with high levels of demand for immigrant labor, and a consequent tendency for planters to substitute blacks for white workers. This was done relatively easily in the unskilled field work that occupied the bulk of colonial labor forces, but could not be done in the colonies' skilled jobs until blacks had been given craft training. The large-scale use of black field hands therefore preceded the use of slaves in craft occupations. Once slaves had been substituted for servants in a colony's field work, the principal use of servants was to perform skilled jobs. Therefore, a colony's initial transition to slavery was followed by an increase in the share of the servants bound for the colony who had occupational skills.

The lag involved in training slaves to do skilled work was typically long because of the lower cost involved in training acculturated American-born slaves than their African-born parents. But as a colony's American-born slave population grew, the relative cost of skilled black labor fell. Rising wages for skilled workers in England between the late seventeenth and mid-eighteenth centuries tended to raise the cost of skilled servants. Although the effect of the latter tendency was uniform across all the colonies, the timing of the decline in the cost of training slaves in a colony depended on the date at which large-scale slavery had been introduced, and therefore varied across colonies. Consequently, the order in which colonies substituted skilled slaves for servants, and ceased to import indentured labor, tended to be the same as the order in which they had earlier substituted unskilled slaves for servants.

This chapter has developed a model of labor supply intended to serve as a framework for analyzing the composition of the labor force of a region of colonial America. The development was done in two parts. The first presented a model of labor supply that considered only the market for unskilled labor, quantitatively by far the more important part of the labor market in the colonies. This version of the model was applied to the development of the labor force of each major colonial region to aid in understanding the significant differences in the relative importance of sustained immigration in general, and of slavery in particular, that existed across regions. In New England, rapid natural increase among the original population of white immigrants combined with low labor productivity to make immigration unimportant to the region after the early colonial period. The Middle Colonies probably had generally higher labor productivity, and because of the higher wages this produced, sustained immigration played a significant role in the region's history. But the immigrants were predominantly white, as Middle Colonies attracted large numbers of Europeans over a long period. It was in the staple-producing colonies farther south that slavery became quantitatively important. In the Chesapeake, white servants satisfied the greatest part of planters' labor needs for more than half a century, but then a decline in the flow of English immigrants to the region in the 1680s forced planters somewhat reluctantly to turn to slaves as their principal source of unskilled labor. The conversion to the large-scale use of slaves in the sugar fields of the West Indies and the rice fields of South Carolina was more rapid after the introduction of those staples, as the unwillingness of whites to work under the conditions created by the southern regions' climates and technologies made slaves the clear economic choice. What the evidence indicates in each of these cases, however, is that some whites were involved in the production of each of these crops in the early years of production, and that it was only after some time that their price rose too high to make their use in the fields profitable. Therefore, it was no inherent characteristic of blacks that made slavery an economic necessity for the southern colonial regions, but rather a choice by whites to avoid the work conditions of these areas that made slavery the economic solution of planters. An interpretation of the perfectly elastic supply of black labor to the colonies suggested by the model of labor supply is simply the recognition that blacks did not share with potential white immigrants their ability to choose.

The second part of the development involved an extension of the model to include the market for skilled labor. This provided a more formal explanation for the sequence of two stages in the process by which slavery replaced indentured servitude in the southern colonial regions. The need to train slaves to do the skilled work of the plantations, and particularly the fact that the cost of training American-born blacks was lower than that for Africans, meant that the substitution of skilled slaves for servants lagged some time behind the initial transition from unskilled servants to slaves. An empirical test based on an implication of this extended version of the model, using the evidence of the English servant registrations on the destinations of servants by skill, provided support for the prediction that

White servitude in the colonial labor market

the share of slaves in a colony's flows of immigrants would be positively related to the share of the colony's white immigrants who possessed skills. The quantitative evidence of the servant registrations, therefore, is consistent with the view that the transition from servants to slaves occurred in two steps, as skilled servants continued to be imported into a region even after slaves had replaced servants in field work.

168

Part V

Indentured servitude in American history

10

Indentured labor in the Americas:
the experience of three centuries

Servitude in colonial British America

The indenture system resulted from the efforts of early British colonizers of America to transplant the English system of service in husbandry to the New World. Under the English system, boys and girls left home in their early teens to work by the year, usually as farm servants. During this period they lived in the households of their employers, typically remaining in the status of life-cycle servants until they married. A significant alteration of the English institution was required to enable many young English men and women to perform their life-cycle service in British America, for the cost of the transatlantic voyage was greater than most could pay out of their savings, and credit for the passage fare was typically unavailable from existing sources in England. The innovation of the colonial system of indentured servitude provided the necessary credit to those who wished to emigrate to British America. The form it took, with the labor of the servants leased for specific periods to the masters who purchased their contracts, meant that the system also supplied colonial planters with a bound labor force.

The longer terms of the servants' contracts in the colonies, together with the conditions of the colonial legislation that came to define the institution, made it more clearly a genuine system of white servitude than its English counterpart. Colonial servitude also came to be distinctly separated from slavery by the legal status of servants as well as their limited terms of service. White servants enjoyed such rights as the ability to sue in court and to give testimony, rights typically denied to black slaves. However, servants were universally subject to strict requirement of specific performance of their contractual obligations by colonial courts, and were subject to harsh punishment for attempts to avoid them.

Little systematic evidence is available on the typical treatment of indentured servants by their masters. Court records provide evidence that in some cases considerable abuses of servants occurred, but few sources concerning normal conditions exist with which to evaluate Richard Ligon's contention concerning Barbados in the mid-seventeenth century:

Slaves and their posterity, being subject to their Masters forever, are kept and preserv'd with greater care than their servants, who are theirs but for five yeers . . . So that for the time, the servants have the worser lives, for they are put to very hard labour, ill lodging, and their dyet very slight.[1]

It has been noted that Ligon's judgment is called into question by his own evidence, which indicates that servants were more carefully fed, clothed, and housed than slaves.[2] Servants were certainly better protected by colonial laws than were slaves. Whereas masters were typically free to punish their slaves in any way they chose, and in many colonies could at worst be fined for killing a slave, corporal punishment for major crimes could be inflicted on servants only by legal authorities, and a master who killed his servant could be tried for murder. Legislation even appeared in the West Indies establishing the minimum standards of food and clothing to be provided for servants.[3] Although these types of evidence again cannot tell us of typical conditions, the protection the servants' basic rights as Englishmen gave them against gross abuses must often have differentiated them from slaves in a significant way. There were, of course, many other factors that influenced the conditions servants encountered during their terms of servitude. For example, the size of the plantation on which they worked probably had a significant effect on their treatment, as small farms, on which servants lived and worked closely with the master and his family, might have been more conducive to treatment of servants as additional members of the family than the large plantations, with their greater regimentation of the labor force.

White servitude was present in British America before slavery, and white servants were the principal source of labor in each of the staple-producing regions before being replaced by slaves. The most intriguing questions about the indenture system therefore have to do with why it declined in importance over time throughout British America, and why slavery gained in importance in most of the areas where servitude had initially been significant. The procedure of this study in approaching these questions was first to look for evidence from an examination of the changing characteristics of the population of indentured servants. The patterns that emerged from this analysis, when combined with evidence from other sources on the population and labor force of British America, led to a systematic description of the way in which servitude interacted with both slavery and free labor in the labor markets of colonial America, and how its relation to these other forms evolved over time. This chapter reviews the principal conclusions that emerged from the quantitative examination of the servant population, and summarizes the characterization of the role of white servitude in the colonial labor market that these produced.

The servant registrations that constituted the basic source of information for this investigation provided evidence about a number of aspects of the composition of the servant population and how it changed over time. With respect to age, throughout the period from the mid-seventeenth century to the American Revolution, the population of migrant servants apparently closely resembled that of English life-cycle servants, as both groups consisted overwhelmingly of individuals in their late teens and early twenties. Unlike their English counterparts, the colonial servants were predominantly male. The share of men among the servants also tended to rise over time, from about three-quarters of the total migrants in the seventeenth century to nine-tenths in the eighteenth.

The occupational distribution of the male servants changed considerably over time. The earliest registrations, from the 1650s, suggest that in that period the men were evenly divided between those with work experience and skills and those without experience and specific occupational skills. In the following decades the servants' average skill levels may have declined, as registrations from the 1680s indicate that perhaps only one-third of the men would be categorized as skilled. The two sets of eighteenth-century registrations point to a reversal of this trend, however, with sharply rising proportions of skilled servants during the last hundred years of the colonial period, as the skilled made up nearly three-fifths of the men registered during the second quarter of the eighteenth century, and 85 percent of those registered in the 1770s. The share of men whose occupational titles indicate agricultural backgrounds also tended to decline over time, so that those with work experience were increasingly drawn from manufacturing and service occupations.

The servant registrations also point to major temporal shifts in the destinations of the servants. A number of West Indian colonies rose to important positions as servant importers, only to decline and later virtually to leave the market for servants. Such was the case most notably for Barbados and Nevis in the seventeenth century, and for Jamaica in the eighteenth. The Chesapeake colonies of Virginia and Maryland were the only British colonies that remained important destinations for servants throughout the period from the 1650s through the 1770s. Pennsylvania also began to import servants in significant numbers during the eighteenth century.

Examination of the servants' patterns of migration to the colonies produced an additional finding involving the destinations of the male servants by occupation. From the 1680s through the middle of the eighteenth century, when the West Indies ceased to import servants, in cross-sectional comparisons of destinations, servants with occupational skills were found to have been more likely to migrate to the West Indian colonies than to the North American mainland. An examination of regional migration estimates for the same period revealed the existence across colonies of a positive relation between the share of slaves in a colony's net immigration and the share of its immigrant servants who were skilled: the more heavily a colony depended on the importation of slaves to satisfy its labor requirements, the higher the proportion of its indentured immigrants who possessed skills.

This evidence on the changing composition and distribution of the servant population over time and space contributed to the construction of a schematic view of the evolution of the role of white servitude in British America, based on an understanding of its functions relative to free and slave labor. In some regions, notably New England and parts of the Middle Colonies, white servitude was never important quantitatively. These areas were characterized by typically low levels of immigration and labor forces made up overwhelmingly of free workers. In other regions, including some of the southern mainland colonies and all the islands of the English West Indies, white servitude was a major source of labor during an initial phase of colonization and development of a staple-producing economy. These colonies typically had consistently high levels of immigration and high shares of the labor force composed of unfree workers. These were the areas in which slavery ultimately grew to quantitative importance, and in each of these colonies sometime during the colonial period slaves came to outnumber servants.

In the latter group of colonies, the process by which slavery replaced servitude occurred in two steps. The first, referred to here as the initial transition to slavery, involved the replacement of servants by slaves in the unskilled field labor of staple-crop cultivation. For some time after this shift occurred, a racial division of labor by skill existed, as white servants continued to be imported as a source of skilled labor and slaves performed the unskilled work of the fields. Finally, in each of these colonies there arose a tendency for slaves to be trained to perform skilled jobs, and this ultimately led planters to cease importing servants altogether.

An economic model of labor supply to the principal regions of British America was used to identify the forces that produced the observed variation in the mix of labor types across colonies, and to explain the timing of the shifts from primary reliance on one type to another. The analysis focused on the labor market as the central mechanism that influenced immigration to a colony. The domestic labor force, those workers already present in a colony, was the most readily available and initially the cheapest source of labor supply. Low levels of the annual marginal productivity of labor therefore tended to be associated with low levels of immigration, as regions where labor productivity appears to have been low did not attract immigrants. Because nearly all the initial colonization of each of the major regions of British America was done by free workers, colonies with persistently low immigration were normally characterized by predominantly free labor forces. The supply of unfree labor was potentially more responsive to differences across regions in labor productivity than that of free labor; because a larger number of Europeans were able to migrate under indenture than as free settlers, over time a given level of economic opportunity tended to attract more indentured servants than free settlers to a region, and high cash bids were sufficient to bring slaves. As a result, there appears generally to have been a positive association between the annual marginal productivity of labor in a colony and the quantitative importance of unfree labor in its labor force. Furthermore, there were significant differences in the supply conditions of the two types of unfree workers. European men and women could exercise choice both in deciding whether to migrate to the colonies and in choosing between possible destinations, and as a result there were differences across individuals in the bargains that would attract servants to a colony. Some white immigrants were usually available to a colony's planters at an implicit annual cost lower than that of slaves. This meant that as a colony's demand for labor rose, the first immigration in response to its rising economic opportunities would be composed of Europeans; at most times, and for most colonies, the bulk of these were indentured servants. Those servants willing to go to a particular colony at the lowest cost to planters would be the first to be carried there, but as the desired volume of immigrant labor rose, the supply of willing recruits tended to be depleted, and increasingly attractive terms of indenture, representing higher costs to colonial planters, became necessary to induce larger flows of servants to the colony. In contrast, slaves obviously lacked the ability to determine their destinations, and slave traders chose their markets largely by the prices offered for their cargoes. The British colonies were only one of the American destinations of African slaves, and no British colony received more than about one-tenth of the total transatlantic flow of slaves over an extended period. Therefore, large numbers of slaves were generally available to colonial planters at a fixed current market price. This implied that once the cost of labor in a colony rose to a level high enough to warrant the importation of slaves at their relatively high price, further increases in the volume of immigration would tend to be made up chiefly of slaves. Because the supply of slaves was more elastic than that of free workers or servants – increasing the volume of the flows of immigrant slaves did not entail the rising labor costs involved in attracting larger numbers of Europeans – it was the colonies with the highest continuing levels of immigration that tended to rely most heavily on slaves.

The patterns of labor force composition described here were reinforced in some degree by differences in the labor supply facing different regions. The nonpecuniary conditions of labor and life in the colonies often tended to reduce the supply of both domestic and white immigrant labor precisely

175

to those colonies where the annual productivity of labor appears to have been highest, and to increase the supply of white immigrants to regions where labor productivity was lower. Thus the high mortality rates and gang labor of the West Indies and South Carolina contributed to making those colonies unattractive to free whites and indentured servants, and the tendencies toward concentration of landholding and rising land prices throughout the staple-producing regions, which restricted the opportunities for freedmen to become landowners, caused many actual and prospective white immigrants to look elsewhere for homes. In contrast, the long-standing availability of land for small farms for freedmen in the Middle Colonies made that region persistently attractive to immigrants, and the same phenomenon may have contributed to the high rate of natural increase among New England's population.

In the terms of the analysis used in this study, the differences in the composition of labor forces across colonies can be traced to different outcomes in their regional markets for labor. Those colonies in which the annual productivity of labor appears to have been relatively low, principally in New England, imported little labor of any kind after the substantial initial migration to the region of the second quarter of the seventeenth century. In other regions, where the annual marginal product of labor was high enough to produce continuing immigration, the new flows of immigrants initially tended to be white workers, primarily indentured servants; only when the demand for labor drove the cost of labor to a higher level did black slaves begin to be imported. Thus the use of servants preceded black slavery chronologically throughout the American colonies. Similarly, slavery was adopted on a large scale first in the West Indies where, as indicated by the analysis of the length of servants' indentures, the annual marginal productivity of labor was persistently above that of the mainland colonies. The greater elasticity of the black than of the white labor supply implied that colonies with high levels of annual net immigration would tend to have immigrant populations composed heavily of slaves. This was the case most strikingly in the West Indies, followed in declining degree with respect to both variables by South Carolina and the Chesapeake. Over time, there was also an additional tendency for the share of blacks in immigration to these regions to rise as the nonpecuniary considerations noted above increasingly made prospective white immigrants look to more recently settled areas as destinations in the colonies. In some cases, as in Pennsylvania, due in large part to the nature of the regional economy, the reputation of a colony or region as a land of opportunity for immigrants would persist, and attract enough Europeans to make possible sizable flows of voluntary immigration to meet the colony's labor needs for an extended period without creating the upward pressure on the cost of labor in the colony that could have led to the large-scale importation of slaves.

The lag observed in both the West Indies and the southern mainland colonies between the initial transition to the use of slave labor in the fields and the later substitution of blacks for whites in skilled jobs was analyzed through an extension of the initial analysis of labor supply, by dividing the labor market into the sectors of unskilled and skilled. The analysis of skilled labor supply was parallel to that of the unskilled, as the potential quantity of white labor available to a colony was less responsive to changes in the price of labor than was that of black labor. The supply of skilled slaves was perfectly elastic at a cost above that of unskilled slaves, with the differential in price equal to the full costs of training a slave in a craft. Consideration of this extended framework indicated that the cost of skilled servants relative to skilled slaves tended to rise over time because of the effects of rising colonial demand for skilled labor under conditions of an inelastic supply of servants and because the cost of attracting skilled white immigrants to America increased over time as English wages for skilled workers rose. The cost of skilled relative to unskilled slaves may have declined over time. Training costs were lower for American-born slaves than for Africans, because of the greater familiarity with English and the generally greater acculturation of the former, and this produced a tendency for the cost of skilled slaves relative to free workers or servants to fall over time, as the share of American-born slaves in a colony's population increased. The combination of the rising price of skilled indentured labor and the declining relative cost of skilled slave labor ultimately resulted in the widespread investment in the training of slaves to replace servants in virtually all the skilled jobs of the British colonies' sugar, tobacco, and rice plantations.

As a result of the operation of these forces, indentured servitude had almost completely disappeared from the British West Indies by the time of the American Revolution. Thus, of 3,359 indentured servants registered upon departing from England during 1773–5, only 12 were bound for the West Indies. By that time, slaves had come to dominate the labor forces of the West Indian colonies: In 1770, blacks made up 84 percent of the population of Barbados, and larger shares of the populations of Jamaica, Antigua, Montserrat, Nevis, and St. Kitts.

Four-fifths of the emigrating English servants registered in the 1770s were bound for the Chesapeake, while one-fifth were bound for Pennsylvania. The servant population was also increased, particularly in Pennsylvania, by the immigration of German redemptioners. Yet by this time neither in the Chesapeake nor in Pennsylvania did indentured servants account for a sizable fraction of the labor force. Thus a sample of

143 probate inventories recorded in ten counties of Maryland and Virginia in 1774 has revealed that whereas 63 percent of the decedents whose estates were inventoried had owned slaves, with an average of more than eight slaves per owner, only 6 percent had owned servants, with a mean of less than two servants per owner. A sample of 163 inventories from three Pennsylvania counties in the same year similarly showed servants to have been present in only 7 percent of the estates probated, with an average of less than two servants in each estate in which any servants were present; even there slaves were present in a slightly higher proportion of the estates in the sample than were servants, and in slightly larger average numbers per owner.[4] The declining relative importance of indentured servitude in the labor forces of both the Chesapeake and Pennsylvania in the third quarter of the eighteenth century is reflected in the generally low estimated levels of net white immigration to both of these regions in the decades after 1750, decades in which rapid growth of the domestic populations of the two regions was also tending to diminish the relative importance of immigrant labor in their work forces.

The principal function of the indenture system examined in this study has been its role as a source of labor to the colonial economy. Although investigation of a number of other dimensions of the system's accomplishment lies beyond the scope of this treatment, one of the more important might briefly be raised here. This concerns the extent to which indentured servitude enabled ambitious Europeans to better themselves economically in the New World. Although such barriers to economic mobility in the New World as seasoning mortality are obviously relevant to this question, in large part its resolution turns on the experience of servants after the completion of their terms of servitude. The most detailed studies of this pertain to the early Chesapeake, and suggest that although economic opportunities for freedmen in that region were substantial from earliest settlement through the third quarter of the seventeenth century, they deteriorated significantly thereafter. Thus the rates of both wealth accumulation and land acquisition fell for freedmen, so that by late in the century the tobacco coast no longer offered former servants the opportunity it had earlier to remain in the region and become prosperous members of its society.[5] The same evolution may have occurred elsewhere in the colonies, perhaps most rapidly in regions where profitable export opportunities led to the dominance of the production of staple crops on large estates, driving up the price of land and raising some types of economic gains for earlier settlers at the expense of newcomers. Yet except in extreme cases of this concentration of production, as perhaps in the smaller sugar islands where freed servants without skills had only the unappealing prospect of gang labor on large plantations, the colonies normally offered work for all, and standards of living for hired laborers after the earliest phases of colonization that probably compared favorably in most places with those the servants had left behind them in Europe.

The American Revolution did not put an end to the use of indentured labor. The war disrupted the operation of the system by temporarily curtailing immigration, but the servant trade revived in the early 1780s.[6] Although the extent of enforcement of English legislation against emigration is not known, an apparent tendency for the postwar indenture system to rely more heavily on German and Irish relative to English immigrants than before the war might have been due in part to an English law of 1785 prohibiting the transport of emigrants on English ships for the purpose of servitude for debt, as well as to other acts of Parliament of the 1780s and 1790s, intended to prevent the emigration of English artisans.[7] Legislation passed by individual American states in the aftermath of the Revolution altered the legal basis of indentured servitude only in minor ways, and the system persisted in use, although on a very limited scale, into the nineteenth century.[8]

The history of the final demise of indentured servitude in the United States remains obscure. Although apparent isolated cases of the indentured servitude of immigrants can be found as late as the 1830s, the system had become quantitatively insignificant in mainland North America much earlier, probably by the close of the eighteenth century.[9] Its end in the United States was not dramatic, and a number of forces might have contributed to its final gradual disappearance. In the Chesapeake, the substitution of black slaves for white servants, already well advanced by the close of the colonial period, might have been accelerated by the temporary disruption of the servant trade during the Revolution and continuing low levels of English migration to the Chesapeake after the war.[10] More fundamentally, the disappearance of indentured servitude as a significant part of the American labor force might have been linked to a general decline in the quantitative importance of immigration in the late eighteenth and early nineteenth centuries. There is evidence suggesting that, as in the nineteenth century, changes in the American rate of economic growth were an important determinant of both levels and trends in migration to British America during the seventeenth and eighteenth centuries.[11] The period between the American Revolution and the War of 1812 may have been marked by initial economic decline and a subsequent period of recovery in America at rates of economic growth lower than those of the periods immediately preceding and following it.[12] Therefore the disruptive effects of the Revolution on immigration might have been succeeded by a continuing low level of economic stimulus to immigration.[13] The beginnings of the large-scale Atlantic migration of the nineteenth century might then have been produced in part by accelerating economic growth after 1820. By this time, the low cost of passage across the Atlantic had

179

apparently eliminated the need for an indenture system for most European immigrants, and the great nineteenth-century transatlantic migration from Europe to the United States was composed of free workers and their families.

Servitude in the Americas in the nineteenth century

Yet the use of the indenture to facilitate long-distance migration in the presence of imperfect capital markets had not ended, for indentured servitude became common in a number of areas in the nineteenth century, and indentures remained in use even for migration to the Americas.[14] At the same time the indenture system was disappearing from the United States, the abolition of slavery in the British sugar colonies in the 1830s produced a renewed demand for indentured labor. Plantation owners, accustomed to a bound labor force, were unhappy with the considerable reduction of black labor supply that typically followed emancipation and the resulting increase in wages, as well as such other aspects of their loss of control over their workers as the irregularity of their work schedules and the perceived lower quality of their labor. These planters formed powerful lobbies in Great Britain to argue for the promotion of immigration to their colonies to lower labor costs and allow them to recapture their positions in international sugar markets. One step toward this goal was government subsidization of immigration, and in some cases the British government guaranteed loans made for the purpose of transporting immigrants to the sugar colonies. But the problem of controlling the geographic mobility of the immigrants after they arrived in the colonies remained, and colonial planters continued to lobby for the right to indenture their workers to prevent them from deserting their estates. After offering considerable resistance to this proposal for fear of creating the appearance of a new slave trade, the British Colonial Office gradually yielded, and ultimately agreed to permit the use of indenture contracts under which immigrants to a colony were imported to work for specific employers for fixed terms.[15]

This revival of the use of indentured labor in the nineteenth-century British sugar colonies and parts of South America constituted a historical episode distinctly different from the earlier use of bound workers in the British colonies of the seventeenth and eighteenth centuries. Whereas the indenture system had earlier involved the immigration of Europeans to America, in the nineteenth century it was principally to Asia that West Indian planters turned for a supply of bound labor. Indentured Indians began to arrive in British Guiana in 1838, and that colony was soon joined as an importer by Trinidad and Jamaica.[16] Shipments of indentured Chinese to Cuba began in 1847, and within a decade British Guiana, Trinidad, and Peru had also received cargoes of bound Chinese laborers.[17]

The form of the contracts commonly used in the migrations to each of these places differed somewhat from that used in the earlier period; for example, wages were generally paid to the Asian servants of the nineteenth century, and the contracts often called for them to be provided with return passage to their country of origin upon completion of their term. Yet the immigrants normally worked for fixed terms of years, without the power to change employers, under legal obligation of specific performance of their contracts, and were therefore bound under contracts of servitude rather than simply contracts of debt that could be terminated by repayment of the principal.

The annual flows of workers migrating to the Americas under indenture in the nineteenth century appear to have been considerably larger in absolute terms than those of the previous two centuries. Precise measurements of the total numbers of immigrants in both periods are unavailable, but estimates suggest that whereas indentured European migration to the American colonies of the seventeenth and eighteenth centuries totaled less than half a million individuals over a period of 150 years, at least half a million Asians, and perhaps considerably more, migrated to the Americas under indenture in a period only about half as long in the nineteenth and early twentieth centuries.[18] Significant qualitative differences also existed in the characteristics of the migrations of the two periods. Unlike the operation of servitude in the earlier era, under which masters imported servants of the same race as themselves, the later movement involved the importation of Asians to work under masters of a different race, and into countries where the bulk of the population was of a different race than the servants. Another difference lay in the fact that whereas indentured migration to the pre-revolutionary American colonies involved movement from economically advanced to relatively backward areas, the opposite was generally the case in the later migration, as Asians moved from less developed to more advanced regions.[19]

These differences resulted from a variety of economic and political forces, and their implications for such comparative features of the systems as the treatment of the workers during their terms and their prospects for economic success after serving their terms are not fully known. Yet a common economic foundation of the use of the device of indentured servitude in these episodes does appear to have existed. In each case the institution appears to have arisen under circumstances in which a sizable difference in labor productivity existed between two regions, and in which a large net flow of labor was therefore warranted by economic conditions but was not feasible under the existing sources of capital to finance the migration. The use of indentures then provided a new source of capital, as the intermediation of merchants allowed prospective immigrants to America to borrow the cost of passage from American farmers and planters in the form of advances against their future labor services. The importance of political considerations has meant, of course, that this economic basis has constituted only a set of necessary, rather than sufficient, conditions for the emergence of an indenture system. However, when used under these circumstances, the indenture system typically provided for the large-scale movement of workers, predominantly male and virtually all in prime work ages, in a single direction.

The use of indentured Asians in the Americas, long under attack by the governments of the sending countries as well as by the same organized groups that had led the campaign to abolish slavery, which opposed servitude in all forms, finally came to an end as the result of a series of political actions that began in the late nineteenth century and were completed in 1917.[20] The revival by planters of a system of servitude after the abolition of slavery had been motivated by the same desire to reduce labor costs that had originally prompted British colonists of the seventeenth century to devise the system of indentured servitude, and the later use of indentured labor was brought to an end by political, rather than economic, considerations.

The legal abolition of the indentured emigration of Indians by the British government in 1917 brought to an end a cycle in the use of bound labor in British America that had lasted almost exactly three centuries. Begun by the introduction of indentured servitude in Virginia within little more than a decade after the settlement of Jamestown, this cycle had seen the rise of slavery initially lead to the abandonment of servitude, and had later seen the abolition of slavery produce a revival of servitude. When legal actions finally brought the use of indentured servants to an end, only legally free workers remained in the labor markets of British America for the first time in more than three hundred years.

The servant registrations

The major source of primary data used in this study consists of six separate collections of legal registrations of indentured servants made in England between 1654 and 1775. These sources vary considerably in both form and content, and a brief survey of some of their characteristics is important to an understanding of their uses and their limitations.

The earliest of the collections, as well as the largest in terms of the number of registrants, was begun in Bristol in September 1654. The indentures of approximately 10,632 servants bound from Bristol for the American colonies were recorded between then and June 1686. Of these, 9,920 are entered in two folio volumes devoted exclusively to the registrations of indentured servants.[1] These appear to be the fair copies of rough entries made between 1654 and 1679 in a series of volumes that contain the accounts of part of the activities of the Bristol Mayor's Court. Additional registrations, which continue from 1679 to 1681, then after a gap resume from 1684 to 1686, are contained among entries relating to other actions of the Mayor's Court, and provide records of another 712 servants.[2]

The registrations were the result of an ordinance of the city of Bristol recorded on September 29, 1654. This ordinance, reproduced in the first volume of the registrations, echoed parts of a parliamentary ordinance made nine years earlier that attempted to prevent the kidnapping of children.[3] However, unlike the parliamentary act, the Bristol ordinance specifically required the registration of servants' indentures. The first entry appears with the same date as the ordinance, with the text of the indenture written out in full, giving details of the servant's destination, term, and freedom dues.[4] Subsequent entries used a shortened version of the contract, giving the same information in summary form. During the following years there was a constant tendency to reduce this formula. The first important change was the substitution of phrases such as "on the like conditions" for the statement of destination and freedom dues. After the end of June 1661, the register rarely recorded either the servant's place of origin or occupation. Following the gap in the registrations during 1681–4, in the final three years there was a partial return to the fuller entries of the earlier period.

Although the apparently systematic omission of some types of information about the servants registered in Bristol in some years makes interpretation of the evidence for some periods difficult, the Bristol registrations are nevertheless valuable for the long period and large number of servants they cover. In recognition of this, one historian has referred to them as "the most important surviving emigration list for the seventeenth century."[5] For the purposes of this study, the Bristol registrations provide important material on the demographic and occupational composition of the servants, while their coverage over time allows an examination of trends in these as well as such other variables as the servants' colonial destinations.

Two separate sets of registrations survive for servants transported from the port of London to the colonies in the mid-1680s. These were also the direct result of legislation, this time a Privy Council order of December 1682 intended to protect merchants against false charges of kidnapping servants. The order provided that merchants who brought their servants to be registered by the proper authorities "shall not be disquieted by any sute on his Majtes behalf."[6] One series of registrations made in response to the order began on January 4, 1683. Between that date and June 1686, records of the indentures of 878 servants were made in two volumes of the "Waiting Books" of the Lord Mayor of London.[7] Although the amount of information varies to some extent between entries, in addition to the names of servant and master, the registrations usually included the servant's colonial destination and the length of the term to be served. Less frequently they gave the servant's place of origin, age, and occupation. The listing is useful for the demographic information it contains about the servants and for that on their colonial destinations.

The other collection of registrations due to the Privy Council order of 1682 is the most important known surviving collection of actual servant contracts from the seventeenth century. These come from the records of the Middlesex County Quarter Sessions. The earliest dated contract was recorded on January 21, 1683. A total of 811 contracts from this series, recording the indentures of 812 servants, are now available, with the latest made in September 1684.[8] The contracts were recorded by filling in blank spaces on forms printed specially for the purpose. Several different formats appear among the contracts in the collection; the differences, and their possible significance, are discussed in Chapter 3. On all types of forms the information normally recorded included the date, the names of servant and master, and the servant's colonial destination. The servant either signed or marked the form at the bottom to indicate agreement, and the contracts were signed by at least one magistrate and at least one witness. Other information about the servant was also frequently entered, most commonly age, place of origin, and occupation or status. Occasional marginal notations on the form were used to denote special provisions of particular contracts, either cash payments or descriptions of the specific work the servant was to perform in fulfilling the contract.

Although the size of the sample obtained from these contracts is relatively small, the Middlesex registrations are important for the large amount of information they provide about individual servants. Only one other set of registrations contains as much detail about the registrants, a collection of eighteenth-century contracts from the London Lord Mayor's Court. These two samples offer a number of opportunities not present in the others. This is due both to their inclusion of an important piece of information not contained in any of the other listings, the ability of the servants to sign their names, and to the large number of variables they contain about each registrant, which gives greater opportunities for multivariate analysis. Together, the two samples gain further in importance for in combination they make possible a number of important comparisons across a period of major changes in the history of the indenture system.

Of the sets of servant registrations used in this investigation, the origins of the fourth in chronological order are the most obscure. A list of 1,443 servants indentured between October 1697 and March 1707 was found among the records of the Corporation of Liverpool.[9] Nothing is known of the process by which these servants were registered; there is no evidence of any national ordinance encouraging servant registrations between the Privy Council order of 1682 and the beginning of the Liverpool registrations, nor are there known surviving lists from other ports in the same period. It would seem likely, therefore, that the Liverpool registrations were due to some local ordinance.[10]

The information given in the Liverpool list is relatively limited. All entries give the name of the servant, and nearly all give the date of registration. The servant's place of origin, age, colonial destination, and term of servitude are frequently given. The list does contain sufficient information about the servants' demographic composition to warrant analysis, and as it is the only sizable set of registrations available from the period between the mid-1680s and the end of the second decade of the eighteenth century, it fills an otherwise considerable gap in time.

The largest surviving set of servant contracts from any part of the colonial period is a collection of 3,187 documents recorded before the Lord Mayor of London between 1718 and 1759.[11] More than 90 percent of these were made during 1718–40, then after a gap several hundred remain from the years 1749–59. These indentures apparently owe their existence to a clause of an Act of Parliament of 1717. The clause, again intended to protect merchants from false charges of kidnapping minors, provided for servants to be brought before magistrates to acknowledge their consent to be bound and transported to the colonies.[12]

Two different types of printed form were used in these London agreements: One, used for minors, was a full contract of servitude, while the other, used for adults, was a declaration by the servant that he had no legal obligations in England and emigrated voluntarily.[13] In spite of this difference, both record the same basic information, including the name of master and servant, the latter's occupation, age, colonial destination, and the date of binding. The servant marked or signed to indicate his agreement, and the contract was signed by the Lord Mayor of London.

The combination of the relatively large sample size and the large number of variables concerning each registrant make these eighteenth-century London registrations the most valuable single data set for several types of analysis. To cite one example, it allows the most detailed multiple regression analysis of the length of indenture, which can be interpreted in the light of an economic model of the market for servants to yield important conclusions concerning the market valuation of the servants' labor.[14]

The latest of the sets of registrations consists of the fair copies of a collection of passenger lists requested from customs officers by the English government in 1773. Worried by discussions of excessive emigration and possible depopulation, the government required lists to be made of all people leaving Great Britain. The surviving transcripts of these lists are now held among Treasury papers.[15] Although the lists include free as well as indentured emigrants, servants can be identified because of the provision for entries specifying the passengers' status. The surviving lists begin in December 1773 and end in March 1776. They include the registrations of 3,709 servants, for whom are listed the date of registration, age, occupation, place of origin, and colonial destination. The lists do not provide information on the specific terms under which individual servants were bound. They are nonetheless useful for the view they give of the demographic and occupational composition of the servant population, and the destinations of the servants on the eve of the American Revolution.

English laws and documents
relating to servant registration

The texts of the following English documents are central to the interpretation of the servant registrations analyzed in this book and are either unavailable or not readily accessible in published form.

The first is a parliamentary ordinance of 1645 calling for the apprehension and punishment of kidnappers. Although the ordinance does not make specific mention of the purpose of the kidnapping, its injunction to search ships "upon the River, and at the Downes" indicates that it was intended to halt the "spiriting" of children to the American colonies. This act clearly constituted a precedent for the later action against spiriting taken by the city of Bristol, for a printed copy of the ordinance was pasted into the earliest volume of servant registrations from Bristol. On the page following the ordinance of 1645 is the handwritten text of an ordinance enacted nine years later by the city of Bristol, the second document presented here. The language of the parliamentary ordinance's condemnation is echoed in the later city ordinance, but the latter went on specifically to identify the problem as the transportation of the kidnapped children "beyond Seas," where they were sold for private gain. This is the earliest ordinance that provided for the registration of servants, which was to be done by the same city officers who normally recorded the indentures of apprentices, as a measure to prevent kidnapping. As noted in Appendix A, this ordinance gave rise to the recording of the terms of individual servant's indentures in Bristol for a period of more than thirty years. The third document is the first indenture recorded as a result of the ordinance; the full terms of Richard Pell's future servitude in Barbados were recorded the day after the ordinance was enacted. Pell's indenture was the prototype of the form of the indentures subsequently recorded in the Bristol registrations, although later entries were considerably abbreviated.

The fourth document is the text of a Privy Council order of 1682 providing for the registration of servants before justices of the peace. As indicated in the order's preamble, the action came in response to considerable lobbying by merchants involved in the servant trade who desired legal registration of their servants as protection against false charges of kidnapping. The order declared that merchants who had their servants' indentures executed before justices of the peace and recorded by clerks of the peace according to the specified procedure would be protected from prosecution on behalf of the king for kidnapping.

Yet the king could not protect the merchants from suits by private individuals, and merchants continued to lobby the Parliament for protection against private legal actions for kidnapping. The fifth document presented here is the text of the clause of an act of Parliament finally obtained by the merchants in 1717, which provided that merchants who took their servants to acknowledge their voluntary consent to the terms of their contracts before magistrates and had the terms of the contracts recorded by clerks of the peace would be safe from any subsequent prosecution for kidnapping.

Text of parliamentary ordinance of 1645[1]

An Ordinance of the Lords and Commons Assembled in Parliament, For the Apprehending and bringing to condigne punishment, all such lewd persons as shall steale, sell, buy, inveigle, purloyne, convey, or receive any little Children. And for the strict and diligent search of all Ships and other Vessels on the River, or at the Downes.

Die Veneris, 9 Maii. 1645.

Whereas the Houses of Parliament are informed, that divers lewd persons doe goe up and downe the City of London, and elsewhere, and in a most barbarous and wicked manner steale away many little Children, It is ordered by the Lords and Commons in Parliament assembled, That all Officers and Ministers of Justice be hereby streightly charged and required to be very diligent in apprehending all such persons as are faulty in this kind, either in stealing, selling, buying, inveigling, purloyning, conveying, or receiving Children so stolne, and to keep them in safe imprisonment, till they may be brought to severe and exemplary punishment.

It is further ordered, That the Marshals of the Admiralty, and the Cinque-Ports, doe immediately make strict and diligent search in all Ships and Vessels upon the River, and at the Downes, for all such Children, according to such directions as they have or shall receive from the Committee of the Admiralty, and Cinque-Ports.

It is further ordered, That this Ordinance be forthwith published in Print, and Proclaimed in the usuall manner as other Proclamations, in all parts of the City of London, within the Line of Communication, and in all Parishes within the Bils of mortality, presently: And in all Churches and Chappels by the Ministers, within the Line of Communication, and Bils of Mortality, on the next Lords day: And in all other Churches and Chappels elsewhere respectively, the next Lords day after the recept hereof, that it may appeare to the World, how carefull the Parliament is to prevent such mischiefes, and how farre they doe detest a crime of so much villany.

Text of Bristol ordinance of 1654[2]

Cittie of Bristoll

At an assembly of the Maior Aldermen and Comon Councell held the 29th day of September in the yeare of our Lord God 1654.

Whereas many complaintes have been oftentimes made to the Maior and Aldermen of the Inveigling, purloining, carrying and Stealing away Boyes Maides and other persons and transporting them beyond Seas and there selling or otherwise disposeing them for private gaine and proffitt and it being a crime of much villany to have children and others in such a Barbarous and wicked manner to be so carried away stollen and sold without any knowledge or notice of the parents or others that have the care and oversight of them for the better preventing of such mischeifes for time to come: It is this day agreed ordeined and enacted by the Maior Aldermen and Comon Councell in Comon Councell assembled that all Boyes Maides and other persons which for the future shall be transported beyond the Seas as Servants, shall before their going a-Ship board have their convenants or Indentures of service and apprentiship inrolled in the Tolzey booke as other Indentures of apprentiship are and have used to bee, and that noe Master or other officer wtsoever of any Ship or vessell shall (before such inrolmt be made) receive into his or their ship or vessell or therein permitt to be transported beyond the Seas such Boyes Maides or other persons as aforesaid; And if any Master or officer of any Ship shall receive or transport any Boy Maid person or persons contrary to this Act and Ordinance Such Master or officer shall forfeit for every such offence some of twenty pounds for such his said offence to be levied either by way of distresse and sale of the offenders goods by some or one of the Serjeants at Mace or Constables of the said Cittie for the time being or Waterbayliffe of the port wherein the Overplus is to be restored to the Owner or to be recovered by Accon of debt to be brought by and in the name of the Chamberlaine of the said Cittie for the time being in the Court of pleas held before the Maior and Aldermen of the said Cittie, the one quarter part of the said forfeiture to be given and paid to such person as shall discover and prove the said offence, and the residue of the said forfeiture to the use of the poore. And it is further ordained and enacted that the Waterbaylife shall from time to time make strict and diligent search in all Ships and vessells after all Boyes Maides and other persons that are to be transported as Servants beyond the Seas and if uppon examination he find any such boy maid or other person which have not their covenants or Indentures of service and apprentiship soe inrolled

189

in the Tolzey booke as aforesaid then the said Waterbaylife shall immediately give an accompt thereof to the Maior or some of the Aldermen who are desired from time to time (as such like occasion shall present) to take such speedy Course therein as by the Law they are enabled to doe And lastly it is ordained that the Maior and Aldermen be intrusted to take order that this Act and Ordinance be published and afterwarde affixed in such convenient places to the intent that all persons concerned may take notice thereof and not in time to come pretend any ignorance of the same.

John Goning Maior.

Text of first indenture recorded in Bristol registrations, 1654[3]

Cittie of Bristoll.

The inrolment of Apprentices and Servants as are Shipped at the port of Bristoll to serve in any of the forreigne plantacons, beginning the 29th of September 1654 John Goninge, Esq. being then Maior.

This Indenture made the thirtieth day of September in the yeare of our Lord God one thousand and six hundred fiftie and foure Between Richard Pell of the one part and Robert Read of the Citty of Bristoll Cooper of ye other part. Witnesseth that the said Richard Pell doth hereby covenant promise and grant to and with the said Robert Read his Executors & assignes from the day of the date hereof untill his first and next arrivall at the Island of Barbadoes and after for and during the term of three yeeres for in such service and imploiment as the said Robert Read or his assignes shall there imploy him according to ye Custome of the Country in the like kinde. In consideration whereof the said Robert Read doth hereby covenant and agree to and with ye said Richard Pell to pay for his passing and to finde and allow him meat & drinke apparell and lodging with other necessaryes during the said terme and at the end of the said terme to pay unto him or his assignes as much good and merchantable Tobacco Indigo goods or cotton as shalbe there worth the some of ten pounds sterling according to the Custome of the Country. In witness whereof the parties above menconed to theis Indentures have interchangeably set their hands & seales the day and yeere abovewritten.

Text of Privy Council order of 1682[4]

Plantations: His Majtes declaracon how merchts may without prejudice send white Servants into Plantacons.

Whereas it has bin represented to his Majte that by reason of the frequent abuses of a lewd sort of People called Spirits in Seducing many of his Majtes subjects to go on shipboard where they have been seized and carried by force to his Majtes Plantacons in America, and that many idle persons who have listed themselves voluntarily to be transported thither, and have received money upon their entring into Service for that purpose, have afterwards pretended they were betrayed, and carried away against their wills and procured their friends to prosecute the merchants who transported them, or in whose Service they are, by Indictmts or Informations in the Crown office in his Majtes name, wch is a great discouragmt to them and an hindrance to the managmt of the Trade of the said Plantations and Navigation of this Kingdom; and severall Merchants and Planters having made humble applications to his Majte that he would be graciously pleased to Direct such methods for their retaining of Servants to Serve in his Majtes Plantacons as in his Royall wisedome, He should think meet, wherby his Majty may be so satisfied of their fair dealing, as to take of all Prosecutions against them at his Majtes Sute, and also that the Scandall that now lyes upon them in generall by reason of such evill disposed persons may not remain upon such as shall for the future follow such Methods as his Majte shall think fit to be pursued.

His Majte taking into his Royall Consideration the said request, is graciously pleased to Declare, that such Merchants, Factors, Masters of Shipps or other Persons that shall use the Method hereafter following in the hiring of Servants for his Majtes Plantations shall not be disquieted by any sute on his Majtes behalf, but, upon certificate thereof, that he will cause all such sutes to be stopped, to the end they may receive no further molestation therby.

1. Such servants are to be taken by Indenture to be executed by the Servant in the presence of the Magistrat or Magistrats herafter appointed, one part therof signed by such servant, and also underwritten and endorsed with the name and hand writing of such Magistrate, wch is to remain with the clerk of the Peace to be returned to the next Sessions there to be filed upon a distinct file, and numbred & kept with the Records.

2. The clerk of the Peace is to keep a fair book, wherin the name of the Person so bound, and the Magistrats name before whom the same was don, and the time and place of doing therof, and the number of the file shalbe entred, and for the more easy finding the same, the Entries are to be made alphabetically according to the first letter of the Surname.

3. All persons above the age of one and twenty yeares or who shall upon view and examination appear to be so in the Judgmt. of the Magistrate may be bound in the presence of one Justice of the Peace, or of the Mayor or Cheif Magistrate of the place where they shall go on shipboard, who is to be fully satisfied from him of his free & voluntary agreemt. to enter into the said service.

4. If any person be under the age of one and twenty years, or shall

appear so to be, he shalbe bound in the presence of the Lord Mayor of London, or One of the Judges, or an Alderman of London being a Justice of the Peace, or the Recorder, or two Justices of the Peace of any other County or place, who shall carefully examin whether the person so to be bound have any Parents or Masters; And if he be not free they are not to take such Indenture unlesse the Parents or Masters give their Consent, and some person that knows the said servant to be of the name and addition mentioned in the Indenture is to attest his said knowledge upon the said Indenture.

5. If the person be under the age of fourteen years, unlesse his Parents shall be present and consent, he is not to be carried on Shipboard till a fortnight at least after he becomes bound, to the intent that if there be any abuse it may be discovered before he be transported, And where his Parents do not appear before the Magistrate, notice is to be sent to them, or where they cannot be found to the Church Wardens or Overseers of the Parish where he was last settled in such manner as the said Magistrate shall think fit and direct.

And because Clerks of the Peace may conceive this not to be any part of the duty of their office; and therefore exact unreasonable Rewards for their trouble and pains therin, His Majte doth declare that if any Merchants or other Persons shall be aggrieved therby, and upon complaint to the Justice, cannot obtein releif, His Majte will take such further care for their ease herein, as in his Royall wisedome, he shall think meet.

And his Majtes futher pleasure is, that this order be printed and published, to the end all persons whom it may Concern take notice therof, and govern themselves accordingly.

Clause of Act of Parliament of 1717[5]

V. And whereas there are many idle Persons who are under the Age of one and twenty Years lurking about in divers parts of *London*, and elsewhere, who want Employment, and may be tempted to become Thieves, if not provided for: And whereas they may be inclined to be transported, and to enter into Services in some of his Majesty's Colonies and Plantations in *America;* but as they have no Power to contract for themselves, and therefore that it is not safe for Merchants to transport them, or take them into such Services; Be it enacted by the Authority aforesaid, That where any Person of the Age of fifteen Years or more, and under the Age of twenty-one, shall be willing to be transported, and to enter into any Service in any of his Majesty's Colonies or Plantations in *America*, It shall be and may be lawful for any Merchant, or other, to contract with any such Person for any such Service, not exceeding the Term of eight Years; Provided such Person so binding him or herself do come before the Lord Mayor of *London* or some other Justice of the Peace of the City, if such Contract be made within the same, or the Liberties thereof, or before some other two Justices of the Peace of the Place where such Contract shall be made if made elsewhere, and before such Magistrate or Magistrates acknowledge such Consent, and do sign such Contract in his or their Presence, and with his or their Approbation; and that then it shall be lawful for any such Merchant or other, to transport such Person so binding him or herself, and to keep him or her within any of the said Plantations or Colonies, according to the Tenor of Such Contract, as aforesaid; any Law or Statute to the contrary in any wise notwithstanding; which said Contract and Approbation of such Magistrate or Magistrates, with the Tenor of such Contract, shall be certified by such Magistrate or Magistrates to the next General Quarter-Sessions of the Peace, held for that County where such Magistrate or Magistrates shall reside, to be registered by the Clerk of the Peace without Fee or Reward.

Possible biases in the age distributions
of the indentured servants

Some comments on the age distributions presented in Chapter 2 for
servants bound in the 1680s and during 1718–59 are necessary, concerning possible biases present in the registrations.

In the Middlesex registrations of 1683–4, the age distributions for both
sexes show a considerable bulge at age 21. Thus about 28 percent of the
men in the sample with stated ages, and 31 percent of the women, were
registered as 21.[1] The suggestion that this concentration was due to entry
into indentures by young tradesmen finishing apprenticeships[2] does not
seem an adequate explanation, both because less than one-fifth of those
men registered as aged 21 were identified as having trades to which youths
could be apprenticed and because the bulge also appears for the age
distribution of the women in the sample.

The Middlesex contracts were apparently recorded as a direct result of
an order of the Privy Council made in 1682.[3] Examination of that order
suggests a hypothesis to explain the irregular distribution of the recorded
ages.

The order's stated intent was to protect merchants from false charges of
"spiriting," or kidnapping, servants. To this end, it specified a process by
which servants who wished to emigrate could be registered before legal
officials. Merchants who so registered their servants would then be
protected against prosecution on behalf of the king for kidnapping. The
order's description of the registration process to be used read in part as
follows:

3. All persons above the age of one and twenty yeares or who shall upon view and
examination appear to be so in the Judgmt. of the Magistrate may be bound in the
presence of one Justice of the Peace, or of the Mayor or Chief Magistrate of the
place where they shall go on shipboard, who is to be fully satisfied from him of his
free & voluntary agreemt. to enter into the said service.
4. If any person be under the age of one and twenty years, or shall appear so to be,
he shalbe bound in the presence of the Lord Mayor of London, or One of the
Judges, or an Alderman of London being a Justice of the Peace, or the Recorder,
or two Justices of the Peace of any other County or place, who shall carefully
examin whether the person so to be bound have any Parents or Masters.[4]

Inspection of the contracts does suggest that different procedures were followed for those whose ages were judged to be less than 21 and those registered as adults. The surviving contracts for adults are normally endorsed by a single Justice of the Peace of Middlesex County. In contrast, the indentures for servants identified as less than 21 are normally signed by two justices. Thus the different treatment prescribed for minors by the Privy Council's order seems to have been followed in practice, and this suggests a possible solution to the apparent puzzle of the large number of 21-year-old servants.

The ages of servants who came to be registered before the magistrates can rarely, if ever, have been established by documentation. The uncertain nature of servants' ages was recognized by the Privy Council order's reference to "persons above the age of one and twenty yeares *or who shall upon view and examination appear to be so in the Judgmt. of the Magistrate"* (emphasis mine). It might be that the magistrate's judgment was affected in the case of the Middlesex Quarter Sessions by the availability of a second Justice of the Peace: When one magistrate was present at a session, some younger servants might have been prematurely promoted to majority.

This hypothesis is speculative, and it is difficult to estimate the extent of the possible distortion of the servants' true ages upon registration. One approach to this problem is to compare the Middlesex age distributions with those of the contemporaneous registrations made in adjacent London.[5] The same incentive to falsify servants' ages would not have been present in the London records because they were made before the Lord Mayor of London, who was specifically authorized by the Privy Council order to bind minors for service in the colonies.

In comparing the age distributions, it is clear that there was a tendency for the ages recorded in London to be lower than those of Middlesex. This can be seen in both the percentage distributions of Table 2.3 and the summary statistics of Table 2.5. Several different explanations could account for this difference. One possibility is that it reflects genuine differences in the age distributions of the servants registered in the two places. Thus, perhaps merchants preferred to take young servants to the Lord Mayor's Court to be legally bound, because of the possible inconvenience if only one justice was present at the Middlesex Quarter Sessions. Another is that the difference resulted from a tendency to pay less attention to the ages of adults than of minors brought before the Lord Mayor and frequently to omit them from the records. This might explain why, as noted in Chapter 2, more than half the servants registered in London in this period had no age recorded. A third possibility is that the true age distributions of the servants registered in the two courts were identical, and that the observed differences were due to the falsification of recorded ages in Middlesex, for the reasons suggested above.

The evidence does not allow conclusive tests of these hypotheses. However, the erratic behavior of the Middlesex age distributions, with a sharp drop in the numbers of men registered between ages 18 and 21 and a similar fall in the number of women registered as 20, suggests that although the servants registered before the Lord Mayor may in fact have been younger on average than those who came before the Middlesex magistrates, it is likely that the difference in the recorded ages was greater than the difference in the actual ages of the servants.

Comparison of the Middlesex and London age distributions does suggest that both effects were present, that is, that the Middlesex registrants tended to be older and that their true ages were distorted to some extent upon registration. Inspection of the Middlesex men's age distribution indicates that it was the men within two years of majority – ages 19 and 20 – who may have been chiefly affected by the hypothetical tendency to falsify recorded ages, as they appear to be underrepresented. Thus 25.6 percent of the London men whose ages were recorded were under 19, compared with 14.9 percent of the Middlesex men, a ratio of 1.72:1. In contrast, 10.9 percent of the London men were 19 or 20, compared with 5.5 percent in Middlesex, giving a higher ratio of 1.98:1. Thus, if the ages recorded for the Middlesex servants are accurate for men of 18 and under, there was apparently a larger proportion of young men in the London sample. However, that the ratio of the shares of men of 19 and 20 between the London and Middlesex samples was higher than the ratio for those 18 and under suggests that the ages of some 19- and 20-year-olds may have been falsely reported in the Middlesex contracts.

The logic of this conclusion is as follows. Let L = proportion of the London sample, and M = proportion of the Middlesex sample, and the subscripts y and o stand for younger and older, respectively. Assume that the servants in the London sample had a lower mean age than those in the Middlesex sample, and that the true ages in both samples were normally distributed with equal variance. Then for a division of the left-hand tails of the distributions (i.e., the area below the means of both), for any specific dividing point between younger and older, it will be true that

$$\frac{L_y}{M_y} > \frac{L_o}{M_o}$$

Above, it was noted that if y = 18 and under, and o = 19 and 20,

$$\frac{L_y}{M_y} = 1.72$$

while

$$\frac{L_o}{M_o} = 1.98$$

so that

$$\frac{L_y}{M_y} < \frac{L_o}{M_o}$$

This indicates that if, as the distributions suggest

$$\left(\text{since } \frac{L_y}{M_y} > 1 \right)$$

the London men were generally younger than those of Middlesex, M_o is too small, that is, men of 19 and 20 may have been underrepresented in the Middlesex registrations. This could have been the result, as suggested above, of the registration of many 19- and 20-year-olds as 21. Similar analysis indicates that 20-year-old women are underrepresented in the Middlesex registrations, suggesting that many of them may also have been registered as 21.

Given the possible biases noted in the age distributions drawn from these two samples – in Middlesex due to the possible falsification of minors' ages, and in London due to possible underrecording of the ages of adults – it is possible that the mean ages obtained from the two are biased in opposite directions. Thus the Middlesex contracts of 1683–4 may yield upward-biased mean ages for servants, whereas the London lists of 1683–6 may give downward-biased means. If this is the case, the true mean ages of servants emigrating from London and Middlesex in the 1680s would lie between those of the two samples.

A further comment on the servants' age distributions concerns those obtained from the London registrations of 1718–59.[6] In both the men's and the women's distributions from that sample, there is a sharp decline at age 21, the age of majority. Thus, for example, while 19- and 20-year-old men accounted for 15.6 percent and 16.2 percent, respectively, of all men whose ages were recorded, 21- and 22-year-olds made up only 6.4 percent and 5.1 percent, respectively. Similarly, whereas women of 19 and 20 made up 23.1 percent and 17.2 percent, respectively, of those with stated ages, those of 21 and 22 comprised, respectively, only 3.6 percent and 4.7 percent. The magnitude of the decline in both distributions makes some consideration of possible registration biases necessary.

Appendix C

These eighteenth-century registrations were apparently due to an Act of Parliament of 1717.[7] Whereas the Privy Council order of 1682 had given English merchants protection from prosecution by the government for kidnapping, it was not until 1717 that Parliament gave them protection from suits by private persons as well. In that year a clause concerning the registration of indentured servants was appended to an act dealing with the transportation of felons. The clause referred specifically only to minors:

[W]hereas there are many idle Persons who are under the Age of one and twenty Years lurking about . . . who want employment . . . [T]hey may be inclined to be transported, and to enter into Services in some of his Majesty's Colonies and Plantations in *America;* but as they have no Power to contract for themselves, and therefore that it is not safe for Merchants to transport them, or take them into such Services; Be it enacted . . . , That where any Person of the Age of fifteen Years or more, and under the Age of twenty-one, shall be willing to be transported, and to enter into any Service in any of his Majesty's Colonies or Plantations in *America,* It shall and may be lawful for any Merchant, or other, to contract with any such Person for any such Service.[8]

Again, the Lord Mayor of London or another London Justice of the Peace was authorized to bind servants, and the surviving London contracts of the following decades were made before a succession of London's mayors and aldermen.

Although the legislation of 1717 referred only to minors, the age distributions of the servants registered show that adults were registered as well. As adults could be registered, it does not seem likely that adults' ages would have been falsified to bring them under the act's jurisdiction, as might have been the case if magistrates had refused to register servants above the age of majority. It might be more likely that merchants felt the risk of prosecution for kidnapping adults was much less than that involved for minors and consequently tended not to bring adults to court for registration. Thus the act may have referred only to minors because it was only for minors that its need was perceived.[9]

Table C.1 presents the ages of the male servants registered in London by date. It shows that adults were not registered at the beginning of the period and that the proportional representation of adults in the records tended to increase over time. Thus the share of adults rose steadily, from none in 1718–19 to 11.1 percent in 1720–4, 30.6 percent in 1725–9, 45.4 percent in 1730–4, and finally to 56.8 percent in 1735–40, before falling to 9.8 percent of the relatively small number of registrations from the period of 1749–59.

It cannot be determined whether the rising share of adults over time was due to some change in the merchants' propensity to register adults. There is no obvious evidence of events, such as frequent lawsuits against merchants, that might have changed their inclination to take their adult as

198

Table C.1. *Ages of male servants registered in London, 1718–58, by period*

Age	(1) 1718–19	(2) 1720–24	(3) 1725–29	(4) 1730–34	(5) 1735–40	(6) 1749–59
12	1	1			1	1
13	1	1		1		
14	9	9	2	3	3	2
15	20	46	27	27	9	7
16	14	64	51	49	19	16
17	25	76	38	52	39	14
18	35	121	54	82	59	21
19	28	127	75	141	59	19
20	19	146	97	102	70	30
21		21	32	59	72	1
22		6	17	70	53	
23		10	18	37	32	1
24		5	9	32	34	2
25		6	22	35	29	2
26		7	6	22	17	2
27		2	11	22	19	1
28		3	8	15	17	
29		2	5	14	14	
30			6	17	8	2
31		4	1	11	10	
32		1	3	9	2	
33		1	3	5	7	
34			2	7	3	
35			4	3	8	
36		1	2	8	4	1
37		1	1	3		
38		1		4	3	
39					2	
40		2		1	2	
42			1	3	1	
43					1	
44					1	
45				2	1	
48		1	1	1		
Total	152	665	496	837	599	122

well as minor servants to be registered before a magistrate. The increasing share of the adults could reflect to some extent both a genuine increase in the relative numbers of adult servants and an increase over time in the percentage of all adult servants brought for registration. If this were the case, the summary statistics of Table 2.6 would overstate the magnitude of the true increase that occurred in the central tendency of the servants' ages over time.

The format of the London registrations of 1718–1759

Two different types of printed form appear in the collection of memoranda that make up the London registrations of 1718–59. One, consistently used only to register minors, was a printed contract, specifying the obligations of both the master and servant. When the blank spaces on the form were filled in by hand, the contract specified the names of those involved, the colony to which the servant was to be sent, and other relevant terms. An example of a contract of this type is illustrated in Figure D.1.

The other form type, used to register adults, was more cursory. It consisted primarily of a declaration by the servant that he had no legal obligations in England, and emigrated voluntarily. An example of this second type is shown in Figure D.2.

The difference between the contracts is potentially of interest for the interpretation of their contents. While the first type appears to constitute the memorandum of a legal labor contract, specifying all terms and conditions of the agreement, the form used for adults appears to be no more than a declaration made by the servant, and would therefore not necessarily be expected to detail all the bargain's terms.

It is of course possible that the apparent difference was not one of substance, and that in practice no distinction was made in the information recorded on the two types of form. However there is direct evidence that suggests that this was not the case, and that the form used for minors was taken seriously as a contract, while that used for adults was not. This evidence comes from the registrations themselves. Approximately 130 of the agreements in the sample contain substantive handwritten additions to the standard form. All of these concern cash payments and salaries to be paid to individual servants.[1] In a number of contracts in which such payments were provided for, the word "cloaths" was struck from the standard agreement, and frequently a handwritten note added, "clothes only excepted," or "to find himself with clothes." The recording of the payments suggests that the documents were taken seriously as contracts rather than simply registrations, and the attention to the detail of clothing indicates that some care was taken in specifying the full terms of contract. But what is most striking is that not a single adult form from the period

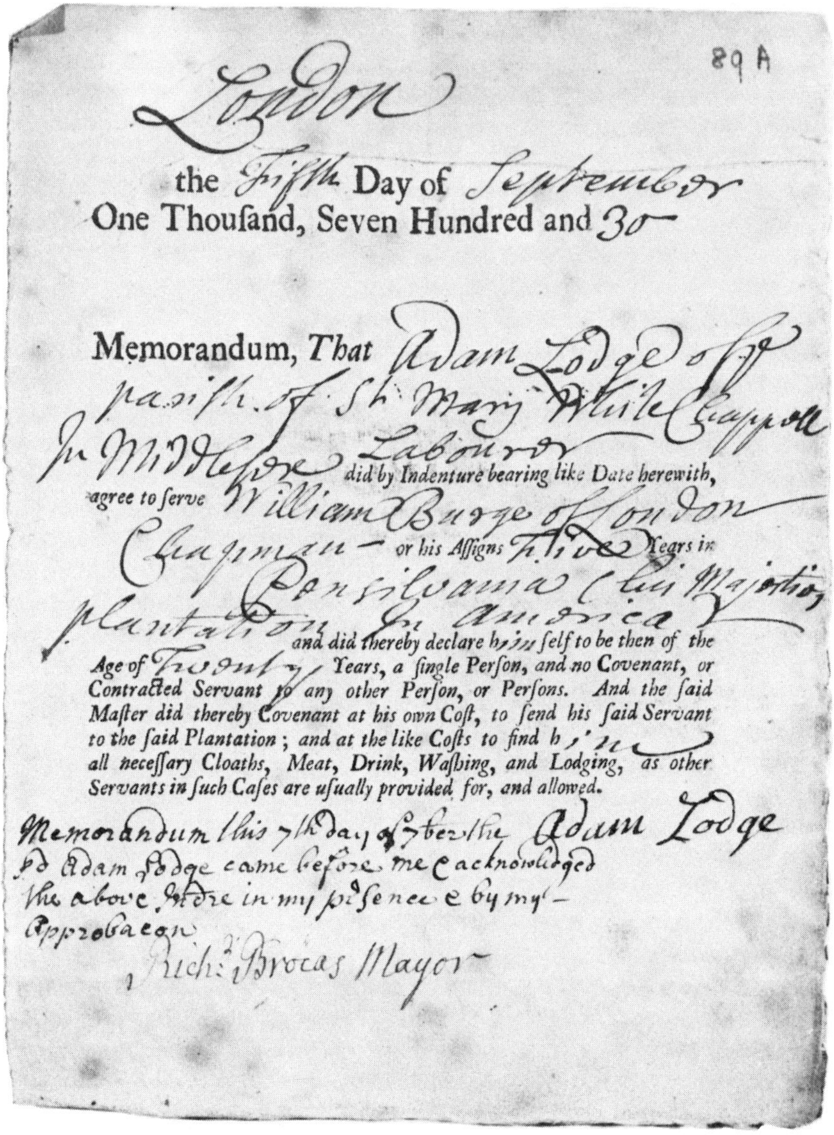

London

the *Fifth* Day of *September*
One Thoufand, Seven Hundred and *30*

Memorandum, That *Adam Lodge off*
pasish of St Mary White Chappell
In Middlesex Labourer did by Indenture bearing like Date herewith,
agree to ferve *William Burge of London*
Chapman — or his Affigns *Five* Years in
Pensilvania (his Majesties
plantation in America) and did thereby declare h *im* felf to be then of the
Age of *Twenty* Years, a fingle Perfon, and no Covenant, or
Contra&ed Servant to any other Perfon, or Perfons. And the faid
Mafter did thereby Covenant at his own Coft, to fend his faid Servant
to the faid Plantation; and at the like Cofts to find h *im*
all neceffary Cloaths, Meat, Drink, Wafhing, and Lodging, as other
Servants in fuch Cafes are ufually provided for, and allowed.

Memorandum this 7th day of 7ber the *Adam Lodge*
to Adam Lodge came before me & acknowledged
the above Indre in my pifence & by my—
Approbacon
Richd Brocas Mayor

Figure D.1 Contract of minor, London registrations of 1718–59

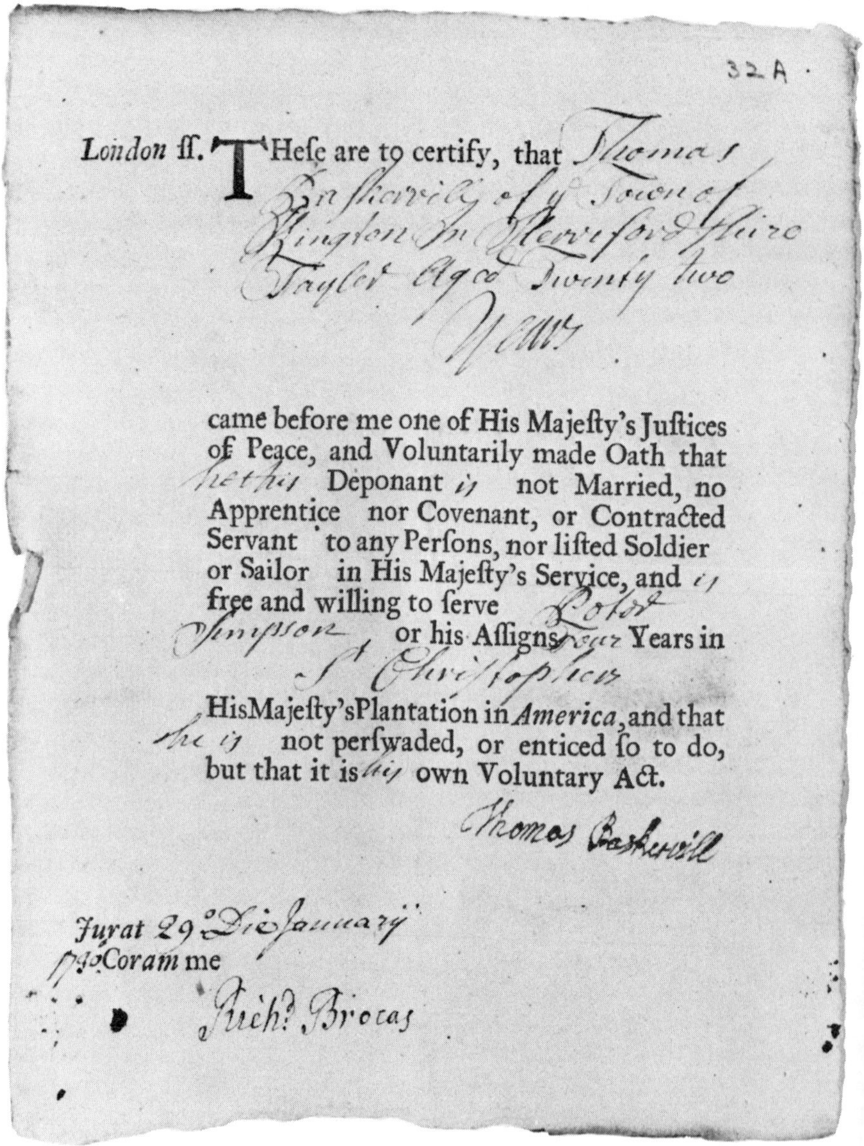

London ff. **T**Hefe are to certify, that *Thomas*
Bashervile of ye Towne of
Kington in Herrifordfhire
Tayler Aged Twenty two
Years

came before me one of His Majefty's Juftices
of Peace, and Voluntarily made Oath that
hethis Deponant *is* not Married, no
Apprentice nor Covenant, or Contracted
Servant to any Perfons, nor lifted Soldier
or Sailor in His Majefty's Service, and *is*
free and willing to ferve *Robert*
Simpson or his Affigns *four* Years in
St Chriftophers

HisMajefty'sPlantation in *America,* and that
he is not perfwaded, or enticed fo to do,
but that it is *his* own Voluntary Act.

Thomas Bashervill

Jurat 29° *Die January*
4° Coram me

Rich? Brocas

Figure D.2 Contract of adult, London registrations of 1718–59

1718–40 contains such a written amendment; all amendments to the surviving agreements from that period are to forms registering minors. The existence of more than one hundred of these amended forms for minors during 1718–40 and none for adults argues strongly against the possibility that it is due to chance that only amended minors' forms survived.

The conclusion drawn here from the evidence concerning the different form types has therefore been that for the period prior to 1740, the registrations for minors specify the full conditions of servitude agreed on by master and servant in England, but that those for adults do not.

As noted in Chapter 4, there is a gap in the surviving agreements in the sample from 1740 through 1748, following which a change in practice is apparent. After the gap, all the surviving forms, including those registering minors, are of the type shown in Figure D.2, previously used only for adults. A number of cash payments to adults were recorded after 1749; the fact that these were recorded, in contrast to the earlier period, further attests to some change in the registration process.

Little can be said with certainty about the implications of this change, but several factors point to a possible deterioration in the quality of the evidence from the 1750s. One is the relatively small number of contracts registered. This of course cannot be conclusive, for it may have been due to an actual decline in the number of servants emigrating. In conjunction with the disappearance of the contract form type earlier used for minors, however, it may be an indication of a decline in interest in servant registration. This might also account for the increased share of the male servants registered without occupations in this later period.

On the colonial destinations of servants registered in Liverpool during 1697–1707 without recorded destinations

The existence of different and relatively stable seasonal distributions of the registrations of servants bound for the Chesapeake and the West Indies, as discussed in Chapter 6, makes possible some inferences concerning the region of destination of the nearly half of the total servants registered in the Liverpool lists of 1697–1707 without stated destinations. The logic behind the procedure is that if the Liverpool registrations followed approximately the same seasonal pattern as those of the other samples examined, inferences about the destinations of the servants whose colonial destinations were not recorded might be drawn from an analysis of the distribution of their registrations over the year.

This procedure would not be valid if the basic assumption of similarity between the seasonality of departures of ships from Liverpool and of those from other ports were incorrect. However, as noted in Chapter 6, the seasonal distribution of Liverpool's Chesapeake registrations was intermediate between the pattern identified in the three earlier seventeenth-century samples and that of the two later eighteenth-century samples. It is therefore possible that the seasonality of servant registrations in Liverpool was the same as that of the other ports in any given year, but that the seasonality of servant shipments to the Chesapeake from all English ports was changing over time in response to changing colonial patterns of demand. It is likely that the seasonality of colonial shipping from Liverpool did resemble that of other English ports, for the length of the voyage was hardly different for Liverpool ships bound for the colonies than for those leaving from Bristol or London.

The monthly distribution of the registrations of the servants from the Liverpool sample with unstated colonial destinations is shown in Table E.1. Statistically, the best sample for systematic comparison is that from Bristol during 1654–86. Its large numbers of registrants bound for both the West Indies and the Chesapeake and its long period of coverage make possible unknown omissions in the registrations a potentially less serious source of distortion than in the smaller samples from shorter periods.

One way of comparing the distributions is by estimation of two regression equations, with the monthly percentage distribution of the

Table E.1. *Month of registration of servants bound at Liverpool with no stated destination, 1697–1707*

Month	Percent of total
January	12
February	19
March	9
April	8
May	1
June	2
July	7
August	8
September	7
October	6
November	15
December	6
Total	100
$N = 673$	

registrations of the Liverpool servants without stated destinations regressed in turn on the monthly percentage distribution of the Bristol servants bound for the West Indies and on that of those bound for the Chesapeake. The results obtained from estimation of these two regressions are presented in Table E.2. These show that the monthly distribution of the Liverpool servants without stated destinations is strongly and positively correlated with that of the Bristol servants bound for the West Indies but is not significantly related statistically to that of the Bristol servants bound for the Chesapeake.

Similar results are obtained from the use of chi-square tests. Thus, a comparison of the monthly percentage distributions of the Liverpool registrants without recorded destinations and the Bristol registrants bound for the Chesapeake yields a chi-square value of 57.32 with 11 degrees of freedom, which rejects the null hypothesis of no difference in the distributions at the .001 level. In contrast, a comparison of the distributions of the Liverpool unknowns and the Bristol registrants bound for the West Indies give a chi-square of only 11.04 with 11 degrees of freedom, which fails to reject the null hypothesis of no difference in the distributions at the .10 level.[1]

It must be emphasized that tests of the sort done in this appendix, based only on observed correlation, cannot be conclusive evidence of destination even if the distributions of the Bristol registrations are appropriate for comparison, because the reason for the omission of the recording of

Appendix E

Table E.2. *Regression results, Liverpool servants*

Equation	Independent variable	Estimated coefficient	Standard error	Constant	R^2	N
(1)	WI_B	1.49	0.48	−4.11	0.49	12
(2)	C_B	−0.08	0.20	8.99	0.01	12

Note: Dependent variable: U_L. Method of estimation: ordinary least squares. Definitions of variables: U_L = percentage distribution by month of Liverpool registrations of servants without stated destinations. WI_B = percentage distribution by month of Bristol registrations of servants bound for the West Indies. C_B = percentage distribution by month of Bristol registrations of servants bound for the Chesapeake.

servants' destinations in the Liverpool lists cannot be determined. In the absence of any independent knowledge of the reason, the evidence of these correlations can only be suggestive. However, bearing in mind this qualification, the results presented here can be taken to suggest that, if the seasonal patterns identified in seventeenth-century registrations persisted to the end of the century, the servants registered in Liverpool without stated destinations may have been predominantly bound for servitude in the West Indies. These distributions cannot identify differences between specific colonies. However, as noted in Chapter 6, Jamaica was the major West Indian servant importer both in the 1680s and in the 1720s and 1730s. It would therefore seem likely that if most of the nearly half of all the servants departing from Liverpool during 1697–1707 were in fact bound for the West Indies, the majority of these probably served their terms in Jamaica. The tentative nature of these inferences needs no further emphasis. Their chief interest lies in the possibility they raise that the apparent sharp decline in West Indian servant imports at the close of the seventeenth century may have been no more than an artifact of the incomplete registration process used to produce a particular document.

Appendix F

Analysis of cash payments and salaries
paid to indentured servants

The length of the term of servitude, analyzed in Chapter 7, was not the only variable dimension of the indenture bargain. Lewis Gray listed other possible variables:

> It was rarely customary to pay wages to the servant or to pay him a sum of money, although occasionally skilled artisans or tutors and clerks stipulated in the indenture for wage payments . . . A practice probably widely pursued is described in an early account of Maryland as follows: "The usuall terme of binding a servant, is for five yeers; but for any artificer, or one that shall deserve more than ordinary, the Adventurer shall doe well to shorten that time and adde encouragements of another nature." In so far as competition influenced the contract, it was manifested mainly in the length of term of service, in agreements with respect to advances of food and clothing, and in amount of freedom dues.[1]

Records of advances of food and clothing and of variation in the amount of freedom dues rarely appear in the documents analyzed in this study. They do not appear to have been used commonly, although they might have been given and simply omitted from the registrations. However, the two sets of registrations analyzed in Chapter 7 consist of actual contracts of servitude and do contain some amendments to the standard provisions of the printed forms.

The earlier of the two samples consists of contracts made in the Middlesex Quarter Sessions during 1683–4. The contracts of 56 servants, just under 7 percent of all those in the sample, were amended to provide for cash payments of varying amounts. Most appear to have been initial lump-sum payments, normally of less than one pound sterling: The most common entries read "5s with him" and "10s with him." Following the analysis of Chapter 7, a regression equation was estimated with the amount of the cash payment made to a servant as the dependent variable. The independent variables – age, sex, literacy, occupation, and destination – were the same ones used in the analysis of the length of indenture. The sample used was that of all servants in the Middlesex sample, minors and adults, whose contracts contained all the necessary information. The results are presented in Table F.1.

Appendix F

Table F.1. *Estimated regression coefficients, Middlesex sample*

Independent variable	Estimated coefficient	Standard error
Age (years)	0.011	0.038
Sex[a]	−0.485	0.456
Literacy[b]	−0.443	0.363
Trade[c]	1.466	0.399
West Indies[d]	0.088	0.354
Constant	0.323	
R^2	0.026	
F	4.03	
N	760	

Note: Dependent variable: amount of cash payment (shillings, sterling). Method of estimation: ordinary least squares.
[a]Male = 0, female = 1. [b]Marked = 0, signed = 1. [c]Laborer or no recorded occupation = 0; all other occupations = 1. [d]West Indian destinations = 1; mainland = 0.
Source: For references to Middlesex sample of 1683–84, see Appendix A.

The results indicate that the hypothesis that all the coefficients are simultaneously equal to zero can be rejected at the .01 level, but the proportion of the variance explained is small, as might be expected in view of the rarity of the payments. Only one coefficient is significant at the .01 level: possession of a skilled trade, which was found in Chapter 7 to have reduced the term of an indenture, significantly raised the amount of the expected cash payment made to a servant.

As noted in Chapter 7 and Appendix D, the registrations made in London during 1718–59 apparently constituted legal contracts only for the minors registered during 1718–40. The contracts of 111 minors, about 6 percent of all minors registered during 1718–40, contain amendments to the standard form. These amendments normally provided for annual salaries to be paid to individual servants during the term of their contract. The salaries were usually stated in terms of the local currency of the colony specified as the servant's destination and varied in amount from as little as £4 per annum to as much as £50 annually. A regression was estimated with the amount of the annual salary as the dependent variable, with the same independent variables used above.[2] The sample used was that of all minors (age less than 21) whose contracts contained all the necessary information. The results obtained are presented in Table F.2.

The overall relationship is again statistically significant, and the proportion of the variance explained is again low. Four of the estimated coefficients, those of age, literacy, possession of a skilled trade, and West Indian destination, are significant at the .01 level. The estimated coefficients indicate that each of these was positively related to the amount

208

Analysis of cash payments and salaries paid to servants

Table F.2. *Estimated regression coefficients, London sample*

Independent variable	Estimated coefficient	Standard error
Age (years)	0.144	0.054
Sex	0.306	0.329
Literacy	0.428	0.167
Trade	1.397	0.190
West Indies	1.291	0.165
Constant	−3.141	
R^2	0.094	
F	42.20	
N	2,046	

Note: Dependent variable: amount of annual salary (pounds colonial currency). Method of estimation: ordinary least squares. All variables defined as in Table F.1.
Source: For references to London sample of 1718–59, see Appendix A.

of a servant's salary, just as in Chapter 7 it was found that all of these were significantly and negatively associated with the length of indenture in this sample.

The results of the analysis of servants' cash payments and salaries presented in this appendix for both samples of contracts are consistent with the hypothesis that these were positively related to the servants' expected earnings in the colonies. These results therefore reinforce the analysis presented in Chapter 7 of the length of indenture, for it has now been seen that in both the available samples of servant contracts, both the length of indenture and the amount of salary to be paid to a servant were adjusted in response to a servant's expected productivity, so that the greater the stock of an individual's human capital, the shorter the term and the greater the size of the cash payment or salary he would be expected to receive, ceteris paribus.

Appendix G

Categorization of occupations

The interest of this study in the kinds of work the servants could perform in the colonies led to the use of a principally functional categorization of the male servants' occupations. The six major functional occupational categories used in the analysis were: agricultural occupations; food and drink processing and distribution; metal and wood crafts; building and construction trades; clothing and textile production; and service occupations. At times some or all of these six categories were combined, and in each case the categories included in a more highly aggregated classification have been indicated. The specific occupations included in each of the six major categories are listed in Table G.1.

In addition to these functional categories, three other classes are often used in discussions of the servants' occupations. One is that of *not given*, which includes all men without recorded occupations. A second is that of *gentleman*, primarily a social rather than an economic or functional category. The third is that of *laborer*, used by contemporaries to designate unskilled workers who worked for hire, primarily but not exclusively in agriculture.

The occupational classifications presented here are similar to some socioeconomic categorizations used by historians of preindustrial England. Thus, for example, although the degree of aggregation sometimes differs, there is general agreement between the occupational classifications used here and those used in studies by associates of the SSRC Cambridge Group for the History of Population and Social Structure.[1] This basic agreement makes possible the type of comparison performed in Chapter 5 between the servant population and other groups in the English population.

Table G.1. *Composition of occupational categories*

Agriculture	Pinmaker	Flaxdresser
Farmer	Potmaker	Fuller
Gardener	Saddler	Furrier
Husbandman	Shipwright	Glover
Ploughman	Smith	Hempdresser
Yeoman	Tinker	Leatherdresser
	Turner	Leatherworker
Food and Drink	Watchmaker	Linen draper
Apothecary	Whitesmith	Mercer
Baker	Wiredrawer	Sergemaker
Brewer		Shearman
Chandler	*Building and Construction*	Shoemaker
Cheesemonger	Bricklayer	Skinner
Cook	Carpenter	Tailor
Distiller	Collier	Tanner
Fisherman	Glazier	Tucker
Grocer	Joiner	Upholsterer
Innkeeper	Mason	Weaver
Merchant	Miner	Woolcomber
Miller	Painter	
Ostler	Pavior	*Services*
Tapster	Plasterer	Accountant
Tobacco worker	Potter	Barber
Victualler	Quarrier	Bookkeeper
Vintner	Sawyer	Butler
	Thatcher	Clerk
Metal and Wood	Tiler	Coachman
Blacksmith		Dancing master
Brazier	*Clothing and Textiles*	Footman
Cooper	Beltmaker	Groom
Coppersmith	Bodicemaker	Hairdresser
Edgetoolmaker	Buttonmaker	Mariner
Farrier	Clothier	Seaman
Founder	Clothworker	Scholar
Hooper	Comber	Schoolmaster
Metalman	Cordwainer	Surgeon
Millwright	Currier	Waterman
Nailer	Draper	Writer
Needlemaker	Dyer	
Pewterer	Feltmaker	

Appendix H

Decennial estimates of white and black net migration by colony, 1650–1780

The estimates of the volume of net migration of whites and blacks to each colony or region by decade presented in this appendix are calculated as a residual, in which changes in a colony's observed population during a decade that are not due to estimated natural increase or decrease are attributed to net migration.[1] The derivation of the estimating equation begins with the identity that net migration to the colony in a decade is equal to the difference in size between the colony's terminal and initial populations less the excess of births over deaths that occurred in the colony during the decade:

$$M = P_1 - P_0 - (B - D), \tag{1}$$

where M = net migration per decade; P_0 = population of the colony at beginning of decade; P_1 = population of the colony at end of decade; B = total births in the colony during the decade; and D = total deaths in the colony during the decade. In this expression positive values of M indicate net immigration, and negative values indicate net emigration.

Because of the virulence in many colonies of seasoning mortality, in which immigrants died as a result of exposure to a new disease environment, mortality rates were often significantly higher for recent immigrants than for other colonists. Equation (1) can be modified to allow for this by recognizing that the colony's population consisted of separate seasoned and unseasoned groups:

$$M = P_1 - P_0 - P_0 R + MS - RM \frac{(1 - S)}{2} \tag{2}$$

where R = decennial rate of natural increase, and S = proportion of immigrants dying in seasoning.[2] Here the estimation of net migration begins with the change in the colony's population over the decade ($P_1 - P_0$) less the natural increase or decrease of the population present at the beginning of the decade ($P_0 R$). In addition, the estimated number of immigrants who died as a result of seasoning during the decade (MS) is added to net migration. And finally, allowance is made for the natural increase or decrease of those new immigrants who survived seasoning

212

$[RM(1 - S)]$; this formulation assumes that once these immigrants had survived seasoning, their natural increase or decrease was the same as that of the population already present in the colony. The final term of the equation is divided by two to obtain an estimate of the natural change of the size of the immigrant population under the assumption that immigrants arrived at a constant rate during any decade, so that on average new immigrants in each decade were present for half the decade.

Solving equation (2) for M yields the estimating equation used here, in which net migration is expressed as a function of P_0, P_1, R, and S:

$$M = \frac{P_1 - P_0 - P_0 R}{(1 - S) \dfrac{2 + R}{2}} \tag{3}$$

This residual method of estimating net migration tends to atttribute to migration all errors in the measurement of the other variables in the equation. Thus, an underestimate of a colony's population in the base year or an overestimate of its population in the terminal year will tend to result in overestimates of net migration in a decade, as will an underestimate of the rate of natural increase in the colony; similarly, overestimates of either base year population or the rate of natural increase, or an underestimate of terminal population, will produce underestimates of net migration. This feature of the method used to estimate net migration makes it important to emphasize that the results presented here are rough, and are intended to serve as broad and preliminary indications of major changes in the composition of flows of immigration to the colonies over time and major differences in this composition across colonies rather than as precise measurements of the volume of immigration.

The population estimates used for the West Indies are those given in John James McCusker, Jr., "The Rum Trade and the Balance of Payments of the Thirteen Continental Colonies, 1650–1775" (Ph.D. dissertation, University of Pittsburgh, 1970), Appendix B, Tables B-84, B-86–89, B-91, pp. 692, 694–7, 699. Population estimates for the mainland colonies were taken from U.S. Bureau of the Census, *Historical Statistics of the United States, Colonial Times to 1970* (Washington, D.C., 1975), Pt.2, Series Z2-17, p. 1168.

The values used for the other variables in the estimating equation are presented in Tables H.1 and H.2. The same rates of natural increase and seasoning mortality are taken to apply to both whites and blacks. This assumption may not be valid in a number of specific cases. In the Chesapeake, for example, the white population may have begun to grow as a result of natural increase by the first decade of the eighteenth century, while the black population may not have done so until as much as two

Appendix H

Table H.1. *Decennial values of* R *and* S *used to estimate net migration, 1650–1700*

	1650–60	1660–70	1670–80	1680–90	1690–1700
West Indies					
R	−.50	−.30	−.30	−.30	−.50
S	.12	.12	.12	.12	.12
Southern colonies					
R	−.15	−.10	−.05	0	.05
S	.10	.05	.05	.05	.05
Northern and middle colonies					
R	.29	.29	.29	.29	.29
S	0	0	0	0	0

Source: Henry A. Gemery, "Emigration from the British Isles to the New World, 1630–1700," *Research in Economic History* 5 (1980), Table A.5., p. 215. Passage mortality has been subtracted from the values given there for *S*.

decades later; see Russell R. Menard, "Immigrants and Their Increase: The Process of Population Growth in Early Colonial Maryland," in Aubrey C. Land, Lois Green Carr, and Edward C. Papenfuse, eds., *Law, Society, and Politics in Early Maryland* (Baltimore, 1977), pp. 97–8; Russell R. Menard, "The Maryland Slave Population, 1658 to 1730: A Demographic Profile of Blacks in Four Counties," *William and Mary Quarterly*, 3d ser. 32, no. 1 (January 1975), pp. 42–3; Allan Kulikoff, "A 'Prolifick' People: Black Population Growth in the Chesapeake colonies 1700–1790," *Southern Studies*, 16, no. 4 (Winter, 1977), p. 394. The evidence is incomplete in this case and lacking in many others. Yet it might be noted that the use of the same value for natural increase for both blacks and whites might tend to overstate white relative to black immigration to the Chesapeake during the period in which their true rates of natural increase differed.

Another approximation which apparently diverges from the actual demographic experience of the colonies is that of a virtually constant rate of natural increase in New England. While available evidence is inadequate to determine the precise extent of variation, a number of indicators suggest that variation in the rate did occur. One significant effect of this variation might be that due to an apparent decline in the actual rate of natural increase, the magnitude of net emigration from New England in the final decade of the seventeenth century and the first decade of the eighteenth may be overestimated here; for discussion of the decline, see Daniel Scott Smith, "The Demographic History of Colonial New

Table H.2. Decennial values of R and S used to estimate net migration, 1700–1780

	1700–10	1710–20	1720–30	1730–40	1740–50	1750–60	1760–70	1770–80
West Indies								
(1) R	−.30	−.30	−.30	−.20	−.20	−.20	−.10	−.10
(2) S	.10	.10	.10	.10	.10	.10	.10	.10
Southern colonies								
(3) R	.05	.05	.05	.15	.15	.28	.28	.28
(4) S	.05	.05	.05	.05	.05	.05	.05	.05
Northern and middle colonies								
(5) R	.28	.28	.28	.28	.28	.28	.28	.28
(6) S	0	0	0	0	0	0	0	0

Source: Line (1): See Table H.1. and Philip D. Curtin, *The Atlantic Slave Trade: A Census* (Madison, 1969), pp. 58–63; Michael Craton, *Sinews of Empire* (Garden City, 1974), pp. 194–9. Line (2): Craton, *Sinews of Empire*, p. 194. Line (3): Russell R. Menard, "The Maryland Slave Population, 1658 to 1730," *William and Mary Quarterly*, 3d ser. 32, no. 1 (January 1975), pp. 42–9; Allan Kulikoff, "A 'Prolifick' People: Black Population Growth in the Chesapeake Colonies, 1700–1790," *Southern Studies* 16, no. 4 (Winter 1977), p. 413, Table 7. Line (4): Kulikoff, "A 'Prolifick' People," pp. 396–7. Line (5): J. Potter, "The Growth of Population in America, 1700–1860," in D. V. Glass and D. E. C. Eversley, eds., *Population in History* (London, 1965), p. 646. Line (6): See Table H.1.

Table H.3. *Decennial estimates of net migration for British mainland colonies, 1650-1780*

Decade	New England		New York and New Jersey		Pennsylvania and Delaware	
	White	Black	White	Black	White	Black
1650–60	3,154	63	−287	−39	254	10
1660–70	8,298	−306	359	−21	2	1
1670–80	1,336	−12	3,568	377	659	24
1680–90	−1,484	300	3,955	274	9,179	217
1690–1700	−17,355	397	3,924	315	3,168	97
1700–10	−3,576	382	−941	158	532	1,186
1710–20	20,110	568	9,473	2,475	299	39
1720–30	−2,146	925	980	−382	14,114	1,524
1730–40	9,461	623	3,699	533	23,409	789
1740–50	−9,526	44	1,382	−645	11,333	352
1750–60	−8,632	−1,175	17,054	1,716	23,235	483
1760–70	5,629	−799	10,810	−1,745	−1,651	−232
1770–80	−22,506	−4,599	−4,570	−3,045	16,539	989

Note: Positive values indicate net immigration; negative values net emigration.

England," *Journal of Economic History* 32, no. 1 (March 1972): 165–83. However, the estimates obtained for New England appear basically to agree with Smith's results, as he concludes, for example, that net migration into New England played only a minor role in the growth of the region's population in the eighteenth century, and that the last three decades of that century were marked by net migration from the region.

Estimates of seasoning mortality rates used here may be conservatively low for some times and places. Direct evidence on seasoning mortality is scarce, but some discussions suggest the possibility of rates considerably higher than those used here; for example, Lorena S. Walsh, "Servitude and Opportunity in Charles County, Maryland, 1658–1705," in Land et al., eds., *Law, Society, and Politics in Early Maryland*, pp. 115–16. Clearly, the use of higher seasoning rates would raise the estimated numbers of immigrants; the rates used here should in general avoid overestimating immigrant flows on this account.

The resulting estimates of net migration, calculated separately for blacks and whites, are presented in Tables H.3 and H.4. It should be remembered that positive values indicate net immigration to the colony, and negative values net emigration from it during the decade.

Extremely high values in Tables 8.3 and 8.4, which are based on the estimates of Tables H.3 and H.4 and the colony population estimates from which these were derived, often appear in the early stages of a

Estimates of net migration by colony, 1650–1780

Maryland and Virginia		North Carolina		South Carolina		Georgia	
White	Black	White	Black	White	Black	White	Black
17,523	1,332						
16,599	1,832	3,122	146				
14,911	1,707	1,841	73	906	186		
9,131	7,259	2,189	95	1,474	1,368		
−302	7,738	2,711	103	760	892		
18,470	10,747	3,492	477	3,451	1,575		
20,924	6,616	3,429	2,110	−2,130	7,902		
38,325	6,376	4,946	2,927	4,827	7,599		
30,282	29,109	12,886	4,015	3,427	6,854		
−16,816	47,262	6,179	7,001	7,589	4,406	1,837	979
19,943	3,785	8,137	7,581	4,377	6,846	576	2,122
−1,573	8,096	26,946	24,608	1,883	1,653	4,681	5,582
−25,212	−19,136	14,594	1,765	18,648	713	17,470	6,677

colony's settlement, and in these cases generally result from large migrations to the colony soon after its initial settlement. A few examples can serve as illustrations. The tremendous net immigration to Jamaica during the 1660s relative to its population at the beginning of the decade reflects the small initial base as well as the substantial immigration of whites resulting from Sir Thomas Modyford's numerous land grants and, even more, the planters' considerable importation of slaves in the decade. During the decades of the 1670s and the 1680s sizable numbers migrated to South Carolina from colonies throughout British America, largely as a result of the colony's proprietors' decision of 1669 to encourage settlement by offering headrights of 150 acres to each new arrival. Similarly, William Penn's promotional efforts and liberal policies of land distribution produced a major migration to his colony immediately after the official foundation of Pennsylvania following the grant of the colony to Penn by Charles II in 1681, and the figure for 1680–90 shown in Table H.3 reflects the impact of this migration on the population of the mid-Atlantic region.

Table H.4. *Decennial estimates of net migration for British West Indies, 1650–1780*

Decade	Antigua White	Antigua Black	Barbados White	Barbados Black	Jamaica White	Jamaica Black	Montserrat White	Montserrat Black	Nevis White	Nevis Black	St. Kitts White	St. Kitts Black
1650–60	1,970	682	16,970	31,364			909	227	5,303	2,500	7,576	4,621
1660–70	1,283	655	5,428	28,650	7,513	9,158	−227	348	−401	−441	−1,671	−802
1670–80	1,390	3,222	6,444	22,219	4,412	17,326	2,259	3,235	762	4,412	0	3,021
1680–90	1,190	5,976	4,746	21,885	3,168	25,936	508	1,484	254	2,674	856	1,123
1690–1700	2,197	10,379	9,773	35,027	4,545	39,394	1,061	2,879	682	4,848	1,212	2,045
1700–10	1,320	8,536	2,902	22,523	2,732	38,954	444	1,725	13	235	2,392	16,248
1710–20	2,183	13,046	11,242	29,007	2,693	49,882	758	1,582	601	3,699	510	−3,817
1720–30	1,320	12,876	7,595	31,556	3,438	59,059	405	5,804	379	2,758	2,366	13,451
1730–40	889	8,025	4,000	24,519	765	45,901	0	395	−74	1,877	173	7,383
1740–50	765	12,543	3,654	26,074	3,630	62,691	296	3,086	222	3,185	148	7,111
1750–60	494	13,432	4,988	29,086	4,148	70,148	543	4,025	593	2,889	642	7,383
1760–70	−94	8,094	1,380	16,444	3,743	53,906	47	2,000	608	1,345	−281	3,895
1770–80	257	3,696	1,661	−468	8,094	72,129	82	456	655	1,263	246	4,140

Appendix I

Colonial destinations of the indentured servants

Tables I.1 and I.2 provide annual listings of the colonial destinations of the 20,657 servants in the six samples of registrations analyzed in this study, which are described in Appendix A. The tabulations are presented separately by sex and have been aggregated across samples.[1]

As mentioned in Chapter 6, in a number of samples some servants had their destination recorded as either of two different colonies; by far the most frequent example of this was the entry "Virginia or Maryland," but other dual entries occasionally appear in the registrations, sometimes involving colonies in different regions. In all such cases, the destination tabulated here is the first of the two mentioned. It should be noted, however, that these cases are not numerous enough to affect the general observations drawn from these data in the text concerning trends and patterns in the servants' colonial destinations.

In the Bristol registrations of 1654–86, the formula phrase "on the like conditions" was often substituted for specific information concerning the terms of particular servants' registrations, particularly during the years between the early 1660s and the beginning of the 1680s. The phrase was here assumed to apply to the servants' colonial destinations, and the destination of each servant was tabulated as the colony last mentioned in preceding registrations.

Appendix I

Table I.1. *Colonial destinations of male servants*

Date	Antigua	Barbados	Jamaica	Mont-serrat	Nevis	St. Kitts	Other West Indies
1654		14					
1655		114			2	1	
1656		156					
1657		370			3	1	
1658		412			23	9	
1659		492		3	29		
1660	1	235			55	11	
1661	1	107			179	9	
1662	1	87	11		144	2	1
1663	4	42		2	99	8	1
1664	8	46			42		
1665		20	1		26	7	
1666		56			2		
1667		78			16		
1668		66			14		
1669		37	6	1	55		
1670		40	9	15	59		
1671	4	35	13		54		
1672		8	7	8	13		
1673		7			5		
1674		38		2	101		
1675	3	18	7	6	35		
1676		19	10		9		2
1677		17	27		11		
1678	1	7			10		
1679		15	9	2	20		
1680	1	10	9	1	15		
1681					1		
1683		99	20		4		4
1684	17	130	162		10		1
1685	3	61	275		9		3
1686	2	23	30	1			5
1697							
1698		19		1			
1699						3	3
1700				9			
1701	2						
1702			1				
1703							
1704							
1705						1	1
1706							1
1707							

Caro-lina	Mary-land	New England	New Jersey & New York	Pennsyl-vania	Virginia	Other main-land	Not Given	Total
					35			49
					76			193
					104			260
		1			76			451
		1			148			593
	1				159			684
	3				140			445
					261			557
	4	22			372			644
	3	24			127			310
		10			86			192
	2	1			173			230
	4	3			182			247
		1			161			256
	1	8			233			322
		11			143			253
	11	8			126			268
	2	7			115			230
	14				155			205
	3				49			64
	4	10			143			298
	9	12			217			307
	8				121	1		170
	4	3			96	5		163
	6	2			97	3		126
	19	11			96	4		176
	17	1			55			109
					1			2
8	59		4	1	67		2	268
10	209	2		27	175		1	744
2	76	4	3	7	86	4	1	534
3	3		2	10	5	1	1	86
					13			13
				3	218		164	405
		34		9	146		64	259
					45	14	43	111
					47		37	86
		4			2		32	39
					1		41	42
							11	11
	2						20	24
					1		32	34
							15	15

continued

Table I.1. *(cont.)*

Date	Antigua	Barbados	Jamaica	Mont-serrat	Nevis	St. Kitts	Other West Indies
1718		9	1				
1719		2	3				
1720		4	18			1	
1721	3	6	15				2
1722			14			55	51
1723	4	1	38			5	1
1724	4		38				
1725	1	2	81			3	
1726							
1727	1		8				
1728	25		6				
1729	8		40				5
1730	1	2	135			3	
1731	11	3	223			7	
1732			7				
1733		4	90				
1734	6		62			1	
1735	2	3	47				
1736	1		162			2	
1737	8		42				
1738	3	1	44			1	
1739	6		64			1	
1740	1		1				
1749			11				
1750	1		20				
1751			7			1	
1752			4				
1753			14			1	
1754	1		9				
1755	9		10			1	
1756	4		8				
1757	2		7				
1758	5						
1759	2		4				
1773							
1774			8				
1775			4				
Total	157	2,916	1,841	51	1,045	134	81

Carolina	Maryland	New England	New Jersey & New York	Pennsylvania	Virginia	Other mainland	Not Given	Total
1	37				5			53
	75			3	16			99
2	82			3	46			156
	20			2	36			84
	39	7		20	6			192
4	48	1		16	4			122
	51	11		5	2			111
3	106			17	5			218
					1			1
	15			1	17			42
	6			84	3			124
	54				4			111
2	59			23	6			231
	37			26	12			319
2	2				1			12
4	39			11	4	3		155
2	24			2	22	3		122
	41			8	6	5		112
19	10			11	4			209
	17				13	1		81
2	14			8	5			78
	27			26	1			125
								2
	1			1				13
	6	2		5	8			42
2	25			6	23			64
	2				2	1		9
1	9				4			29
		1		1	3			15
	3			1				24
1	11				1			25
	1					3		13
				1		8		14
								6
	55				133			188
17	1,103			475	432	30		2,065
	848		29	142	83			1,106
85	3,332	201	38	955	5,461	86	464	16,847

223

Appendix I

Table I.2. *Colonial destinations of female servants*

Date	Antigua	Barbados	Jamaica	Nevis	St. Kitts	Other West Indies	Carolina
1654		2		1			
1655		37					
1656		41					
1657		118					
1658		123		4	6		
1659		151		3			
1660	1	88		20	6		
1661		21		32	2		
1662		19	1	38	1		
1663	2	18		30	3		
1664	2	14		7			
1665		4		3	3		
1666		13					
1667		32		6			
1668		17		4			
1669		7	1	20			
1670		12	1	15			
1671	1	6	1	10			
1672		3		8			
1673	5	2	4		2		
1674		9		14			
1675		5	3	13			
1676	2	6	2				
1677		5	6				
1678		5		5			
1679		5		10			
1680	1			2			
1681							
1682							
1683		3	7			3	2
1684	1	12	40	2			6
1685	3	13	68	8		7	1
1686		9	9			5	
1697							
1698							
1699							
1700							
1701							
1702							
1703							
1704							
1705							
1706							
1707							

224

Maryland	New England	New Jersey & New York	Pennsyl-vania	Virginia	Other mainland	Not given	Total
				12			15
				37			74
				34			75
				43			161
	1			50			184
				61			215
1				44			160
				103			158
1	5			135			200
1	4			29			87
	1			35			59
				69			79
				70			83
				61			99
1	1			56			79
				60			88
5	1			28			62
2	1			29			50
2				36			49
				16			29
1	1			44			69
1				65			87
5				38			53
4				25			40
1	5			35			51
6				31			52
5				9			17
							0
							0
24			2	20		1	62
80	1		1	63		1	207
37	1	1		58			197
	1	3	4	10			41
				3			3
				63		41	104
	10		7	54		18	89
				26		2	28
				19		13	32
				1		22	23
						26	26
						26	26
						15	15
				3		49	52
						6	6

continued

Table I.2. *(cont.)*

Date	Antigua	Barbados	Jamaica	Nevis	St. Kitts	Other West Indies	Carolina
1718	.					2	
1719							
1720						1	
1721						1	
1722						2	
1723			1			1	
1724							
1725						1	
1727			1				
1728							
1730			5				
1731			11			1	
1732							
1733			2				
1734							
1735							
1736			4				
1737							
1738							
1739			2				
1749							
1750			2				
1751			1				
1756						1	
1757			1				
1773							
1774							1
1775							
Total	18	800	173	255	23	25	10

Colonial destinations of the indentured servants

Maryland	New England	New Jersey & New York	Pennsyl-vania	Virginia	Other mainland	Not given	Total
6				1			9
6			5	7			18
4			2	10			17
3				7	1		12
2					1		5
4			1		1		8
3			3		1		7
4			5				10
2				4			7
			10				10
1							6
5			5				22
					1		1
3			1		2		8
					1		1
1					2		3
1			2		4		11
			1				1
2							2
2			2	1			7
					1		1
			2				4
			1				2
							1
							1
6				2			8
68			51	33	5	12	170
162			3	7			172
462	33	4	105	1,650	20	232	3,810

Notes

Preface

1 The full references to these papers are: "Immigration and the Colonial Labor System: An Analysis of the Length of Indenture," *Explorations in Economic History* 14, no. 4 (October 1977): 360–77; "British Servants and the Colonial Indenture System in the Eighteenth Century," *Journal of Southern History* 44, no. 1 (February 1978): 41–66; " 'Middling People' or 'Common Sort'?: The Social Origins of Some Early Americans Reexamined, "*William and Mary Quarterly,* 3rd ser. 35, no. 3 (July 1978): 499–524; "Literacy and the Social Origins of Some Early Americans," *Historical Journal* 22, no. 1 (March 1979): 75–91; "The Social Origins of Some Early Americans: Rejoinder," *William and Mary Quarterly,* 3rd ser. 36, no. 2 (April 1979): 264–77; "Demographic Aspects of White Servitude in Colonial British America," *Annales de Démographie Historique* (1980): 239–52; "White Servitude and the Growth of Black Slavery in Colonial America, "*Journal of Economic History,* 41, no. 1 (March 1981): 39–47; "The Market Evaluation of Human Capital: The Case of Indentured Servitude, "*Journal of Political Economy,* 89, no. 3 (June 1981): 446–67.

1. The significance and origins of the colonial indenture system

1 Abbot Emerson Smith, *Colonists in Bondage: White Servitude and Convict Labor in America, 1607–1776* (Chapel Hill, N.C., 1947), p. 13.

2 Ibid.

3 Ibid., p. 336; Wesley Frank Craven, *White, Red and Black: The Seventeenth-Century Virginian* (Charlottesville, Va., 1971), p. 5.

4 Ulrich B. Phillips, *Life and Labor in the Old South* (Boston, 1963), pp. 25–6.

5 Eric Williams, *Capitalism and Slavery* (New York, 1966), p. 19.

6 Russell Menard, "From Servants to Slaves: The Transformation of the Chesapeake Labor System," *Southern Studies,* 16, no. 4 (Winter, 1977): 360.

7 Ibid.; Gloria L. Main, "Maryland and the Chesapeake Economy, 1670–1720," in Aubrey C. Land, Lois Green Carr, and Edward C. Papenfuse, eds., *Law, Society, and Politics in Early Maryland* (Baltimore, 1977), p. 140.

8 Lewis Cecil Gray, *History of Agriculture in the Southern United States to*

1860 (Gloucester, Mass., 1958), 1:349–51; Alice Hanson Jones, *Wealth of a Nation to Be: The American Colonies on the Eve of the Revolution* (New York, 1980), pp. 115–16.

9 London, 1583.

10 Ibid. The pamphlet is not paginated; the passage quoted occurs in the seventh chapter.

11 Marcus Jernegan, *Laboring and Dependent Classes in Colonial America, 1607–1783* (Chicago, 1931), pp. 46–7.

12 Eugene I. McCormac, *White Servitude in Maryland, 1634–1820* (Baltimore, 1904), p. 7; Smith, *Colonists in Bondage*, p. 8; Carl Bridenbaugh, *Vexed and Troubled Englishmen, 1590–1642* (London, 1967), p. 240; Richard Hofstadter, *America at 1750: A Social Portrait* (New York, 1971), p. 49.

13 Smith, *Colonists in Bondage*, p. 8.

14 E.g., see Thomas Smyth, *De Republica Anglorum* (1583; reprint ed., Menston, 1970), pp. 113–14.

15 David Beers Quinn, *The Voyages and Colonizing Enterprises of Sir Humfrey Gilbert* (London, 1940), 1:6, 74, 91.

16 E.g., McCormac, *White Servitude in Maryland*, p. 13; Sigmund Diamond, "Values as an Obstacle to Economic Growth: The American Colonies," *Journal of Economic History* 27, no. 4 (December 1967): 564, 570. On the colonial use of English institutions in devising a legal framework, see J. R. T. Hughes, *Social Control in the Colonial Economy* (Charlottesville, Va., 1976).

17 Perry Miller, *Errand into the wilderness* (Cambridge, 1956), p. 134.

18 Smith, *Colonists in Bondage*, pp. 10–16.

19 Peter Laslett, *The World We Have Lost*, 2nd ed. (London, 1971), p. 13.

20 Ann Sturm Kussmaul, "Servants in Husbandry in Early-Modern England" (Ph.D. diss., University of Toronto, 1978), pp. 1, 42.

21 Laslett, *World We Have Lost*, p. 15.

22 Kussmaul, "Servants in Husbandry," pp. 99–122.

23 Laslett, *World We Have Lost*, p. 259, n. 4. For additional evidence on the relative numbers of apprentices and farm servants, see R. E. Chester Waters, "A Statutory List of the Inhabitants of Melbourne, Derbyshire, in 1695," *Journal of the Derbyshire Archaeological and Natural History Society* 7 (1885): 24–5; A. J. and R. H. Tawney, "An Occupational Census of the Seventeenth Century," *Economic History Review* 5 (1934): 47, 59–61; Philip Styles, "A Census of a Warwickshire Village in 1698," *University of Birmingham Historical Journal* 3 (1951): 39–40; K. J. Allison, "An Elizabethan Village 'Census,'" *Bulletin of the Institute of Historical Research* 36 (1963): 91–103; Peter Laslett and John Harrison, "Clayworth and Cogenhoe," in H. E. Bell and R. L. Ollard, eds., *Historical Essays, 1600–1750* (London, 1963), p. 169; C. W. Chalklin, *Seventeenth-Century Kent* (London, 1965), pp. 246–7.

The status of apprentice in husbandry, created by the Statute of Artificers in 1563, was apparently rarely used; S. T. Bindoff, "The Making of the Statute of Artificers," in S. T. Bindoff, J. Hurstfield, and C. H. Williams, eds.,

Elizabethan Government and Society (London, 1961), p. 92; O. Jocelyn Dunlop, *English Apprenticeship and Child Labor* (London, 1912), pp. 97–8.

24 Laslett, *World We Have Lost,* pp. 21, 259, n. 4.

25 Ibid., p. 263, n. 17; Peter Laslett, *Family Life and Illicit Love in Earlier Generations* (Cambridge, 1977), pp. 13, 31–5, 83–6.

26 Laslett, *World We Have Lost,* p. 2.

27 The terms of the contracts might be written down in unusual circumstances, so examples exist; e.g., see "Thomas Clarke and John Hill's Security for the faithful service of Ambrose Clarke, whom Mr. Paul D'Ewes had taken for his Gardener, 1627," British Museum, Harleian MS 98, f. 25.

28 Michael Dalton, *The Countrey Justice* (London, 1677), pp. 121–30; Kussmaul, "Servants in Husbandry," p. 54; J. S. Cockburn, ed., *Western Circuit Assize Orders, 1629–1648,* Camden Fourth Series, 17 (London, 1976) no. 993, p. 229.

29 R. Keith Kelsall, *Wage Regulation Under the Statute of Artificers* (London, 1938), p. 65; J. Tait, ed., *Lancashire Quarter Sessions Records,* Chetham Society, n.s., 77 (1917): 216; Kussmaul, "Servants in Husbandry," p. 55, n. 10.

30 Passage to the colonies was £6, apparently from the beginning of the colonial period; e.g., John Smith, *The Generall Historie of Virginia, New England, and the Summer Isles* (London, 1624), p. 162; Samual Purchas, *Purchas His Pilgrimes* (London, 1625), 4: 1791. In addition, particularly during the seventeenth century, the servant was frequently supplied with a complete set of clothing before leaving England. Estimates of the costs involved in this vary, but include William Bullock's of £3 7s 10d per servant in 1649 and Edward Littleton's of a little less than £5 in 1689; Bullock, *Virginia Impartially examined, and left to publick view, to be considered by all Iudicious and honest men* (London, 1649), p. 36; Littleton, *The Groans of the Plantations* (London, 1689), p. 17. For further evidence on all these costs, see Chapter 7. The important point here is simply that the sum was considerable, beyond the budget of many Englishmen who wished to emigrate to America. Thus, for crude comparison, in 1688 Gregory King estimated the annual income per person of a family headed by a freeholder of the better sort as £13, by a freeholder of the lesser sort as £10, by a farmer as £8.5, by an artisan or handicraftsman £9.5, and by a laborer or out servant £4.3; Laslett, *World We Have Lost,* pp. 36–7.

31 Although the length of the term received by a particular servant varied with the servant's personal characteristics and choice of colonial destination, four years was generally the minimum term given. Shorter terms could be and occasionally were given, but terms of three years were rare, and few records remain of indentures of two years or less. What these terms represent is the time necessary for the servant to repay the passage fare out of his implicit net wages in the colonies–i.e., out of the difference between the value of his marginal product in the colonies and the cost of the maintenance he received there. More formally, the value of the labor the servant promised to perform, discounted to the date at which the contract was signed, was equal to the

present discounted value of the sum of his passage fare to the colonies, the cost of all the food, clothing, lodging, and other maintenance provided there, and the freedom dues he received at the end of his term. For further evidence on the length of indenture and analysis of its determinants, see Chapter 7.

32 Smith, *Colonists in Bondage,* pp. 264–70.

33 This statement is not intended to imply that servants in the colonies were always treated more harshly by their masters and with less consideration for their welfare than were servants in England. Indeed, one would not expect most masters to have physically abused workers in whom they had a considerable investment. Yet the evidence of both court records and contemporaries' comments suggests that harsh treatment of servants, unlike that typically given to members of the master's family, including the sale of servants from one master to another, was more common in the colonies than in England, and that this occurred because servants were a valuable form of property in America. It is possible that such treatment of immigrants affected the whole institution of service in the colonies to the extent of applying equally to American-born servants. One statement that suggests this appears in the autobiography of a former servant, Solomon Mack, who was born in Connecticut in 1732: "My parents became poor, and when I was four years old, the family, then consisting of five children, were obliged to disperse . . . I was bound out to a farmer in the neighborhood. As is too commonly the case, I was rather considered as a slave than a member of the family, and, instead of allowing me the privilege of common hospitality, and a claim to that kind protection due to the helpless and indigent children, I was treated by my master as his property and not as his fellow mortal; he taught me to work, and was very careful that I should have little or no rest from labour." Archibald F. Bennett, "Solomon Mack and His Family," *The Improvement Era*, 58, no. 9 (September 1955): 631.

34 Edmund S. Morgan, *American Slavery, American Freedom: The Ordeal of Colonial Virginia* (New York, 1975), pp. 128–9.

35 Dunlop, *English Apprenticeship,* pp. 57, 127–8.

36 E.g., see Henry Best, *Rural Economy in Yorkshire in 1641,* Publications of the Surtees Society (1857), 33:132–5, 163–4; Kussmaul, "Servants in Husbandry," pp. 70–3, 281–5.

37 Morgan, *American Slavery, American Freedom,* p. 128.

38 This conclusion refers to the indenture system as it functioned in the vast majority of cases. Exceptions can be found. Thus the agreement of 1618 by which the Virginia Company contracted with the Common Council of the City of London for one hundred boys and girls between the ages of 8 and 16 to be "taken up and transported [under indenture] to Virginia there to be educated and brought up . . . in such trades and professions as the said company shall think fitt," with the costs of transportation to be paid by the Council, is a clear example of the exercise of the compulsory apprenticing power of the parish to provide indentured servants for the colonies; Corporation of London Records Office, "Journal of the Common Council," September 24, 1618, 30, f. 396; Dalton, *The Countrey Justice,* p. 128; E. M. Leonard, *The Early History of English Poor Relief* (London, 1965), pp.

55–7, 76. However, this method was soon abandoned; Robert C. Johnson, "The Transportation of Vagrant Children from London to Virginia, 1618–1622," in H. S. Reinmuth, Jr., ed., *Early Stuart Studies* (Minneapolis, 1970), pp. 137–51. Quantitatively, the most important exception to the voluntary indenture system was the transportation of convicts, which apparently began early in the colonial period and reached sizable dimensions after 1718; see Smith, *Colonists in Bondage,* pp. 89–135. Rogues and vagabonds could be sentenced to transportation to the colonies but apparently seldom were; ibid., pp. 136–51.

39 Smith, *Colonists in Bondage,* p. 287.

40 Tawney quoted in Miller, *Errand into the Wilderness,* p. 133; George Alsop, *A Character of the Province of Mary-Land* (London, 1666), pp. 30–1.

41 William Wood, *New England's Prospect,* 1635, ed. Alden T. Vaughan (Amherst, Mass., 1977), p. 73; Anonymous, *A Brief Description of the Province of Carolina on the Coasts of Floreda* (London, 1666), p. 9.

42 Smith, *Colonists in Bondage,* pp. 5–6.

43 James Curtis Ballagh, *White Servitude in the Colony of Virginia* (Baltimore, 1895), pp. 11–12. Ballagh contends that the length of term to be served before receipt of a share of the divided profits apparently increased from five years in 1606 to the seven quoted in a Virginia Company broadside in 1609. The broadside is reprinted in Alexander Brown, ed., *The Genesis of the United States* (London, 1890), 1:248–9; also see R. I., *Nova Britannia: Offering Most Excellent fruites by Planting in Virginia* (London, 1609), reprinted in Peter Force, ed., *Tracts and Other Papers, Relating Principally to the Origin, Settlement, and Progress of the Colonies in North America* (Washington, D.C., 1836), pp. 23–4.

44 Smith, *Colonists in Bondage,* p. 10; Morgan, *American Slavery, American Freedom,* pp. 21, 81–2; Ballagh, *White Servitude,* pp. 20–1.

45 Morgan, *American Slavery, American Freedom,* p. 94; Sigmund Diamond, "From Organization to Society: Virginia in the Seventeenth Century," *American Journal of Sociology,* 58, no. 5 (March 1958): 469.

46 Corporation of London Records Office, "Journal of the Common Council," vol.30, f. 396; Susan Myra Kingsbury, ed., *The Records of the Virginia Company of London* (Washington, D.C., 1906), 1: 270–1, 3: 115, 313, 493–4, 505–6; Ballagh, *White Servitude,* pp. 28–9; Smith, *Colonists in Bondage,* pp. 12, 147–9; Robert C. Johnson, "The Transportation of Vagrant Children from London to Virginia, 1618–1622," in H. S. Reinmuth, Jr., ed., *Early Stuart Studies* (Minneapolis, 1970), pp. 137–51.

47 Kingsbury, *Records of the Virginia Company,* 3: 313; Smith, *Colonists in Bondage,* pp. 12–13. An actual indenture for the service of an Englishman in Virginia survives from 1619, but the agreement was not carried out. However, the existence of the contract suggests that the basic form may have been in common use before 1620; ibid., pp. 14–15.

48 Ibid., pp. 15–16.

49 Ibid., p. 16. A similar system was also put into use by the French during the second quarter of the seventeenth century. Although various forms of contract were used for workers bound for the French New World colonies, the

earliest example of a contract of the type described in the text, in which a servant was bound to an intermediary for transfer to another master not identified in the contract upon arrival in the colonies, apparently dates from 1645. On the development of contract forms in the French servant trade, see G. Debien, "Les Engagé Pour Les Antilles (1634–1715)," *Revue d'Histoire des Colonies,* 38 (1951): 47–68.

50 Lance E. Davis and Douglass C. North, *Institutional Change and American Economic Growth* (Cambridge, 1971), p. 211.

51 For an interpretation of the length of the terms assigned under this legislation, see David W. Galenson, "British Servants and the Colonial Indenture System in the Eighteenth Century," *Journal of Southern History,* 44, no. 1 (February 1978): 60–5.

52 Karl Frederick Geiser, *Redemptioners and Indentured Servants in the Colony and Commonwealth of Pennsylvania* (New Haven, 1901), p. 53; Frank Ried Diffenderfer, *The German Immigration into Pennsylvania Through the Port of Philadelphia, 1700 to 1775; Part II, The Redemptioners* (Lancaster, Pa., 1900), pp. 215–18, 192–4; Gottlieb Mittelberger, *Journey to Pennsylvania* (Cambridge, Mass., 1960), pp. 17–19; Smith, *Colonists in Bondage,* p. 22.

53 For apparent examples of this, see Geiser, *Redemptioners and Indentured Servants,* pp. 74, 114–15.

54 And, indeed, any other members of a family of redemptioners would be responsible for the fare of one who died at sea if more than half the voyage had been completed before the death occurred; Cheesman A. Herrick, *White Servitude in Pennsylvania* (Philadelphia, 1926), p. 187.

55 Although evidence is scarce, it appears that the infamous "Newlanders," who traveled in Germany recruiting servants, did not themselves typically enter into agreements for transportation with prospective servants but rather received commissions from ships' captains when the latter entered agreements with redemptioners in Rotterdam or Amsterdam. This is suggested by the accounts of Mittelberger, Muhlenberg, and Saur, quoted in Diffenderfer, *German Immigration into Pennsylvania,* pp. 192, 196, 243.

56 It might be argued that in a competitive market the redemptioner would be compensated for bearing this risk, perhaps by means of a shorter indenture than an English servant of equal expected productivity. It would be difficult to test for this effect because of the need to allow for the possible lower initial productivity of Germans in colonial America resulting from language difficulties, which would have had an opposite tendency, to lengthen the term of a German servant relative to an English immigrant alike in other respects. It has been noted that very short terms of one or two years appear more frequently for redemptioners than for indentured servants (e.g., Smith, *Colonists in Bondage,* p. 232), but this may have been due in many cases to the partial payment of the fare in advance by redemptioners.

57 These include Ballagh, *White Servitude;* John Spencer Bassett, *Slavery and Servitude in the Colony of North Carolina* (Baltimore,1896); Geiser, *Redemptioners and Indentured Servants;* McCormac, *White Servitude in Maryland;* and Herrick, *White Servitude in Pennsylvania.*

58 Smith, *Colonists in Bondage.*
59 K. G. Davies, *The North Atlantic World in the Seventeenth Century* (Minneapolis, 1974), p. 343.
60 Carter Goodrich, "Indenture," in *Encyclopaedia of the Social Sciences* (New York, 1932), 7:646.
61 Smith, *Colonists in Bondage,* p. 336.
62 See Appendix H.

2. The age and sex distributions of the indentured servants

1 Herbert Moller, "Sex Composition and Correlated Culture Patterns of Colonial America," *William and Mary Quarterly,* 3rd ser. 2, no. 2 (April 1945): 118.
2 Ibid., pp. 114–22; Richard S. Dunn, *Sugar and Slaves* (New York, 1973), p. 327; Robert V. Wells, *The Population of the British Colonies in America before 1776* (Princeton, 1975), pp. 272–5; Russell R. Menard, "Immigrants and Their Increase: The Process of Population Growth in Early Colonial America," in Aubrey C. Land, Lois Green Carr, and Edward C. Papenfuse, eds., *Law, Society, and Politics in Early Maryland* (Baltimore, 1977), p. 98.
3 See Chapter 7.
4 George Alsop, *A Character of the Province of Mary-Land* (London, 1666), p. 38; William Bullock, *Virginia Impartially examined, and left to publick view, to be considered by all Iudicious and honest men* (London, 1649), p. 54. In some places the imbalance between the sexes was apparently so great that even a poor background was no bar to an English woman's social advancement. E.g., an Englishman wrote of Barbados in 1654 that "a Baud brought over putes on a demuor comportment; a whore if hansume makes a wife for some rich planter"; Henry Whistler, "Voyage to the West Indies, 1654," British Museum, Sloane MS 3926, f. 9. On the purchase of female servants as wives in the colonies, also see Susan Myra Kingsbury, ed., *The Records of the Virginia Company of London* (Washington, D.C., 1933), 3:115, 313, 493–4, 505–6; Francesco Giavarina to the Doge and Senate, March 3, 1656, in Allen B. Hinds, ed., *Calendar of State Papers, Venetian,* (London, 1930), 33:184; "Report of England of Giovanni Sagredo," 1656, in ibid., p. 309; Edward Nicholas to Joseph Jane, Cologne, March 4, 1656, Public Record Office, London, State Papers 18/25, f. 9; Robert Beverley, *The History and Present State of Virginia* (London, 1750), Bk. 4, p. 51.
5 This would be consistent with the decline in the size of the premium for females (see Chapter 7) that occurred between the 1680s and the second quarter of the eighteenth century. If this motive had been an important determinant of the demand for female servants, it could also account for the apparent discrepancy between the evidence of a positive premium for females implied by the analysis of the servant contracts presented in Chapter 7 and that of a positive premium for males shown in Virginia probate inventories of the late seventeenth century; see Philip Alexander Bruce, *Economic History of Virginia in the Seventeenth Century* (New York, 1907), 2: 51–2. The

evidence of the servant contracts reflects the (expected) values of servants newly arrived in the colonies, whereas that of the probate records indicates the values of servants who had already been purchased and placed on estates. Female servants were freed from their indentures if they married the owners of their contracts. Therefore if some women had been highly valued as wives, and had married shortly after arriving in the colonies, and if these had constituted a sizable proportion of all female indentured arrivals, the average price of women relative to men based on the group of all new arrivals in the colonies, which included these women, could have been higher than the average relative price of female servants based on the group inventoried in the probate records of those women remaining in indentures some time after arrival, which did not include those valued as wives.

6 See Chapter 7.

7 Steve Crawford, "The Aggregate Structure of the Slave Family," University of Chicago Workshop in Economic History, Report 7980-4, October 1979, pp. 33–4.

8 The possible existence and effects of systematic biases in the age distributions of three samples – those from Middlesex and London in the 1680s and London in 1718–59 – resulting from the legal processes that generated the data are discussed in Appendix C.

9 The full underlying frequency distributions of age by sex for each sample are presented in David Walter Galenson, "The Indenture System and the Colonial Labor Market," (Ph.D. diss. Harvard University, 1979) Tables III-4–III-8, pp. 51–5.

10 I am grateful to the Cambridge Group for the History of Population and Social Structure for permission to use these data drawn from their files.

11 R. S. Schofield, "Age-Specific Mobility in an Eighteenth-Century Rural English Parish," *Annales de Démographie Historique* (1970), p. 264.

12 Ibid., p. 266; Peter Laslett, *Family Life and Illicit Love in Earlier Generations* (Cambridge, 1977), p. 34.

13 This difference would be reduced somewhat if the comparison were made between those living in service in England and in the colonies, for it must be remembered that the registrations of indentured servants are not censuses of those in service, as are the English village listings, but rather records of the ages of entry from which those registered were bound to serve fixed terms of years.

14 For discussion of the Privy Council order of 1682 that authorized the registrations of the 1680s, and its possible effect on the evidence of the London and Middlesex registrations, see Appendix C.

15 For discussion of the possible age bias of the registrations in the London sample of 1718–59, see Appendix C.

16 It might be noted that pairwise comparisons of the differences in mean ages of men across sequential samples over time indicate that the differences are statistically significantly different than zero; the results for women are weaker. Thus two-tailed t-tests indicate that the difference in the mean ages of men were significant at the .01 level between the following chronologically sequential pairs of samples: London (1683–6) and Liverpool; Middlesex

(1683–4) and Liverpool; Liverpool and London (1718–59); and London (1718–59) and London (1773–5). The differences in the mean ages of women across samples were significant at .01 only between Liverpool and London (1718–59), and London (1718–59) and London (1773–5).

3. The occupations of the seventeenth-century indentured servants

1 These same two samples formed the basis for an influential study by Mildred Campbell, "Social Origins of Some Early Americans," in James Morton Smith, ed., *Seventeenth-Century America: Essays in Colonial History* (Chapel Hill, N.C., 1959), pp. 63–89. Although based on the same evidence, my interpretations differ significantly from those of Campbell. A statement of the differences of interpretation, and subsequent discussion, is contained in David W. Galenson, " 'Middling People' or 'Common Sort'?: The Social Origins of Some Early Americans Reexamined," *William and Mary Quarterly,* 3d ser. 35, no. 3 (July 1978): 499–524; Campbell, "Response," ibid., pp. 525–40; Galenson, "The Social Origins of Some Early Americans: A Rejoinder," ibid., 36, no. 2 (April 1979): 264–77; Campbell, "Reply," ibid., pp. 277–86. The discussion of the present chapter is based upon my interpretation of this evidence.

2 See Appendix A for a description and full references to the Bristol registrations.

3 The first period in Table 3.1 has been restricted to the years before 1661; the latter year is excluded because during nearly half the year no occupational descriptions were recorded in the registrations.

4 W. G. Hoskins found that 1657 was the first of five successive years of bad wheat harvests; "Harvest Fluctuations and English Economic History, 1620–1759," *Agricultural History Review,* 16 (1968): 18, 29. This may have been a factor, perhaps an important one, contributing to both the increase in total registrations and the increased share of yeomen in the Bristol registrations beginning in 1657. Although no generalizations can be documented concerning the motives for emigration of large numbers of servants, historians have stressed the importance of dislocations of normal life, of which bad harvests were a leading type, as a determinant of flows in the seventeenth-century servant trade. See K. G. Davies, *The North Atlantic World in the Seventeenth Century,* vol. 4, *Europe and the World in the Age of Expansion* (Minneapolis, 1974), p. 104, and Edmund S. Morgan, *American Slavery, American Freedom: The Ordeal of Colonial Virginia* (New York, 1975), p. 236.

The possible importance of this factor however, might be undercut by another of Hoskins's findings, that the wheat harvests of 1655–6 had been deficient in western England. The Bristol lists were dominated by natives of the west: Of more than 2,500 English servants whose places of origin are given, more than 88 percent came from Bristol and the fourteen counties that together made up the western and Oxford assizes circuits in the seventeenth century. Therefore, the change in the relevant western conditions was apparently less sharp than that in overall English agricultural conditions between the period 1654–6 and that of 1657–61. See Hoskins, "Harvest Fluctuations," p. 29, and J. S. Cockburn, *A History of English Assizes 1558–1714* (Cambridge, 1972), pp. 19, 23.

5 The full text of this ordinance appears in manuscript in the first volume of registrations, Bristol Record Office, Bristol, B.A.O. 04220(1), f. 27.

6 Probably a quarter or more of the males in the Bristol list during 1654–6 were minors. In these years, 24% of the males received terms of servitude of five or more years; in other samples in which both the servant's age and length of indenture are available, this proportion tends to be a downward-biased estimator of the proportion of males under 21, because at most times and places the number of minors indentured who received terms of four years tended to be greater than the number of adults who received terms of five or more years. This relation holds in the servant registrations of the Middlesex Quarter Sessions from 1683–4, as well as in the London registrations from 1682–6 and 1718–59. An exception is the Liverpool registrations from 1697–1707.

7 One implication of this hypothesized shift can be tested. If it is correct that a significant number of those males without occupational designations in the first few years of registration were minors and that beginning in 1657 adult laborers were combined with this group, then the age composition of the males without recorded occupations should have shifted upwards between the periods 1654–6 and 1657–60. As the length of indenture tended to be negatively related to age for minors, a shift in the age composition of the servants without occupations toward adults should have been reflected in a decline in the proportion of the group receiving terms of more than the adult's usual term of four years and an increase in the mean age of the group in a decline in the mean length of indenture received by those in the category. These changes did occur. The portion of the group receiving terms of five or more years fell from 38% in 1654–6 to 33% in 1657–60. The mean length of indenture fell from 4.96 years in the first period to 4.65 years in the second, with the difference significantly different than zero at the .05 level. For systematic evidence on the relationship between age and length of indenture from later periods, see Chapter 7.

8 See Appendix A for references to the Middlesex registrations.

9 This hypothesis and the suggested implication are offered by Campbell, "Social Origins of Some Early Americans," p. 71, n. 17.

10 Cregoe D. P. Nicholson, *Some Early Emigrants to America* (Baltimore, 1965), pp. 1–3.

11 Campbell's description, on which this hypothesis is based, is not specific; this statement is based on inspection of the forms. In fact, as the illustrations show, it is not strictly accurate to say that any of the form types contained a separate blank for the servant's occupation or status.

12 Peter Laslett, *The World We Have Lost,* 2nd ed. (London, 1971), pp. 46–7. This is one of the two factors cited by Mildred Campbell in defense of the validity of the status terms; the other was the large number and variety of the skills listed; "Social Origins of Some Early Americans," p. 72. There may have been another factor of even greater importance. Colonial courts could

invalidate an indenture in the case of fraud by a merchant or recruiting agent. See Richard B. Morris, *Government and Labor in Early America* (New York, 1946), p. 312. There is also evidence that courts paid careful attention to details of form and substance of servants' indentures (ibid., p. 311) and that colonial courts could lengthen the terms of servants as punishment for a number of offenses; Morgan, *American Slavery, American Freedom*, pp. 216–18; Abbot Emerson Smith, *Colonists in Bondage: White Servitude and Convict Labor in America, 1607–1776* (Chapel Hill, N.C., 1947), pp. 265–7. Given these facts, it seems likely that fraud by a servant in claiming a skill he did not possess could have been cause for extension of his term of service.

If claims of false occupations by servants had been a significant problem in this period, qualifications would probably have been placed on some of the indentures. It was customary in a later period for London merchants to make payments of salaries to skilled servants conditional on their understanding of their stated trades, and the same could be done by the purchasers of skilled redemptioners in eighteenth-century Philadelphia. See "Memoranda of Agreements to Serve in America and the West Indies," Corporation of London Records Office, and *Record of Indentures of Individuals Bound Out as Apprentices, Servants, etc.*, Pennsylvania-German Society, *Publications* (Lancaster, 1907), 16:321–3. Though cash payments were made to some of the servants in the samples considered here, no such conditions appear in either the Bristol or Middlesex registrations.

13 Richard Vann, "Quakerism and Social Structure in the Interregnum," *Past and Present*, no. 43 (May 1969): 74; David Cressy, "Describing the Social Order of Elizabethan and Stuart England," *Literature and History*, 3 (1976): 35. There is abundant evidence that this was particularly true of the type of registration process under consideration here. The Bristol servants' indentures were to be recorded "as other Indentures of apprenticeship are and have used to bee" (see earlier in this chapter), apparently in the Mayor's Court, and the rough copies were kept with those of the indentures of apprentices. For the latter, see manuscript volumes of "Actions and Apprentices," B.A.O. 04354, 04355(1)–(6), and 04356(1); also Elizabeth Ralph, *Guide to the Bristol Archives Office, City and County of Bristol* (Bristol, 1971), p. 52; William Dodgson Bowman, ed., *Bristol and America: A Record of the First Settlers in the Colonies of North America, 1654–1685* . . . (London, 1929), pp. viii–ix; and C. M. MacInnes, *A Gateway of Empire* (Bristol, 1939), p. 161. Similarly, in the Middlesex sessions records servants' indentures apparently were recorded by the same process as those of apprentices; W. L. Grant and James Munro, eds., *Act of the Privy Council of England, Colonial Series* (London, 1910), 2:41–3; E. G. Dowdell, *A Hundred Years of Quarter Sessions: The Government of Middlesex from 1660 to 1760* (Cambridge, 1932), pp. 144–6. Although apprentices normally did not have occupations, their fathers' occupations were a standard entry in registrations of apprentices in Bristol and elsewhere. For example, see D. Hollis, ed., *Calendar of the Bristol Apprentice Book, 1532–1565,* I (Bristol, 1949); Patrick McGrath, ed., *Merchants and Merchandise in Seventeenth-Century Bristol* (Bristol, 1955), pp. 1–19; Arthur J. Willis and A. L. Merson,

eds., *A Calendar of Southampton Apprenticeship Registers, 1609–1740* (Southampton, 1968), p. xvi; and William West, *The First Part of Symboleographie* ... (London, 1657), sec. 582. When apprentices did have occupations, they apparently were recorded upon registration; Christabel Dale, ed., *Wiltshire Apprentices and Their Masters, 1710–1760* (Devizes, 1961), pp. xvi, 16, 95, 150, 158. The occupation of the father was recorded on the contracts of servants bound to craftsmen, as well as those of apprentices; J. A. Twemlow, ed., *Liverpool Town Books: Proceedings of Assemblies, Common Councils, Portmoot Courts, etc., 1550–1862,* (Liverpool, 1935), 2:930–62. And finally, servants who had specific occupations would have them recorded when they appeared before justices in such proceedings as quarter sessions; see, e.g., S. C. Ratcliff and H. C. Johnson, eds., *Warwick County Records* (Warwick, 1941), 6:47. Thus, servants' occupations were recognized and the registration of servants was like that of apprentices in the recording of the father's occupation (or presumably that of the servant). This being so, and given the general similarity of the registration of the indentures of apprentices and of the servants of the Bristol and London records, the customs followed in recording apprentices' covenants were very likely carried over to the registration of servants bound for the colonies. It would therefore have been routine for the clerks to record either the occupation of the servant's father or that of the servant himself.

14 "Privy Council Registers, 69," P.C. 2/69, p. 596, P.R.O., London; C.O. 324/5, "Entries Relating to Plantations in General," 2:90, P.R.O.; or Grant and Munro, eds., *Acts of Privy Council,* 2:42.

15 The difference in the proportion of minors among those without additions and among the tradesmen and craftsmen is significant at the .01 level for a two-tailed t-test, as is the difference between the proportions of minors among those without additions and among the farmers; the difference in the share of minors among those without additions and the laborers is significant at the .02 level.

16 For a discussion of the measure, see Chapter 5.

17 A suggestive finding on a problem similar to the one considered here might be cited from D. V. Glass's analysis of the London poll-tax returns of 1692. Glass found that "the vast majority of the individuals whose occupations were not stated were within the lower income groups"; thus 89% of those without recorded occupations paid only the minimum tax, compared with only 40% of those with specified occupations; "Socio-Economic Status and Occupations in the City of London at the End of the Seventeenth Century," in Peter Clark, ed., *The Early Modern Town: A Reader* (London, 1976) pp. 223–4. Similarly, in her analysis of colonial probate records, Alice Hanson Jones found that male decedents without recorded occupations had the lowest mean wealth of any group. Jones, *Wealth of a Nation to Be: The American Colonies on the Eve of the Revolution* (New York, 1980), p. 224.

18 Similar examples can be found in other contemporary registrations. Thus eight youths indentured before the Lord Mayor of London in July 1684 were described as "pilfering boys that lie day and night in the marketts and streets of this city, and haveing no friends or relations to take care or provide for

them"; Michael Ghirelli, *List of Emigrants from England to America* (Baltimore, 1968), p. 34.

19 Smith, *Colonists in Bondage*, p. 287.

20 Josiah Child, *A New Discourse of Trade* (London, 1693), pp. 170–3; Charles Davenant, *Discourses on the Publick Revenues, and on the Trade of England* (London, 1698) 2:196–7.

21 Henry Whistler, "Voyage to the West Indies," 1654, Sloane MS 3926, f. 9, British Museum; William Berkeley, *A Discourse and View of Virginia* (London, 1662), p. 4; William Bullock, *Virginia Impartially examined, and left to publick view, to be considered by all Iudicious and honest men* (London, 1649), p. 14. For examples of other similar contemporary comment see *A Publication of Guiana's Plantation* (London, 1632), pp. 13–14; Charles I, *A Proclamation against the disorderly Transporting His Maiesties Subjects to the Plantations within the parts of America* (London, 1637); Customer of London, "Concerning Passes and Passing out of this Kingdome," 1637, C.O. 1/9, f. 190, P.R.O., London; Thomas Fuller, *The Holy State* (Cambridge, 1642), p. 193; John Hammond, *Leah and Rachel, or the two fruitful sisters, Virginia and Mary-Land; Their present condition, impartially stated and related* ... (London, 1656), pp. 3, 9; Edward Nicholas to Joseph Jane, Cologne, Mar. 4, 1655/6, S.P. 18/125, f. 9v, P.R.O., London; Richard Ligon, *A True and Exact History of the Island of Barbados* (London, 1657), p. 13; Marcellus Rivers and Oxenbridge Foyle, *Englands Slavery, or Barbados Merchandize* ... (London, 1659), p. 22; Committee to the Council of Foreign Plantations, "Certain Propositions for the better accomodating the Forreigne Plantations with Servants," 1662, Egerton MS 2395, f. 277, proposition 5, British Museum; "Petition of the Mayor of Bristol to the King," July 16, 1662, S.P. 29/57, f. 146, P.R.O., London; Richard Head, *The English Rogue described, in the life of Meriton Latroon,* Part II (London, 1665), p. 3; "Petition of the Council and Assembly of Barbados to the King," November 24, 1675, C.O. 1/35, f. 237v, P.R.O., London: Nicholas Spencer to Lord Culpeper, August 6, 1676, quoted in Morgan, *American Slavery, American Freedom,* p. 236; Johnathan Atkins to Lords of Trade and Plantations, Barbados, August 15, 1676, C.O. 1/37, f. 173, P.R.O., London; Richard Beale Davis, *William Fitzhugh and His Chesapeake World* (Chapel Hill, N.C., 1962), p. 82; J. C. Jeaffreson, ed., *A Young Squire of the Seventeenth Century, From the Papers (A.D. 1676–1686) of Christopher Jeaffreson* (London, 1878), 1:259; Thomas Lynch to Lords of Trade and Plantations, Jamaica, August 29, 1682, C.O. 1/49, f. 127v, P.R.O., London; "Some few Consideracons offered to yor Majtie on the Subject of the present severe prosecution of Sundry Merchants, and Masters of Shippes in the Crowne Office for transporting Servants ... " November 3, 1682, C.O. 1/50, f. 304v, P.R.O., London; "A moderate calculacon of the annuall charge and produce of a Plantacon in Barbados," (1688) Sloane MS 3984, f. 218v, British Museum; Edwyn Stede to Lords of Trade and Plantations, Barbados, August 30, 1688, C.O. 29/4, p.9, P.R.O., London; Dalby Thomas, *An Historical Account of the rise and growth of the West Indian Collonies* ... (London, 1690), p. 11; "Journal of the General

Assembly of Virginia," June 2, 1699, C.O. 5/1411, pp. 139–40, P.R.O., London; Edward Ward, *The London-Spy Compleat . . .* , 2nd ed. (London, 1704), pp. 54–5; and Hugh Jones, *The Present State of Virginia* (London, 1724), p. 114.

22 On the tendency of unskilled laborers and vagrants to migrate to London, see M. Dorothy George, *London Life in the Eighteenth Century* (New York, 1965), pp. 109–10; Carl Bridenbaugh, *Vexed and Troubled Englishmen, 1590–1642* (London, 1967), pp. 166–8; Carl Bridenbaugh and Roberta Bridenbaugh, *No Peace beyond the Line: The English in the Caribbean, 1624–1690* (New York, 1972), p. 27; L. A. Clarkson, *The Pre-Industrial Economy in England, 1500–1700* (London, 1971), p. 32; Robert C. Johnson, "The Transportation of Vagrant Children from London to Virginia, 1618–1622," in Howard S. Reinmuth, Jr., ed., *Early Stuart Studies: Essays in Honor of David Harris Willson* (Minneapolis, 1970), pp. 137–8; Paul A. Slack, "Vagrants and Vagrancy in England, 1598–1664," *Economic History Review,* 2nd ser. 27 (1974):371; Peter Clark and Paul Slack, *English Towns in Transition, 1500–1700* (London, 1976), p. 64; and F. J. Fisher, "London as an 'Engine of Economic Growth,'" in Clark, *Early Modern Town,* p. 210.

23 For examples of this view, see Abbot Emerson Smith, "Indentured Servants: New Light on Some of America's 'First' Families," *Journal of Economic History,* 2 (1942):46; Smith *Colonists in Bondage,* pp. 287–8, 300; Marcus Wilson Jernegan, *Laboring and Dependent Classes in Colonial America, 1607–1783* (1931; reprint ed., New York, 1965), p. 51; and Thomas J. Wertenbaker, *Patrician and Plebeian in Virginia* (1910; reprinted ed., New York, 1959), pp. 162–3.

24 Campbell, "Social Origins of Some Early Americans," pp. 73, 76, 89; Wesley Frank Craven, *White, Red, and Black: The Seventeenth-Century Virginian* (Charlottesville, Va., 1971), p. 8.

25 Lawrence Stone, "Social Mobility in England, 1500–1700," *Past and Present,* no. 33 (April 1966);18–20.

4. Occupations of the eighteenth-century indentured servants

1 All of the surviving registrations are contained in the "Memoranda of Agreements to Serve in America and the West Indies" held at the Corporation of London Records Office, London Guildhall. These have been abstracted and published by Jack Kaminkow and Marion Kaminkow, *A List of Emigrants from England to America, 1718–1759* (Baltimore, 1964) and David Galenson, "Agreements to Serve in America and the West Indies, 1727–31," *Genealogists' Magazine* 14, no. 2 (June 1977):40–4.

2 This evidence is presented and discussed in Chapter 5.

3 For the regression evidence on which these statements are based and discussion of its interpretation, see Chapter 7.

4 The nature and possible implications of the change are discussed in Appendix D.

5 For discussion, see Appendix C.

6 M. Dorothy George, *London Life in the Eighteenth Century* (Harmonds-

worth, 1976), p. 150. The lists are held in the Public Records Office, London, Treasury 47/9–11.

7 Mildred Campbell, "English Emigration on the Eve of the American Revolution," *American Historical Review* 61, no. 1 (October 1955):4. On the distinction between indentured servants and redemptioners, see Chapter 1.

8 The total of 68% is the sum of the 63% "craftsmen and tradespeople" and the 5% clerical workers and schoolmasters; Campbell, "English Emigration," pp. 6–7.

9 Ibid., p. 6. In addition to the figures quoted in the text, Campbell found that 3% of the male passengers were described as planters or gentlemen; ibid., p. 7.

10 The major problem is the frequent combination by individuals of farming with manufacturing or service occupations, without clear economic priority of either. For discussions of this overlap of individuals' occupations in pre-industrial England, see J. C. K. Cornwall, "The Agrarian History of Sussex, 1540–1640" (M.A. thesis, University of London, 1953), pp. 377–8; Margaret Gay Davies, *The Enforcement of English Apprenticeship* (Cambridge, 1956), pp. 97–8; Joan Thirsk, "Industries in the Countryside," in F. J. Fisher, ed., *Essays in the Economic and Social History of Tudor and Stuart England* (London, 1961), pp. 70–88; D. C. Coleman, *The Economy of England, 1450–1750* (Oxford, 1977), p. 71. However, in support of the validity of the basic distinction, see, e.g., Gordon Batho, "Noblemen, Gentlemen, and Yeomen," in Joan Thirsk, ed., *The Agrarian History of England and Wales, Vol. IV, 1500–1640,* (Cambridge, 1967), p. 302.

11 Peter Laslett, *The World We Have Lost,* 2nd ed. (London, 1971), p. 47; D. C. Coleman, "The Economy of Kent Under the Later Stuarts" (Ph.D. diss., University of London, 1951), Appendix 3, Table B, p. 427.

12 Laslett, *World We Have Lost,* p. 13; K. J. Allison, "An Elizabethan Village Census," *Bulletin of the Institute of Historical Research* 36 (1963):91–103; A. J. and R. H. Tawney, "An Occupational Census of the Seventeenth Century," *Economic History Review* 5 (1934):47, 59–61; Philip Styles, "A Census of a Warwickshire Village in 1698," *University of Birmingham Historical Journal,* 3 (1951):39–40; and R. E. Chester Waters, "A Statutory List of the Inhabitants of Melbourne, Derbyshire, in 1695," *Journal of the Derbyshire Archaeological and Natural History Society* 7 (1885):24–5.

13 Laslett, *World We Have Lost,* p. 47. Even laborers might have some specific skills; e.g., see Peter Laslett, *Family Life and Illicit Love in Earlier Generations* (Cambridge, 1977), p. 61; Alan Everitt, "Farm Labourers," in Thirsk, *Agrarian History,* pp. 397, 432–4. Nonetheless, it will be assumed here that men described as laborers did not have skills that differentiated their productivity from that of the least skilled workers in agriculture.

5. Literacy and the occupations of the indentured servants

1 In the case of the adults in the later sample, the surviving documents are declarations of voluntary consent rather than actual contracts. However, they

were legal memoranda of agreements and were to be signed or marked by the servants, and are therefore as useful as contracts for the present investigation of the servants' literacy.

2 R. S. Schofield, "The Measurement of Literacy in Pre-Industrial England," in Jack Goody, ed., *Literacy in Traditional Societies* (Cambridge, 1968), pp. 311–25; Lawrence Stone, "Literacy and Education in England 1640–1900," *Past and Present*, no. 42 (February 1969):98. Schofield specifically suggested: "For the early nineteenth century . . . a measure based on the ability to sign probably overestimates the number able to write, underestimates the number able to read at an elementary level, and gives a fair indication of the number able to read fluently; "Measurement of Literacy." p. 324. An extended discussion of this relationship, with additional evidence for the first half of the nineteenth century, is contained in R. S. Schofield, "Some Dimensions of Illiteracy in England, 1600–1800" (unpublished paper, no date), pp. 2–5. Based on an investigation of the history of school curricula, Schofield further concluded that "the structure of education was basically the same at least from the sixteenth century, and it is therefore probable that the relationships between ability to sign, ability to read, and ability to write remained the same throughout this period"; "Measurement of Literacy," p. 324. I am grateful to Roger Schofield for access to the unpublished paper cited above.

3 Stone, "Literacy and Education in England," pp. 103–12; R. S. Schofield, "Dimensions of Illiteracy, 1750–1850," *Explorations in Economic History* 10, no. 4 (Summer 1973):449–51; Richard Vann, "Literacy in Seventeenth-Century England: Some Hearth-Tax Evidence," *Journal of Interdisciplinary History* 5 (1974):292; David Cressy, "Literacy in Pre-industrial England." *Societas* 4, no. 3 (Summer, 1974):234–40; David Cressy, "Levels of Illiteracy in England, 1530–1730," *Historical Journal* 20, no. 1 (1977):5–10.

4 Cressy, "Levels of Illiteracy in England," Table 1, p. 5. The rate in London was apparently considerably higher, particularly late in the century; Cressy, "Literacy in Pre-industrial England," p. 233.

5 Schofield, "Dimensions of Illiteracy," pp. 445–6.

6 The number of observations is small, and this difference is not statistically significant at the .10 level. However, for discussion of a similar finding for men in the sample, in which the increase is significant, see later in this chapter.

7 Cressy, "Literacy in Pre-industrial England," Table 3, p. 234; Cressy, "Levels of Illiteracy in England," Table 1, pp. 5, 8.

8 Cressy, "Literacy in Pre-industrial England," p. 238; Cressy, "Levels of Illiteracy in England," Table 1, pp. 5,8.

9 Cressy gives the figure cited for "tradesmen and craftsmen" in the 1680s in "Literacy in Pre-industrial England," Table 4, p. 235, and for "tradesmen" in "Levels of Illiteracy in England," Table 3, p. 11; he gives the same rate as an average for the category "tradesmen and craftsmen" for 1580–1700 in ibid., Table 1, p. 5.

10 For a discussion of some of the factors relevant to such a comparison, see Cressy, "Levels of Illiteracy in England," p. 4.

11 Because of this temporal difference, some consideration might be given to its

effect on the comparison; were significant changes occurring in the extent of literacy in England during the mid-eighteenth century? Schofield found male literacy to have been roughly stable during the second half of the century; "Dimensions of Illiteracy," p. 446. No comparable time series evidence is available for the English population in the first half of the century. Within the London registrations, there is some evidence of an upward trend in literacy over time. A comparison of the men registered in the two periods 1718–29 and 1730–40 indicates that the overall male literacy rate rose from 62% to 76%. To a large extent this increase was due to shifts in both the occupational and age distributions of the men registered over time. A comparison of the literacy rates separately for the minors and adults in each of the eight occupational categories considered in the two periods reveals increases in the literacy rates of twelve of the sixteen resulting groups, decreases for three, and no change for one; for the tabulation, see David Galenson, "Literacy and the Social Origins of Some Early Americans," *Historical Journal,* 22, no. 1 (March 1979): Table A, p. 82. However, only three of the changes are statistically significant at the .10 level or better.

The results of regression analysis of the ability to sign in the London sample indicate that, controlling for age, sex, occupational category, and place of origin, the date of a servant's registration had a statistically significant, but relatively small, effect on the probability that an individual would sign his contract. Thus the estimated average increase in the probability obtained with both linear and nonlinear estimators was just under one-half of one percentage point per year, ceteris paribus. These findings are presented and discussed in David W. Galenson, "Literacy and Age in Preindustrial England: Quantitative Evidence and Implications," *Economic Development and Cultural Change* 29, no. 4 (July 1981), Tables 1 and 2, pp. 818–22. Because little is known of the degree to which the servants were representative of all Englishmen, no generalization of these results can be made regarding changes in English literacy in the period. However, the relatively small changes indicate the absence of major changes in literacy over time for the men registered and make aggregation for the entire period useful for comparison to Schofield's rates.

12 This and the following figures are taken from Schofield, "Dimensions of Illiteracy," Table 1, p. 450. As was done in using Cressy's rates, Schofield's "illiteracy" rates have been transformed into "literacy" rates by subtracting them from 100%. Statistically, the information conveyed is precisely the same.

13 The weights used in this and the calculation reported in the following sentence are the reported numbers of observations on which Schofield's rate for each of the respective groups is based.

14 That the farmers and laborers among the indentured servants may actually have been more highly literate on average than other Englishmen of the same occupations might have resulted from the selection by merchants of the more skilled men from these groups to be indentured; however, it would seem more likely that it was the more educated from these groups who were aware of the opportunities offered by the indenture system and chose to emigrate.

15 A two-tailed *t*-test shows the difference to be significant at the .01 level.

16 Using two-tailed *t*-tests, the differences are statistically significant at the .001 level for two of the categories, at .01 for one, and at .10 for two; three fail to be significant at the .10 level.

17 An interesting implication is the possibility that, though boys generally began to train for skilled trades at about 14, they did not begin to be identified with the trade until they had had as many as three or more years of training.

18 This is suggested, e.g., by J. H. Plumb, "How Freedom Took Root in Slavery," *New York Review of Books,* 22, no. 19 (November 27, 1975):4.

19 The use of the terms *formal* and *informal* education throughout this discussion follows the usage of Schofield, "The Measurement of Literacy," p. 315.

The normal school-leaving age in this period was not above 15; Stone, "Literacy and Education in England," p. 99; Cressy, "Levels of Illiteracy in England," p. 11; R. S. Schofield, "Age-Specific Mobility in an Eighteenth Century Rural English Parish," *Annales de Démographie Historique* (1970), p. 266. The youngest servants included in the two categories of husbandmen and laborers were 15, and there was only one of that age in each. The minor–adult differentials might therefore be estimates of the numbers of men who learned to sign after the school-leaving age and may constitute lower-bound estimates of the number who learned to sign through means other than formal instruction in school. As noted above, Schofield's investigation of the relationship between the abilities of signing, reading, and writing for the period before the nineteenth century was based on the structure of formal education, specifically the order in which the skills were normally taught in schools; "The Measurement of Literacy," p. 324. Schofield recognized the problem posed by informal education, as neither its structure nor its extent has been systematically investigated (ibid., p. 315). If it was widespread, and its order of instruction of literacy skills often significantly different from that of the schools, it could upset the general validity of the relationships suggested by Schofield in ibid., p. 324. Victor E. Neuberg has suggested that the ability to read was more common than the ability to write among the eighteenth-century poor, but, as he notes, quantitative evidence is lacking; "Literacy in Eighteenth Century England: A Caveat," *Local Population Studies,* no. 2 (Spring 1969):44–6. The minor–adult differentials of Table 5.3 may give some indication of the extent of informal education in teaching the ability to sign to men from their mid-teens on.

Regression analysis of the Middlesex and London samples indicates that, holding constant sex, occupation, place of origin, and date of registration, the average effect of an increase in age of one year was to raise the probability that a servant would sign by nearly one percentage point in the earlier, and two percentage points in the later, sample; Galenson, "Literacy and Age in Preindustrial England," Table 2, p. 820. Further analysis of the later sample also indicates the presence of significant differences in the effect of age across occupational groups; ibid., Table 3, p. 823.

20 Evidence of variation by county for the mid-seventeenth century is given by Schofield, "Some Dimensions of Illiteracy in England," p. 12 and Table 5.

These differences were persistent: for an indication of their magnitude in the first half of the nineteenth century, see Schofield, "Dimensions of Illiteracy," p. 444.

21 Cressy, "Literacy in Pre-industrial England," pp. 235, 238; Schofield, "Dimensions of Illiteracy," p. 444.

22 For complete tabulations by county of the recorded places of origin of the servants in these samples, see David Walter Galenson, "The Indenture System and the Colonial Labor Market" (Ph.D. diss., Harvard University, 1979), Tables VII-3 and VII-5, pp. 184, 186.

23 This might be plausible in view of the fact that the 1680s was a period of intensive recruitment for indentured labor. Thus in the Chesapeake region a decline in the supply of white labor contributed to a sharp increase in the cost of English servants relative to African slaves; for discussion, see Chapter 9. The shift in the supply of white servants may have resulted in a decline in the average productivity of the workers bound, as planters accepted less desirable servants in order to maintain a white labor force. Seventeenth-century London attracted many vagrants and unskilled workers, and during the 1680s many less productive and less skilled workers might have been drawn by recruiting agents from the immediate area of the port as the agents attempted to increase the supply of servants to the colonies. If present, this recruiting of less skilled workers from London could have tended to lower the literacy rate of servants from the city relative to that which would be obtained from a random sample of Englishmen of the period. The particular circumstances of the 1680s may therefore account for the absence of a positive metropolitan effect on the servants' literacy rates in the 1680s.

24 The latter difference is significant at the .01 level for a two-tailed t-test.

25 On the basis of two-tailed t-tests, the rate for the tradesmen and craftsmen is significantly higher than that of those without additions at the .01 level, whereas the difference between the rates for those without additions and for the husbandmen and laborers fails to be significant at the .10 level.

26 Again using two-tailed t-tests, the rate for the tradesmen and craftsmen is significantly higher than that for those without additions at the .01 level, whereas that of the husbandmen and laborers is significantly greater than that of the men without additions at the .05 level.

27 On the basis of the two-tailed t-tests, the literacy rate of the men with additions is significantly higher than that of those without additions at the .05 level in the Middlesex sample and at the .01 level in the London sample.

6. Patterns of servant migration from England to America

1 Richard S. Dunn, *Sugar and Slaves: The Rise of the Planter Class in the English West Indies, 1624–1713* (New York, 1973), p. 164.

2 Aubrey Land wrote of Maryland and Virginia: "Both were part of a single economic region which political boundaries could not split asunder and were treated as a unit in contemporaneous British commercial records"; "Economic Base and Social Structure: The Northern Chesapeake in the Eighteenth Century," *Journal of Economic History* 25, no. 4 (December 1965):641.

3 Abbot Emerson Smith, *Colonists in Bondage: White Servitude and Convict Labor in America, 1607–1776* (Chapel Hill, N.C., 1947), pp. 36–7.

4 Philip Alexander Bruce, *Economic History of Virginia in the Seventeenth Century* (New York, 1907), 1:622–4. William Bullock wrote in 1649 that "the ordinary time of going [to Virginia] is about *September* or *October*, which times Ships have made choice of, in respect the Crop of Tobacco will be ready for the homeward fraught, which is always in, or about *December*," and George Alsop noted in 1666 that "between *November* and *January* there arrives in this Province [Maryland] Shipping to the number of twenty sail and upwards, all Merchant-men loaden with Commodities to Trafique and dispose of, trucking with the Planter . . . for Tobacco"; *Virginia Impartially Examined, and left to publick view, to be considered by all Iudicious and honest men* (London, 1649), p. 46; Alsop, *A Character of the Province of Mary-Land* (London, 1666), p. 51.

5 Bruce, *Economic History of Virginia*, 1:623.

6 Edmund S. Morgan, *American Slavery, American Freedom: The Ordeal of Colonial Virginia* (New York, 1975), p. 184.

7 The concentration of these seventeenth-century registrations in late summer and fall provides evidence against Abbot Emerson Smith's contention that British servants were shipped without regard to season even though it was known that they should be landed in early winter to protect their health; Smith, *Colonists in Bondage*, pp. 254–5.

8 Virginians were aware of the declining severity of seasoning mortality before the end of the seventeenth century; Morgan, *American Slavery, American Freedom*, p. 182.

9 Gerald W. Mullin, *Flight and Rebellion* (London, 1972), p. 15.

10 Quoted in ibid., p. 15.

11 Dunn, *Sugar and Slaves*, pp. 191–6; Carl Bridenbaugh and Roberta Bridenbaugh, *No Peace Beyond the Line* (New York, 1972), pp. 88–91.

12 Little is known of the typical method of payment for servants in the West Indies. Of the problem of collecting payments for slaves delivered that plagued the Royal African Company in this period, K. G. Davies wrote: "It was seldom if ever possible to realize the proceeds of the sale of a cargo of slaves in the West Indies quickly enough to provide that same ship with a return cargo of sugar"; *The Royal African Company* (New York, 1970), p. 187. Whether delayed payment for servants was also the rule is not known. However, it does seem likely that the practices of ships' captains and merchants, operating independently on a relatively small scale, in extending credit would have been very different from those of a joint stock company as large as the Royal African Company.

On the seasonality of sugar production and shipping, see Bryan Edwards, *The History, Civil and Commercial, of the British Colonies in the West Indies* (London, 1794), 2:212; Michael Craton and James Walvin, *A Jamaican Plantation: The History of Worthy Park, 1670–1970* (Toronto, 1970), pp. 100–15; Elsa V. Goveia, *Slave Society in the British Leeward Islands at the End of the Eighteenth Century* (New Haven, 1965), p. 127; Ralph Davis, *The Rise of the English Shipping Industry* (London, 1962), p. 279.

13 For tabulations by sex of the mean ages of servants bound for every major colonial destination in each of the five samples in which age was recorded, see David Walter Galenson, "The Indenture System and the Colonial Labor Market" (Ph.D. diss., Harvard University, 1979), Tables VIII-25–VIII-29, pp. 225–8.

14 For tabulations of the destinations of the male servants in each sample for which occupational information was recorded, using the same nine occupational categories as in Chapters 3 and 4, see ibid., Tables VIII-30–VIII-34, pp. 259–63.

15 Analysis of the Bristol registrations of 1654–61 is complicated here by issues of periodization similar to those considered in Chapter 3. The most serious of the problems for the present purpose is apparently the incomplete occupational registrations of 1661. Sometime during 1661 servants' occupations ceased to be recorded systematically. It cannot be determined precisely when this occurred. Although a servant's addition was recorded as late in 1661 as November 25, few additions appear after July, and it may be that July was the dividing line at which, for unknown reasons, occupations generally began to be omitted from the records.

When the whole period 1654–61 is considered, 48.8% of the 1,900 men bound for Barbados were skilled, compared with 40.8% of the 999 bound for Virginia, but when the sampling period is ended with June 1661, as is done in Table 6.6, 49.7% of the male registrants for Barbados were skilled, compared with 50.6% of Virginia's. The specification of the period chosen here therefore yields results less favorable to the finding of a skill differential between servants bound for the West Indies and the Chesapeake than would the inclusion of the whole year of 1661. For annual tabulations of the shares of skilled men bound for Barbados, Virginia, all West Indian, and all mainland destinations during 1654–61, with separate breakdowns for the first and last six months of 1661, see Galenson, "Indenture System and the Colonial Labor Market," Table VIII-A-1, p. 279.

16 The difference in proportions in the Bristol registrations of 1684–6 of 5.3 percentage points fails to be statistically significant at the .10 level. However, the 10.7 point difference in the Middlesex sample is significant at the .01 level for a two-tailed t-test, and the difference of 17 points in the London sample of 1718–59 is significant at .001.

17 Both differences in proportions, of 7.2 percentage points in the Barbados – Chesapeake comparison and 6.2 points in that of Jamaica and the Chesapeake, are significant at the .10 level for two-tailed t-tests.

18 The 22.7 percentage point difference in the proportions is significant at the .001 level for a two-tailed t-test.

19 These differences also appear within particular occupational categories. The mean age of men bound for the West Indies was higher than that of men bound for the mainland in four of the six skilled categories in the Middlesex sample of 1683–4 and in all of the six categories in the London sample of 1718–59. For tabulations of the mean ages of men in each occupational category by region of destination, see Galenson, "Indenture System and the Colonial Labor Market," Tables VIII-41 and VIII-42, pp. 272–3.

20 Evidence of a steep relationship between age and net earnings for the skilled servants is presented and discussed in Chapter 7.

21 Lois Green Carr and Lorena S. Walsh, "The Planter's Wife: The Experience of White Women in Seventeenth-Century Maryland," *William and Mary Quarterly,* 3rd ser. 34, no. 4 (October 1977):547.

22 The difference in proportions between Barbados and the Chesapeake during 1654–61 of 2.3 percentage points is not significant at the .10 level for a two tailed *t*-test. The differences in the proportions of skilled laborers bound for Barbados and the Chesapeake (12.8 percentage points) and for Jamaica and the Chesapeake (8.9 points) in the pooled samples from the 1680s are significant at .01, as is that of 24.3 points between the proportions bound for Jamaica and the Chesapeake in the eighteenth-century registrations.

23 The effects of two other possible sources of bias are more speculative. Servants who arrived in the colonies from England without written agreements were purchased by masters who then took them before a colonial court where a magistrate would bind them to a term of servitude. The length of the term was typically determined by a schedule, fixed by each colony's legislature, which assigned terms on the basis of the servant's age and sex (for discussion and references to these, see Smith, *Colonists in Bondage,* pp. 229–30, and Richard B. Morris, *Government and Labor in Early America* [New York, 1965], pp. 390–1). Servants bound in this way were said to serve according to the custom of the country. Little quantitative evidence is available concerning the servants in this category, and little is known about either their numbers or their characteristics relative to those bound by contract in England. However, a study of one Maryland county in the last four decades of the seventeenth century has suggested that servants bound by the custom of the country were numerous, comprising more than two-fifths of all servants in the county, and that they were younger on average and less often skilled than servants who worked in the county under written indentures; Lorena S. Walsh, "Servitude and Opportunity in Charles County, Maryland, 1658–1705," in Aubrey C. Land, Lois Green Carr, and Edward C. Papenfuse, eds., *Law, Society, and Politics in Early Maryland* (Baltimore, 1977), pp. 112, 129, 131. More evidence from other times and places is necessary before conclusions can be drawn about the quantitative implications of these customs-of-the-country servants. However, if servants bound by the custom were generally less skilled than those with contracts, and if they migrated disproportionately to mainland colonies, to the extent that they were quantitatively important in total servant flows, their presence would tend to reinforce the skill differentials found among the servant registrations by lowering the share of the skilled among servants bound for the mainland relative to the West Indies.

Similar analysis, and similarly tentative conclusions, apply to the involuntary white servants transported from England to the colonies. Although these included a number of groups, including rogues and vagabonds and military and political prisoners, probably the most important members of this class quantitatively were reprieved convicts, who were typically sentenced to seven years' servitude in America (for information about involuntary servants, see Smith, *Colonists in Bondage,* Chaps. 5–9). The greatest numbers of felons were transported during the eighteenth century and virtually all were taken to Maryland or Virginia. Little is known of the skills of these involuntary servants, but if they were on average less skilled than voluntary servants with written indentures, their disproportionate migration to the Chesapeake relative to the servants included in the samples of registrations analyzed here would tend to reinforce the skill differentials between destinations found in the servant registrations by lowering the share of all servants bound for the mainland who had skilled occupations.

7. The market for indentured servants

1 Abbot Emerson Smith, *Colonists in Bondage: White Servitude and Convict Labor in America, 1607–1776* (Chapel Hill, N.C., 1947), pp. 221–2; Eugene I. McCormac, *White Servitude in Maryland 1634–1820* (Baltimore, 1904), p. 42; Philip Alexander Bruce, *Economic History of Virginia in the Seventeenth Century* (New York, 1907), 1:633; William Eddis, *Letters from America* (Cambridge, Mass., 1969), p. 40; Edmund S. Morgan, *Virginians at Home* (New York, 1952), p. 56.

2 Bruce, *Economic History of Virginia,* 1:622; Smith, *Colonists in Bondage,* p. 39; Arthur Pierce Middleton, *Tobacco Coast: A Maritime History of Chesapeake Bay in the Colonial Era* (Newport News, Va., 1953), pp. 145–56; K. G. Davies, *The North Atlantic World in the Seventeenth Century* (Minneapolis, 1974), pp. 96–7; J. R. T. Hughes, *Social Control in the Colonial Economy* (Charlottesville, Va., 1976), p. 108. Thus a Glasgow merchant wrote to a correspondent in 1749, concerning servants to be bound and shipped from Glasgow, that "I assure you they are the Best Commoditie goes to Jamaica from this place"; William Gordon to Baillie Gilbert Gordon, Glasgow, November 3, 1749; Scottish Record Office, Bught Papers, GD 23/6/98/19.

3 Smith, *Colonists in Bondage,* pp. 37–9, 42, 209. That the market for servants was competitive is further supported by Smith's conclusion that the profit made in the trade by merchants was "a comfortable profit, despite the large risks that sickness or death might scale down the value of the cargo, but it was not exorbitant, for the time involved in these transactions was long and the total value of any shipload was not great"; ibid., p. 39.

Although the large numbers of merchants who bound servants in all periods and the relatively low barriers to entry into the industry of binding and delivering servants to the colonies suggest that the English market for servants was probably highly competitive throughout the period spanned by the samples analyzed here, significant changes in the structure of the industry might have occurred over time. The mean number of servants per master in the three seventeenth-century samples from Bristol, London, and Middlesex ranged from 2.2 to 3.9, whereas the figure for the eighteenth-century London sample, 18.7, was considerably higher. Because little is known of the relation of these samples to the overall populations of masters and servants, this evidence can be only suggestive; however, if it does represent a genuine change in the organization of the industry, it might point to an increasing specialization by some merchants in this industry over time. Another change over time that would appear consistent with this possibility is that the evidence analyzed here suggests that the quality of information in the market for servants might have improved during the period spanned by the two samples analyzed in this chapter. Thus, the coefficient of variation of the length of indenture among men of a given age was considerably lower in the London registrations of 1718–59 than in the Middlesex sample of 1683–4 for six of the eight age groups of minors above the age of 12. On the relation of wage dispersion to information, see George J. Stigler, "Information in the Labor Market," *Journal of Political Economy,* 70, no. 5, part 2, Supplement (October 1962):94–105.

4 Gary S. Becker, *Human Capital,* 2nd ed. (New York, 1975), p. 223.
5 This assumes a solution to the problem of monitoring the servant's work in which the productivity gains from the master's control over the servant's time and effort were not offset by shirking.
6 In a world in which futures contracts for free wage labor could be made with certain fulfillment, the present value of an indenture for a given number of years and of a series of contracts for hires for the same years would differ only by a premium that would reimburse the servant for the loss of freedom resulting from his residence in the master's household and other legal provisions governing servitude. However, in the absence of these guaranteed futures contracts, in some cases the master might also have been willing to pay more for an indenture because of the assurance it gave him of labor supply in peak seasons or in future years; similarly, workers might sometimes have been willing to accept lower implicit wages in return for the guarantee of employment the indenture represented.

The relative cost of this insurance to master and servant could vary, and the relation between the implicit wage paid to servants and the hire rate for free workers is therefore indeterminate. Yet, that these considerations may shed light on a related puzzle is suggested by Adam Smith's contention that the ratio of (bound) servants to independent workers in the English labor force varied inversely with the real wage rate; *An Inquiry Into the Nature and Causes of the Wealth of Nations* (New York, 1965), pp. 83–4. If Smith's argument is correct, the apparent infrequency with which freed servants in America reindentured themselves may be an indication that the cost of subsistence was rarely a large share of the normal earnings of workers in the colonies.

7 Smith, *Colonists in Bondage,* p. 57.
8 Although £6 was the fare cited in the early colonial period, after the middle of the seventeenth century £5 was the fare normally quoted for passage to all colonies. For references to quotations of passage charges from England to a number of colonies, see Susan M. Kingsbury, ed., *The Records of the Virginia Company of London* (Washington, D.C., 1906), 1:227–8; John Smith, *The Generall Historie of Virginia, New-England, and the Summer Isles* (London, 1624), p. 162; Samuel Purchas, *Purchas His Pilgrimes* (London, 1625), 4:1791; Maryland Historical Society, *The Calvert Papers,*

Peabody Publication Fund, No. 28 (Baltimore, 1889), 1:206; Somerset Record Office, Taunton, "Helyar Manuscripts," January 4, 1670; John Cordy Jeaffreson, ed., *A Young Squire of the Seventeenth Century, From the Papers (A.D. 1676–1686) of Christopher Jeaffreson* (London, 1878), 2:102; William Bullock, *Virginia Impartially examined, and left to publick view, to be considered by all Iudicious and honest men* (London, 1649), p. 47; Samuel Wilson, *An Account of the Province of Carolina in America* (London, 1682), p. 19; E. Littleton, *The Groans of the Plantations* (London, 1689), p. 17; Edward P. Alexander, ed., *The Journal of John Fontaine* (Charlottesville, Va. 1972), p. 45; Smith, *Colonists in Bondage*, p. 35. A qualification to the statement in the text is the possible seasonal variation in the cost of delivering servants to some colonies, discussed later in this chapter.

Children under the age of 13 were sometimes charged less than a full fare; e.g., see Marion Balderston, ed., *James Claypoole's Letter Book, London and Philadelphia, 1681–1684* (San Marino, Calif., 1967), p. 197; A. D. Chandler, ed., *The Colonial Records of the State of Georgia* (Atlanta, 1904), 1:143, 168,191,209; 2:115, 117; Smith, *Colonists in Bondage* pp. 210–11. This practice does not contradict in any significant sense the claim that for the British servants considered here fares were charged on a per head basis, equal for all, for very few English servants were under 13. Therefore, virtually all British servants would have been charged full fares.

On the costs of equipping and clothing servants before their departure, see Littleton, *Groans of the Plantations,* p. 17; Bruce, *Economic History of Virginia,* 1:630; Smith, *Colonists in Bondage,* pp. 36–7; Bullock, *Virginia Impartially examined,* p. 36. On maintenance costs at the port before departure, see Smith, *Colonists in Bondage,* pp. 37, 346; Bullock, *Virginia Impartially examined,* p. 47.

9 This statement neglects one potential element of cost. The marginal cost of delivery, and therefore auction prices, would have included any costs the merchant incurred in recruiting servants in England. These could clearly vary across individual servants, producing differences in expected auction prices. These costs could have been correlated with individual productivity, as in some instance skilled servants were given lump-sum payments at the time of binding. For some evidence of this practice, see the analysis of the Middlesex sample in Appendix F.

10 Both sets of accounts are held in the P.R.O., London: "Booke of Accompte for the Shippe called ye Tristam and Jeane of London wch came from Virginia Anno Dm 1637," H.C.A. 30/635; "A Journall taken ye . . . of Januarye by me T.H. of all my dealings in Merchandize at Barbados, for Shipp Abraham," H.C.A. 30/636.

11 The full frequency distributions of the prices paid for men and women in each auction are given in David Walter Galenson, "The Indenture System and the Colonial Labor Market" (Ph.D. diss., Harvard University, 1979), Table IX-13, p. 303. The proportions of total sales that occurred at the modal price were 49% for the Virginia auction and 79% for that in Barbados.

12 The two free passengers each paid 450 pounds of tobacco; P.R.O., H.C.A.

30/635. For the 1637 Chesapeake farm price of tobacco, see Russell R. Menard, "Economy and Society in Early Colonial Maryland," (Ph.D. diss., University of Iowa, 1975), p. 475. The fare quotation, of £6 sterling per person, is in Maryland Historical Society, *The Calvert Papers*, 1:206.

13 I am grateful to the St. Mary's City Commission, Annapolis, Maryland, for transcriptions of the price quotations from probate inventories held at the Hall of Records, Annapolis. Most of the quotations are from the early decades of the period; on the later devaluation of Maryland currency and its reflection in probate valuations, see John J. McCusker, *Money and Exchange in Europe and America, 1600–1775: A Handbook* (Chapel Hill, N.C., 1978), pp. 189–204, and Gloria Lund Main, "Personal Wealth in Colonial America: Explorations in the Use of Probate Records from Maryland and Massachusetts, 1650–1720" (Ph.D. diss., Columbia University, 1972), pp. 14–18.

14 Smith, *Colonists in Bondage*, p. 37. A precise analysis would include a positive premium in the probate valuations, for these servants had normally been seasoned, i.e., had spent a year in the new colonial disease environment, and consequently had a longer life expectancy than the new arrivals, ceteris paribus.

It might be noted that the auction prices quoted here conflict with Smith's contention that servants were typically sold for considerably more than the cost of their delivery to the colonies and therefore with his conclusion that servants were generally "grievously exploited"; ibid., p. 39. The evidence of the probate valuations also casts doubt on Smith's contention, by indicating that the typical value of servants in the colonies would not have warranted auction prices far above delivery costs.

15 Mortality rates differed across colonies, and the effects of this on the length of indenture will be discussed later in this chapter. The assumption here is that mortality rates among servants both during passage and in the colonies were not systematically related to individual productivity.

16 For references to laws relating to runaways, see Smith, *Colonists in Bondage*, pp. 264–70; Raphael Semmes, *Crime and Punishment in Early Maryland* (Baltimore, 1938), pp. 116–18.

17 On freedom dues, see Smith, *Colonists in Bondage*, pp. 238–41; Robert O. Heavner, "Economic Aspects of Indentured Servitude in Colonial Pennsylvania" (Ph.D. diss., Stanford University, 1976), pp. 50–1. For a discussion of an analogous provision, nonvested pensions as a firm's insurance against quits, see Becker, *Human Capital*, p. 34.

The nature of freedom dues has some implications for other dimensions of the servant contract. The dues were normally specified by colonial law and in these cases were equal for all servants in a given colony. Therefore, the discounted cost of the dues to the planter at the time he purchased a contract varied inversely with the length of the contract. One effect of the fixed value of the freedom dues may therefore have been to tend to reduce the amount of variation in the length and other dimensions of the contracts, as the variations in the latter were intended to equalize the net present values of all contracts. This point should not obscure another basic effect of the existence of freedom dues for, ceteris paribus, they raised the cost of servants to planters, and therefore tended to lengthen the term of indenture.

18 On the fear of the islands among British servants, see Smith, *Colonists in Bondage*, p. 57.

19 For an account of these acts, see ibid., pp. 30–4.

20 For a discussion of the reasons for this in the later sample, see Appendix D.

21 This analysis is presented in Appendix F.

22 Terms of less than four years do occur, but they appear to have been rare, particularly after the mid-seventeenth century; thus the share of indentures of less than four years fell from 14% of the Bristol registrations of the 1650s to 6% of those of the 1660s and 2% of those from both the 1670s and 1680s, whereas they accounted for only 0.5% of all indentures of known length in the Middlesex registrations of the 1680s and 1.2% of those in the London registrations of 1718–59. The reasons for the rarity of these shorter terms are not known. Four years may have been the term required at most times and places for the average adult to repay the cost of passage out of his net earnings, but it is unclear why shorter terms were not more often given to highly skilled servants like the accountant James Corss, whom Walter Tullideph sent to the manager of his plantation in Antigua in 1759 with a note stating that he "hath bound himself to serve me four years agreeable to the Laws of Antigua, but as he is 22 years of Age, he thought it hard to serve so long and for that reason, I have given him a Certificate that he is to be absolved from the last year's Service"; "Letter Books of Dr. Walter Tullideph" (MSS, Dundee, Scotland), vol. 3. (I am grateful to Richard Sheridan for this reference.) That planters normally preferred to substitute salaries for reductions of the term below four years suggests the possibility that fixed costs of hiring and/or a desire to capture the returns from a servant's general training in the colony may have been important considerations.

Regarding the adjustment of the terms of minors, it might be noted that the considerable amount of variation in the length of term that remains when age is held constant appears to contradict David Souden's conclusion that "the length of indenture seems generally to have been socially rather than economically determined, reflecting prevailing ideas of when young people could be expected to have come of age"; " 'Rogues, whores, and vagabonds'? Indentured servant emigrants to North America and the case of mid-seventeenth-century Bristol," *Social History*, 3, no. 1 (January 1978), p. 26. If the length of indenture had simply been set with reference to a specified age at which the servant should be freed, it would seem that all servants of a single age should have received the same term. In fact, e.g., 16-year-old servants bound in Middlesex during 1683–4 received terms ranging from four to nine years, whereas servants of the same age bound in Liverpool during 1697–1707 received from four to ten, and those bound in London during 1718–59, from three to eight; for frequency distributions of the length of indenture for men and women by age in four samples, see Galenson, "Indenture System and the Colonial Labor Market," Tables IX-2–IX-9, pp. 283–90. Nor, by this hypothesis, should the length of indenture have been affected by economic variables other than age, such as sex, skill, and literacy; evidence that it was is presented later in this chapter.

23 The hedonic approach to the analysis of prices is based on the hypothesis that price differences among variants of a particular commodity can be explained by a limited number of observable characteristics of these variants. The estimation of regression equations which express the prices of commodity variants as a function of their characteristics can therefore indicate which characteristics are in fact associated with price differences, and in each case what the relationship is. If the relevant characteristics have been identified, the estimated coefficients from the equation can be interpreted as prices for the characteristics. On the use of the hedonic method, see Zvi Griliches, ed., *Price Indexes and Quality Change* (Cambridge, Mass., 1971).

24 On the interpretation of coefficients in hedonic price indexes, see Sherwin Rosen, "Hedonic Prices and Implicit Markets: Product Differentiation in Pure Competition," *Journal of Political Economy*, 82, no. 1 (February 1974):24–5.

25 The difference in the sex coefficients of the two samples in Table 7.1 is significant at the .01 level. On the decline in colonial sex ratios over time, see Chapter 2.

26 Robert William Fogel and Stanley L. Engerman, *Time on the Cross: The Economics of American Negro Slavery* (Boston, 1974), p. 77. For additional evidence, see Jacob Metzer, "Rational Management, Modern Business Practices, and Economies of Scale in the Ante-Bellum Southern Plantations," *Explorations in Economic History*, 12, no. 2 (April 1975):136–7.

27 The differentiation of occupational categories in regression analysis of the later sample is made possible by the much larger number of skilled minors in that sample.

28 None of the four coefficients is significantly different from any of the other three at the .10 level.

29 Christopher Jeaffreson to William Poyntz, St. Christopher, June 5, 1676; in Jeaffreson, *A Young Squire of the Seventeenth Century*, 1:186. In a later letter, Jeaffreson offered better terms of indenture, in the form of extraordinary freedom dues, to "a good carpenter . . . and the like to a good cooper, and soe to a mason," explaining "for it is but just, such workemen should have some consideration for their tyme, more than others"; ibid., 1:207–8. Earlier in the century, the anonymous author of a pamphlet intended to attract settlers to Maryland noted in a section entitled "A direction for choice of seruants": "The usuall time of binding a servant, is for five yeers; but for any artificer . . . the Adventurer shall doe well to shorten that time, and adde encouragement of another nature . . . rather then to want such usefull men," *A Relation of Maryland* (London, 1635), p. 54.

For other examples of requests by colonial planters for skilled servants, see Richard Beale Davis, ed., *William Fitzhugh and His Chesapeake World* (Chapel Hill, N.C., 1963), p. 92; Balderston, *James Claypoole's Letter Book*, pp. 147, 151, 153, 156, 197; J. Eston to Colonel Samuel Eston, London, March 1, 1684, University of London Library, Newton Papers, MS 523/1055/1; Samuel Clay to Colonel Samuel Newton, London, March 29, 1684, ibid., 523/1055/2; Colonel Richard Scott (to R. Bates?), Barbados, August 8, 1702, ibid., 523/1103; Walter B. Edgar, ed., *The Letterbook of Robert Pringle* (Columbia, S.C., 1972), 1:282; Walter Tullideph to Thos.

Martin, Antigua, March 21, 1741, and Walter Tullideph to Wm. Dunbar, Antigua, July 24, 1746, in "Letter Books of Walter Tullideph," vols. I, II; Messrs. Lascelles and Maxwell to Thos. Fox, London, February 24, 1744, in "Messrs. Lascelles & Maxwell Letter Book from September 1743 to 19 February 1745" (MSS, London), f. 238 (I am grateful to Richard Sheridan for the latter two references); British Museum, Martin Papers, vol. 4, Add MSS 41,349, ff. 32–4, 45, 72, 97, 107.

30 Samuel Martin to Messrs. Codrington & Miller, Antigua, March 26, 1761, Martin Papers, 4, Add MSS 41,349, f. 97v. Also see the comments in Martin's letter to his son, Samuel Martin, Jr., in ibid., 1, Add MSS 41,346, ff. 23, 211v; 2, Add MSS 41,347, f. 182. For other statements of usefulness of servants with agricultural skills in the colonies, see Anonymous, *A Relation of Maryland* (London, 1635), p. 52; Anonymous, *A Brief Description of the Province of Carolina on the Coasts of Floreda* (London, 1666), p. 9; Anonymous, *A Publication of Guiana's Plantation* (London, 1632), p. 22; Balderston, *James Claypoole's Letter Book*, pp. 147, 151, 153, 156.

31 The coefficient of laborer for the London sample in Table 7.1 is significantly different from that of farmer at the .10 level for a one-tailed t-test, from those of metal-construction and clothing-textiles at .05, and from that of services at .025. It is significantly different than zero at the .10 level for a two-tailed t-test.

32 It might be noted that the erratic behavior of the coefficients of higher ages in Table 7.1 for the Middlesex sample may have been due to the falsification of the ages of some servants. The latter may have resulted from the legal requirements under which the registrations were made; for discussion and evidence, see Appendix C.

33 Possible seasonal variation in delivery costs has been controlled for in the equation reported in Table 7.2 on which these estimates are based.

34 No wages were recorded for unskilled servants. The average wage payments received by the skilled servants in the London sample by age were:

Age	Mean annual wage (£)
15	0.00
16	0.40
17	0.79
18	1.45
19	1.52
20	3.02

Source: Corporation of London Records Office, "Memoranda of Agreements to Serve in America and the West Indies."

The present value of freedom dues at the time of binding varied across colonies and over time, according to differences and changes in legislation and with changes in the value of colonial currencies and commodities. No explicit allowance has been made for the dues in the calculation because of the difficulty of estimating their typical value; inclusion of the effect of the lump-sum payments would lower the estimates of the net annual earnings of servants without changing their relative values by age.

35 Becker, *Human Capital,* p. 221.
36 Fogel and Engerman's estimates of net earnings by age for unskilled male slaves were:

| | Old South, 1790–1860 | | Louisiana, 1838–1860 | |
Age	Annual net earnings ($)	Relative net earnings (age 23 = 1.0)	Annual net earnings ($)	Relative net earnings (age 23 = 1.0)
19	58	.763	76	.776
20	64	.842	82	.837
21	68	.895	88	.898
22	72	.947	94	.959
23	76	1.000	98	1.000

Source: Robert William Fogel and Stanley L. Engerman, "The Market Evaluation of Human Capital: The Case of Slavery" (Paper presented to Cliometrics Conference, Madison, Wis., 1972), Charts III and IV.

37 Jeaffreson, *A Young Squire of the Seventeenth Century*, 1:257.
38 The difference between the coefficients of literacy in the two samples is significant at .10 for a two-tailed *t*-test. For discussion of the servants' literacy, see Chapter 5.
39 Jeaffreson, *A Young Squire of the Seventeenth Century*, 2:61.
40 P.R.O., London, "Petition of the Council and Assembly of Barbados to the King," 1675, C.O. 1/35, f. 237v.
41 Smith, *Colonists in Bondage,* p. 57.
42 On English wages, see Elizabeth Gilboy, *Wages in Eighteenth Century England* (Cambridge, Mass., 1934), pp. 219–25; E. H. Phelps Brown and Sheila V. Hopkins, "Seven Centuries of the Price of Consumables, Compared with Builders' Wage-Rates," *Economica,* 23 (November 1956):302–13. On changes in colonial mortality rates, see, e.g., Russell R. Menard, "Immigrants and Their Increase: The Process of Population Growth in Early Colonial Maryland," in Aubrey C. Land, Lois Green Carr, and Edward C. Papenfuse, eds., *Law, Society, and Politics in Early Maryland* (Baltimore, 1977), pp. 99–100.
43 On the seasonality of sugar production and shipping, see Michael Craton and James Walvin, *A Jamaican Plantation: The History of Worthy Park, 1670–1970* (Toronto, 1970), pp. 100–15; Elsa V. Goveia, *Slave Society in the British Leeward Islands at the End of the Eighteenth Century* (New Haven, 1965), p. 127; Ralph Davis, *The Rise of the English Shipping Industry* (London, 1962), p. 279. On tobacco, see Bruce, *Economic History of Virginia* 1:622–4; Bullock, *Virginia Impartially examined,* p. 46; George Alsop, *A Character of the Province of Mary-Land* (London, 1666), p. 51; Davis, *Rise of the English Shipping Industry*, pp. 285–7. On the costs of maintaining

servants between binding and sailing, see Smith, *Colonists in Bondage*, pp. 36–7, 59–65; Scottish Record Office, Bught Papers, GD 23/6/98, nos. 4, 14, 18; on maintenance costs also see Bristol Record Office, "Depositions, 1654 to 1657," B.A.O. 04439(2), ff. 12–13.

For factors relevant to seasonality in the colonial demand for labor, see Gerald W. Mullin, *Flight and Rebellion: Slave Resistance in Eighteenth-Century Virginia* (London, 1972), p. 15, and Edmund S. Morgan, *American Slavery, American Freedom: The Ordeal of Colonial Virginia* (New York, 1975), p. 158.

44 Similar analysis of the contracts of servants bound for the Chesapeake during 1718–40 indicates that the lagged annual farm price of Maryland tobacco had no significant effect on the length of indenture, as in a regression equation that included the variables of Table 7.2 the estimated coefficient of an interaction term between the price of tobacco, lagged one year, and Chesapeake destination was statistically insignificant. Because of a greater continuing reliance on production of a single staple in the West Indies in the eighteenth century, it is likely that the price of sugar serves as a better index of the West Indian demand for labor than does the price of tobacco for the Chesapeake. On the diversification of agricultural production in the Chesapeake, see Paul G. E. Clemens, *The Atlantic Economy and Colonial Maryland's Eastern Shore: From Tobacco to Grain* (Ithaca, N.Y., 1980), pp. 168–205; Gregory A. Stiverson, *Poverty in a Land of Plenty: Tenancy in Eighteenth-Century Maryland* (Baltimore, 1977), pp. 65–103. The tobacco prices used were those of Russell R. Menard, "Economy and Society in Early Colonial Maryland" (Ph.D. diss., University of Iowa, 1975), p. 478.

45 Sir George Peckham, *A True Reporte, of the late discoveries, and possessions, taken in the right of the Crowne of Englande, of the Newfound Landes, By that valiaunt and worthy Gentleman, Sir Humfrey Gilbert Knight* (London, 1583), Chapter 7, not paginated.

8. The role of the indenture system in the colonial labor market

1 Because of the quantitative importance in many areas of colonial America of production by families or other units, such as plantations, of a wide variety of goods and services for consumption by the family or on the plantation, a broad definition of the labor force is used in this study to allow an analysis that will lead to an understanding of the significant differences between regions in the composition of labor forces by the categories of free, indentured, and slave labor. Specifically, throughout the discussion of this study the labor force is defined to have been composed of all individuals engaged in the production of goods and services, without regard to whether the individual's labor or output was bought and sold in the market. This definition therefore includes in the labor force such individuals as farmers who produced solely for the consumption of their own families, as well as such other family members as wives and children who helped in the cultivation of crops or with other types of work in the household; it would clearly also include all servants and slaves involved in the production of goods and services, regardless of the ultimate use of the latter.

the Subscribers at Howels Point," Testamentary Papers, Box 55, Folder 42. I am grateful to Lorena Walsh for this evidence.

18 Samuel Martin, *An Essay upon Plantership,* 5th ed. (London, 1773), p. xv.

19 Samuel Martin to Samuel Martin, Jr., Antigua, June 25, 1751; British Museum, Martin Papers, vol. 1, Add MS 41,346, f. 23.

20 Quoted in Carl Bridenbaugh, *The Colonial Craftsmen* (Chicago, 1961), pp. 15–16. On the training of slaves by white servants, also see ibid., pp. 13, 17.

21 The description of the development of Bybrook plantation and the quotations are drawn from J. Harry Bennett, "Cary Helyar, Merchant and Planter of Seventeenth-Century Jamaica," *William and Mary Quarterly,* 3d ser. 21, no. 1 (January 1964): 53–76, and Bennett, "William Whaley, Planter of Seventeenth-Century Jamaica," *Agricultural History* 40, no. 2 (April 1966): 113–23.

22 Richard S. Dunn, *Sugar and Slaves: The Rise of the Planter Class in the English West Indies, 1624–1713* (New York, 1973), pp. 198, 319; Carl Bridenbaugh and Roberta Bridenbaugh, *No Peace Beyond the Line: The English in the Caribbean, 1624–1690* (New York, 1972), pp. 302–3.

23 William Hay to Archibald Hay, Barbados, September 10, 1645; Scottish Record Office, Hay of Haystoun Papers, GD 34/945.

24 Christopher Jeaffreson to William Poyntz, St. Kitts, May 11, 1677, May 6, 1681; in John Cordy Jeaffreson, ed., *A Young Squire of the Seventeenth Century, From the Papers (A.D. 1676–1686) of Christopher Jeaffreson* (London, 1878), 1:207–8, 255.

25 William Fitzhugh to John Cooper, June 7, 1681; Fitzhugh to Nicholas Hayward, January 30, 1687; in Richard Beale Davis, ed., *William Fitzhugh and His Chesapeake World* (Chapel Hill, N.C., 1963), pp. 92, 202.

26 William Gordon to Baillie Gilbert Gordon, Glasgow, May 31, 1732; Scottish Record Office, Bught Papers, GD 23/6/98, 98/4.

27 William Gordon to Baillie Gilbert Gordon, Glasgow, August 4, 1732; December 3, 1733; ibid., GD 23/6/98, 98/6, 98/14.

28 Lascelles and Maxwell to Thos. Fox, London, February 24, 1744; "Messrs. Lascelles and Maxwell Letter Book from September, 1743, to February, 1745" (MS, London), f. 238. I am grateful to Richard Sheridan for this reference.

29 Samuel Martin to John Browning, Antigua, November 2, 1757; British Museum, Martin Papers, vol. 4, Add MS 41,349, f. 32.

30 Samuel Martin, "Some instructions to my eldest son" (Antigua, 1767); ibid., vol. 2, Add MS 41,347, ff. 302v–3.

31 Walter Tullideph to David Tullideph, Antigua, May 19, 1735; "Letter Books of Dr. Walter Tullideph" (MSS, Dundee, Scotland), vol. 1; Walter Tullideph to David Tullideph, Antigua, July 12, 1735; ibid. Walter Tullideph to Thos. Martin, Antigua, March 21, 1740/1; ibid. I am grateful to Richard Sheridan for this reference.

32 Walter Tullideph to James Russell, Dundee, November 12, 1759; ibid., vol. 3.

33 Walter Tullideph to Duncan Grant, Tullideph Hall (near Dundee), February 22, 1760; ibid.

34 Jack P. Greene, ed., *The Diary of Colonel Landon Carter of Sabine Hall, 1752–1778* (Charlottesville, Va., 1965), 1:200, 202.
35 Robert Pringle to Andrew Pringle, Charleston, November 22, 1740; in Walter B. Edgar, ed., *The Letterbook of Robert Pringle* (Columbia, S.C., 1972), 1:272.
36 Petition of the Council and Assembly of Barbados to the King, Barbados, November 24, 1675; P.R.O., London, C.O. 1/35, f. 237v.
37 Edward Littleton, *The Groans of the Plantations* (London, 1689), p. 14.
38 Quoted in Bridenbaugh, *The Colonial Craftsman*, pp. 15–16.
39 "An Account of the English Sugar Plantacons," ca. 1660–85; British Museum, Stowe MS 324, f. 6.
40 Governor Sir Jonathan Atkins to Lords of Trade and Plantations, Barbados, October 26, 1680; P.R.O., London, C.O. 29/3, pp. 92–3.
41 "To the Kings most Excellent Matie.: The humble Petition of the Persons who have Estates in your Maties. Plantations in America," November 3, 1682; P.R.O., London, C.O. 1/50, f. 303.
42 Greene, *The Diary of Colonel Landon Carter*, 2:1055.
43 Menard, "The Maryland Slave Population, 1658 to 1730," pp. 36–7, 51–3; Mullin, *Flight and Rebellion*, pp. 7, 11–13, 17–19, 39, 84–7, 94–7; Kulikoff, "Tobacco and Slaves," pp. 235–42.
44 Richard B. Sheridan, "Planter and Historian: The Career of William Beckford of Jamaica and England, 1744–1799," *Jamaican Historical Review*, 4 (1964):48, 51–4.
45 Eric Williams, *Capitalism and Slavery* (New York, 1966), p. 19.
46 Lewis Cecil Gray, *History of Agriculture in the Southern United States to 1860* (Gloucester, Mass., 1958), 1:350; Richard Pares, *Merchants and Planters, Economic History Review*, Supplement No. 4 (1960), p. 19.

9. The indenture system and the colonial labor market: an overview

1 See Zvi Griliches, "Hybrid Corn and the Economics of Innovation," in Robert William Fogel and Stanley L. Engerman, eds., *The Reinterpretation of American Economic History* (New York, 1971), pp. 207–13; also Edwin Mansfield, "Technical Change and the Rate of Imitation," *Econometrica*, 29 (October 1961):741–66.
2 The price elasticity of labor supply measures the percentage change in the quantity of labor provided relative to the percentage change in the price of labor (i.e., the wage rate). A low price elasticity indicates that the quantity supplied is relatively insensitive to changes in price, while a high elasticity indicates that even small changes in price will result in large changes in the amount of labor supplied. At the extremes, a perfectly inelastic supply curve indicates that the amount of labor supplied in some period is fixed, without any response to changes in price, whereas a perfectly elastic (or infinitely elastic) supply curve indicates that any desired level of labor will be supplied at a constant price.
3 Given the quantitative importance of slaves in many British colonies, as well as in other countries' New World possessions, and the international nature of

the African slave trade, it appears that the concept could be extended more widely among American colonies. However, this is not necessary for the purposes of the present study.

4 Philip D. Curtin, *The Atlantic Slave Trade: A Census* (Madison, 1969), pp. 119, 216.

5 Abbot Emerson Smith, *Colonists in Bondage: White Servitude and Convict Labor in America, 1607–1776* (Chapel Hill, N.C., 1947), pp. 30–4, 57.

6 Smith, *Colonists in Bondage,* pp. 58–64; William Bullock, *Virginia Impartially examined, and left to publick view, to be considered by all Iudicious and honest men* (London, 1649), p. 47.

7 Thus a Glasgow merchant wrote to a recruiting agent in Inverness concerning the bargains of servants to be bound for service in Jamaica that they were to have "Eight pence Each day after they Indent until they be Shipped from this port"; William Gordon to Baillie Gilbert Gordon, May 31, 1732, Scottish Record Office, Bught Papers, GD 23/6/98/4.

Evidence that the supply of indentured labor was less than perfectly elastic can be drawn from a result presented in Chapter 7: Ceteris paribus, the length of the indentures of servants bound for the West Indies in the eighteenth century was negatively related to the lagged price of sugar. This correlation indicates that increases in the price of sugar were associated with increases in the cost of indentured labor to West Indian planters. Because high sugar prices were normally due to high demand for sugar, and therefore produced a high demand for labor in the sugar colonies, the result implies that the supply curve for indentured labor was less than perfectly elastic, because the cost of servants rose as the demand for them increased.

For a different analysis of inelastic white labor supply to the colonies, see Henry A. Gemery and Jan S. Hogendorn, "The Atlantic Slave Trade: A Tentative Economic Model," *Journal of African History,* 15, no. 2 (1974): 223–46. The four arguments they give for the inelasticity – the cost of transportation to the colonies relative to English workers' savings, English hostility to emigration after 1660, high mortality rates in the southern colonies, and the presence of large numbers of slaves in the same regions – would all appear more likely to affect the levels of the supply curves facing some or all colonies than to affect their elasticities.

8 See Chapter 8, notes 35 and 39, and quotations in text for evidence from Barbados; also Eric Williams, *Capitalism and Slavery* (New York, 1966), p. 23.

9 Richard S. Dunn, *Sugar and Slaves: The Rise of the Planter Class in the English West Indies, 1624–1713* (New York, 1973), p. 200; Edmund S. Morgan, *American Slavery, American Freedom: The Ordeal of Colonial Virginia* (New York, 1975), p. 298. For evidence of the aversion to gang labor among free workers in the nineteenth century, see Robert William Fogel and Stanley L. Engerman, *Time on the Cross* (Boston, 1974), pp. 236–8; Roger L. Ransom and Richard Sutch, *One Kind of Freedom* (Cambridge, 1977), p. 76.

10 Gloria Lund Main, "Personal Wealth in Colonial America: Explorations in the Use of Probate Records from Maryland and Massachusetts, 1650–1720"

(Ph.D. diss., Columbia University, 1972), Table III-15, p. 175; Lorena S. Walsh, "Servitude and Opportunity in Charles County, Maryland, 1658–1720," in Aubrey C. Land, Lois Green Carr, and Edward C. Papenfuse, *Law, Society, and Politics in Early Maryland,* (Baltimore, 1977), Table 5-2, p. 119.

11 On English attitudes toward blacks in the seventeenth century, see Winthrop D. Jordan, *White Over Black* (Baltimore, 1969), Chap. 1.

12 Because of the nature of surviving records, it is difficult to find direct evidence of these preferences. The preference for freedom is suggested by various popular expressions in England, including warnings to potential servants of the dangers of becoming slaves, and outcries against "spirits," or kidnappers involved in the servant trade; e.g., see Marcellus Rivers and Oxenbridge Foyle, *Englands Slavery, or Barbados Merchandize* (London, 1659), p. 22; Richard Head, *The English Rogue Described, in the Life of Meriton Latroon* (London, 1665), Pt. 2, pp. 1–3; and, in general, Smith, *Colonists in Bondage,* pp. 67–86.

An illustration of the opposition to long-term contracts as well as the preference for freedom appears in the letters of George Haworth, an Englishman who emigrated to Pennsylvania in 1699. He found work at good wages and in 1701 wrote to his mother: "So if any of my relations have a mind to come to this country, I think it is a very good country and that they may do well, but be sure to come free, but if you come servants, they must be sold for 4 or 5 years and work hard, so be sure to come free"; "Early Letters from Pennsylvania, 1699–1722," *Pennsylvania Magazine of History and Biography,* 37, no. 147 (July 1913):332–4.

13 One implication of the formulation of supply price given here might be noted, specifically, that statements concerning the supply price of slave or servant labor cannot be based solely on the price at which slaves or servants were sold. Richard Bean and Robert Thomas have argued that slaves were adopted on a large scale earlier in the West Indies than in the Chesapeake because of differences in the relative supply prices of the two types of labor to the two regions: The cost of transportation for slaves from Africa to the islands was substantially lower than to the mainland, whereas the cost of transporting servants from England was approximately equal for both of the regions. As a result, they argue, the cost of slaves relative to servants was always lower in the West Indies than in the Chesapeake, and this can explain why the use of slaves became advantageous earlier in the islands than on the mainland; Richard N. Bean and Robert P. Thomas, "The Adoption of Slave Labor in British America," in Henry A. Gemery and Jan S. Hogendorn, eds., *The Uncommon Market: Essays in the Economic History of the Atlantic Slave Trade* (New York, 1979), pp. 394–8. Yet Bean and Thomas neglect the fact that the relevant supply price for capitalized stocks of labor must allow not only for initial purchase price but also for the expected longevity of the worker. In fact, the islands' extremely high mortality rates may have made the annual cost of slave labor substantially higher to West Indian than to Chesapeake planters in the seventeenth century; see Morgan, *American Slavery, American Freedom,* pp. 300–1. This would be consistent with a

result presented in Chapter 7, as analysis of the length of servants' indentures indicated that servants bound for the West Indies received shorter terms than those bound for the Chesapeake, ceteris paribus. This finding implies that the relevant supply price of servant labor, the annual implicit rental cost, was higher in the islands than on the mainland. That the equilibrium rental costs of all types of labor were higher in the West Indies than in the Chesapeake would be consistent with a higher marginal productivity of labor in sugar than in tobacco production; another implication of the result concerning the cost of servants, to be considered later in this chapter, is that the preference of servants for the mainland over the islands made their price relative to slaves higher in the West Indies than in the Chesapeake, and produced an earlier and more complete transition to slavery in the islands.

14 K. G. Davies, *The North Atlantic World in the Seventeenth Century* (Minneapolis, 1974), pp. 180–6; Dunn, *Sugar and Slaves;* Richard B. Sheridan, *Sugar and Slavery: An Economic History of the British West Indies, 1623–1775* (Barbados, 1974); Jordan, *White Over Black,* pp. 63–6. The introduction of sugar into Barbados in the early 1640s provided West Indian planters with a highly profitable staple crop that rapidly replaced tobacco, cotton, and the other crops with which the planters had earlier experimented.

15 This discussion draws on Dunn, *Sugar and Slaves,* pp. 59–72, 110–16, 301–34; and Sheridan, *Sugar and Slavery,* pp. 131–3, 164, 194, 237–8.

16 Dunn, *Sugar and Slaves,* pp. 76–7. It is difficult to determine whether whites generally found slave societies distasteful and therefore avoided them or whether it was the type of labor to be done in those regions that they disliked. That disproportionate numbers of skilled servants were bound for colonies with large slave populations is consistent with the latter, and it suggests the possibility that it was not the presence of slaves but, rather, the gang labor of the unskilled that whites disliked. Some whites may have found the presence of slaves a positive attraction, in that the presence of a less advantaged group raised the relative social status of poor whites. However, some evidence suggests that potential emigrants worried about their reception in slave societies. An extreme example occurs in a letter from a London merchant to a Barbados planter in 1684: Concerning his efforts to recruit a white servant for the latter, the merchant wrote that "Mrs. Tilly is a white Livord . . . [words missing] . . . comes now with strange storyes that she is fearful her son shoulde worke for the Negroes . . . she is resolved to keep him at home"; J. Eston to Colonel Samuel Newton, London, March 1, 1683/4; University of London Library, Newton Papers, MS 523/1055/1.

Richard Bean and Robert Thomas have stressed the importance of rising wages in England during 1640–5 in reducing the supply of indentured servants to Barbados in their explanation of the substitution of slaves for servants; "The Adoption of Slave Labor in British America," pp. 391–3. However, if this effect had been a major one, it should have reduced British emigration in general, so the apparent failure of total British migration to the American colonies to fall during the 1640s and 1650s appears to cast some doubt on this argument; see Henry A. Gemery, "Emigration from the British

Isles to the New World, 1630–1700: Inferences from Colonial Populations,"
Research in Economic History 5 (1980):215. That improving economic
conditions in England may have played a significant part in the later rise of
slavery in the Chesapeake by reducing white labor supply, as is argued later in
this chapter, is suggested by estimates which indicate that a considerable
decline in total migration from England to the American colonies did occur in
the final two decades of the seventeenth century; ibid., p. 215.

17 The quotation is from Bryan Edwards, *The History, Civil and Commercial,
of the British Colonies in the West Indies* (London, 1794), 2:244; also see
pp. 221–62; Davies, *North Atlantic World*, pp. 184–6. On the consolidation
of small farms and the growth of large plantations, see Dunn, *Sugar and
Slaves*, pp. 91–6, 169–77; Sheridan, *Sugar and Slavery*, pp. 119–22.

18 Richard Pares, *Merchants and Planters, Economic History Review*, Supple-
ment No. 4 (1960), pp. 19–20, 23; Dunn, *Sugar and Slaves*, p. 69; Davies,
North Atlantic World, p. 183; Morgan, *American Slavery, American
Freedom*, p. 298.

19 An example is Morgan, *American Slavery, American Freedom*, pp. 297–9.

20 The expected present value of a servant and slave to a planter at the time of
purchase can be formulated:

$$PV_i = \sum_{j=1}^{n_1} (1-p)\frac{NP_{ij}}{(1+r)^j}$$

$$PV_s = \sum_{j=1}^{n_2} (1-p)\frac{NP_{sj}}{(1+r)^j}$$

where PV = expected present value; i = indentured servant; s = slave; n_1 =
term of servant in years; n_2 = life expectancy of slave who did not die in
seasoning; NP = net annual product of labor; r = discount rate; and p =
probability that an immigrant would die in seasoning. This formulation
indicates why changes in seasoning mortality cannot affect the relative value
of a servant and a slave to a planter, for changes in p change PV_i and PV_s in
the same proportion.

A possible qualification to this analysis results from the consideration of
output produced by a servant or slave before dying in seasoning. The presence
of this output would have tended to raise the value of servants relative to
slaves in periods of high seasoning mortality, with the magnitude of the effect
on relative prices positively related to the typical value of the output.
Although evidence on the magnitude of this output remains to be analyzed, it
appears unlikely that those who died in seasoning would normally have been
healthy long enough to contribute significantly to production.

It might be noted that declining seasoning mortality could have had some
effect on the composition of the labor force as a result of supply side
differences: Thus, if the supply of slaves was considerably more elastic than
the supply of servants, an increase in the demand price of both in the same
proportion could have produced a larger increase in slave than servant
imports. As noted in the text, however, this is not likely to have caused the

large-scale adoption of slave labor in the Chesapeake in the 1680s, for the decline in seasoning mortality has been dated as complete at least two decades earlier.

For a fuller discussion of the effects of changing seasoning mortality on the demand for servants and slaves, see David Walter Galenson, "The Indenture System and the Colonial Labor Market" (Ph.D. diss., Harvard University, 1979), pp. 408–11. For additional discussion of changing seasoning mortality, see Morgan, *American Slavery, American Freedom*, pp. 160–2, 175–6, 297–9, 308–10. Morgan makes no mention of the possibility of unequal incidence of seasoning mortality by race, and appears to assume there was no difference; *American Slavery, American Freedom*, pp. 297–8.

Much remains unknown concerning both the precise causes of seasoning mortality in the early Chesapeake and secular trends in its importance, and the analysis of its implications for labor choice offered here must therefore be considered provisional. There has recently been considerable debate over the specific diseases responsible for seasoning; see Darrett B. Rutman and Anita H. Rutman, "Of Agues and Fevers: Malaria in the Early Chesapeake," *William and Mary Quarterly*, 3d ser. 33, no. 1 (January 1976):31–60; and Carville V. Earle, "Environment, Disease, and Mortality in Early Virginia," in Thad W. Tate and David L. Ammerman, eds., *The Chesapeake in the Seventeenth Century* (Chapel Hill, N. C., 1979), pp. 96–125. To the extent that seasoning mortality resulted from contact with an unfamiliar disease environment, the numerical predominance of whites in the early seventeenth century could have produced generally greater risks for blacks entering the Chesapeake, and higher seasoning mortality for blacks. A decline in seasoning mortality rates could then have had the effect Morgan suggests, of increasing the relative demand of Chesapeake planters for slaves. However, insofar as seasoning mortality was caused by malaria, it would apparently have fallen more heavily on white Europeans than on black Africans; see Rutman, "Of Agues and Fevers," p. 35. A decline in seasoning mortality due to malaria would therefore have tended to raise the demand of Chesapeake planters for servants relative to slaves.

21 Morgan, *American Slavery, American Freedom*, pp. 180–4.
22 Gloria L. Main,"Maryland and the Chesapeake Economy, 1670–1720," in Aubrey C. Land, Lois Green Carr, and Edward C. Papenfuse, eds., *Law, Society, and Politics in Early Maryland* (Baltimore, 1977), pp. 139–40; Russell Menard, "From Servants to Slaves; The Transformation of the Chesapeake Labor System," *Southern Studies*, 16, no. 4 (1977):360–9: Main, "Personal Wealth in Colonial America," pp. 175–6; Carville V. Earle, *The Evolution of a Tidewater Settlement System: All Hallow's Parish, Maryland, 1650–1783*, University of Chicago, Research Paper No. 170 (1975), pp. 44–6; Russell R. Menard, "Economy and Society in Early Colonial Maryland" (Ph.D. diss., University of Iowa, 1975), pp. 156–9. Some fluctuation occurred in the number of servants in the Chesapeake's labor force after 1700, but even in absolute terms the number of servants did not subsequently reach the levels of the period before 1680.
23 For estimates of demand elasticities and additional discussion, see Galenson,

"The Indenture System and the Colonial Labor Market," pp. 414–16. For the view that declining servant supply forced a switch to slaves in the Chesapeake, see Menard, "From Servants to Slaves," p. 389; Main, "Maryland and the Chesapeake Economy," pp. 139–40. In the long-run, the elasticity of demand for servants may have increased. Thus a comparison of the hire rates for indentured servants calculated in Chapter 7 for the early eighteenth century with hire rates implied by Maryland slave prices in the same period suggests they were approximately equal. The calculation for slaves assumed a thirty-year life expectancy for a male aged 20; e.g., see Darret B. Rutman and Anita H. Rutman, " 'Now-Wives and Sons-in-Law': Parental Death in a Seventeenth-Century Virginia County," in Thad W. Tate and David L. Ammerman, eds., *The Chesapeake in the Seventeenth Century* (Chapel Hill, N.C., 1979), p. 178. If a 20-year-old slave had had the same annual net earnings as a 20-year-old unskilled servant, of about £2.20 (see Chapter 7), with a subsequent age/net-earnings profile of the shape estimated by Robert William Fogel and Stanley L. Engerman, "The Market Evaluation of Human Capital: The Case of Slavery" (unpublished paper presented to Cliometrics Conference, Madison, Wis., 1972), Charts III and IV, with a 10% discount rate the present value of the slave would have been approximately £26. This is close to the actual price of prime-aged males in early eighteenth-century Maryland (Menard, "From Servants to Slaves," p. 372), indicating that the implicit hire rates on unskilled servants and slaves were similar. The interpretation of this could be that by the third decade of the eighteenth century planters had found slaves to be close substitutes for unskilled servants, and of roughly equal productivity.

24 Menard, "From Servants to Slaves," pp. 359, 367–8.

25 Charles Calvert to Lord Baltimore, April 27, 1664; Maryland Historical Society, *The Calvert Papers*, Peabody Publication Fund, No. 28 (Baltimore, 1889), 1:249.

26 Support for this position comes from evidence on the price of slaves over time. If an inelastic supply of slaves had been increasing less rapidly than the Chesapeake demand for them, as Menard implies "From Servants to Slaves," (pp. 367–8), the result should have been increasing slave prices. However, the data show no significant upward trend in slave prices between 1674 and 1698 and in fact exhibit very little variation of any kind (ibid., p. 372).

27 On trends in sugar and slave prices, see Davies, *North Atlantic World,* pp. 188–9; Sheridan, *Sugar and Slavery,* pp. 252–3, 392, 401; Dunn, *Sugar and Slaves,* pp. 72, 102; Menard, "From Servants to Slaves." p. 372; David Galenson, "The Slave Trade to the English West Indies, 1673–1724," *Economic History Review,* 2nd ser., 32, no. 2 (May 1979):242–4.

28 Menard, "From Servants to Slaves," pp. 368–9.

29 E. H. Phelps Brown and Sheila V. Hopkins, "Seven Centuries of the Prices of Consumables, Compared with Builders' Wage-Rates," *Economica,* n.s., vol. 23, no. 92 (November 1956):302–6; Russell R. Menard, "From Servant to Freeholder: Status Mobility and Property Accumulation in Seventeenth-Century Maryland," *William and Mary Quarterly,* 3d ser. 30, no. 1 (January 1973):37–64; Walsh, "Servitude and Opportunity in Charles County," pp. 123–8; Menard, "From Servants to Slaves," p. 380; Lois

Green Carr and Russell R. Menard, "Immigration and Opportunity: The Freedman in Early Colonial Maryland," in Tate and Ammerman, *Chesapeake in the Seventeenth Century*, pp. 206–42. The last paper cited clearly indicates that the Chesapeake's high demand for hired labor meant that freedmen who remained in the region need never lack employment at relatively high wages, at least in the seventeenth century. However, it also shows that their chances of becoming independent landowners began to decline significantly after 1660. For immigrants and prospective immigrants whose aim in coming to the New World was to own land, this restriction of the available economic opportunities would have had a considerable importance.

The account offered here of the Chesapeake's initial transition to slavery differs from the recent interpretation of T. H. Breen in *Puritans and Adventurers: Change and Persistence in Early America* (New York, 1980) in a number of respects. Specifically, my explanation disagrees with Breen's contentions that it was only after 1680 that Chesapeake planters gained access to direct shipments of slaves from Africa (ibid., p. 142), that servants immigrating to Virginia during the 1680s were of a higher social rank than the indentured servants who came to the colony in the middle of the seventeenth century (ibid., p. 142), that economic opportunities for freedmen improved in the last three decades of the seventeenth century (ibid., pp. 143–4), and that the initial transition to slaves in Virginia resulted from the dissatisfaction of planters with the indenture system (ibid., p. 150). On the first of these points, see, e.g., Menard, "From Servants to Slaves," pp. 366–7; on the second, see the discussion of trends in the composition of the servant population, based on the registrations, in Chapters 4 and 6 above; on the third, see Menard, "From Servant to Freeholder," passim, and Carr and Menard, "Immigration and Opportunity," passim; and on the last, see the discussion of the text in this chapter, and the references cited there.

30 Peter H. Wood, *Black Majority: Negroes in Colonial South Carolina from 1670 through the Stono Rebellion* (New York, 1975), pp. 36, 53–62. Wood has also pointed to a second factor which he believes contributed to the rise of slavery in South Carolina, the possibility that blacks may have been more resistant than whites to yellow fever and malaria, the two diseases most responsible for South Carolina's high mortality rates; ibid., pp. 89–91. As in the case of skill in rice cultivation, if these diseases had been specific to South Carolina, blacks' greater immunity would have raised the demand for slaves relative to servants in comparison with other colonies and therefore speeded the transition to slavery and increased the final degree of reliance on slaves. However, this is not the case, as malaria and yellow fever were present in other American regions that entered the market for servants and slaves, and a relative advantage in the resistance of slaves to the diseases would already have been reflected in the slaves' market prices. Blacks' greater immunity would not have raised the likelihood of slavery being adopted in South Carolina unless malaria and yellow fever were quantitatively more important there than elsewhere in the Americas.

31 Ibid., p. 62; Lewis Cecil Gray, *History of Agriculture in the Southern United States to 1860* (Gloucester, Mass, 1958), 1:283.

32 Wood, *Black Majority*, pp. 64–9.

The case of Georgia appears to have paralleled that of South Carolina in a number of respects, as rice was grown on large plantations under conditions unattractive to white servants. The more rapid substitution of slaves for servants in Georgia after the legal prohibition of slavery in the colony was removed in 1750 might indicate the importance of increases over time in the relative supply price of English servants. For a consideration of the relative costs of white and black labor in Georgia, see Ralph Gray and Betty Wood, "The Transition from Indentured to Involuntary Servitude in Colonial Georgia," *Explorations in Economic History* 13, no. 4 (October 1976): 353–70.

33 "Certaine Notes and Informations concerning New England," ca. 1660–4, British Museum, Egerton MSS 2395, f. 415v.
34 Percy Wells Bidwell and John I. Falconer, *History of Agriculture in the Northern United States, 1620–1860* (New York, 1941), pp. 33–4, 37–9, 115–17; Kenneth A. Lockridge, *A New England Town: The First Hundred Years* (New York, 1970), pp. 69–73; Philip J. Greven, Jr., *Four Generations: Population, Land, and Family in Colonial Andover, Massachusetts* (Ithaca, N.Y., 1970), p. 49.
35 J. Potter, "The Growth of Population in America, 1700–1860," in D. V. Glass and D. E. C. Eversley, eds., *Population in History: Essays in Historical Demography* (London, 1964), pp. 648–52; Daniel Scott Smith, "The Demographic History of Colonial New England," *Journal of Economic History,* 32, no. 1 (March 1972):165–83; Greven, *Four Generations,* Chaps. 2,5,7; Lockridge, *New England Town,* pp. 65–8.
36 It might be noted that although many references can be found in New England's "high wages," the annual marginal productivity of labor was probably kept below the level at which bound labor would have been profitable in most parts of New England by the seasonality of agriculture. This is suggested by Ralph V. Anderson and Robert E. Gallman, "Slaves as Fixed Capital: Slave Labor and Southern Economic Development," *Journal of American History* 64, no. 1 (June 1977):24–9. For an indication of seasonal variation of wages in colonial New England, see Bidwell and Falconer, *History of Agriculture in the Northern United States,* pp. 117–18.
37 Bidwell and Falconer, *History of Agriculture in the Northern United States,* pp. 42, 48.
38 E.g., Paul Boyer and Stephen Nissenbaum, *Salem Possessed: The Social Origins of Witchcraft* (Cambridge, 1974), p. 94.
39 Lorenzo Johnston Greene, *The Negro in Colonial New England* (New York, 1942), pp. 81–2, 88, 104–8; Bidwell and Falconer, *History of Agriculture in the Northern United States,* pp. 109, 116.
40 James T. Lemon, *The Best Poor Man's Country: A Geographical Study of Early Southeastern Pennsylvania* (New York, 1976), p. 14; Smith, *Colonists in Bondage,* pp. 57–8.
41 Lemon, *Best Poor Man's Country,* pp. 27–9, 151–67, 180–1, 216.
42 Potter, "The Growth of Population in America," pp. 652–60. Lemon, *Best Poor Man's Country,* p.xiii; also see, e.g., "Early Letters from Pennsylvania, 1699–1722," pp. 330–40.

43 Smith, *Colonists in Bondage,* pp. 117–19, 317–28.
44 Gray, *History of Agriculture in the Southern United States,* 1:467–8; Morgan, *American Slavery, American Freedom,* p. 298.
45 E.g., see Gerald W. Mullin, *Flight and Rebellion* (London, 1972), pp. 17–18.
46 John Oldmixon, *The British Empire in America* (London, 1708), 2:121–2.
47 Russell R. Menard, "The Maryland Slave Population, 1658 to 1730," *William and Mary Quarterly,* 3d ser. 32, no. 1 (January 1975):36–7; Mullin, *Flight and Rebellion,* pp. 39, 47. It might be noted that there is evidence from South Carolina of African-born slaves possessing craft skills; John Donald Duncan, "Servitude and Slavery in Colonial South Carolina, 1670–1776" (Ph.D. diss., Emory University, 1971), p. 436. Duncan concludes, however, that most black tradesmen in South Carolina were born in the colony; ibid., pp. 436–7.
48 Exceptions to this general tendency may have existed, particularly in the case of the Chesapeake. Wesley Frank Craven has suggested that the magnitude of the trade in slaves between the West Indies and Virginia in the seventeenth century may have been greater than has generally been recognized. As Barbados had one of the older black populations among the British colonies, slaves brought to Virginia from Barbados might already have become acculturated; Wesley Frank Craven, *The Colonies in Transition, 1660–1713* (New York, 1968), p. 292; Wesley Frank Craven, *White, Red, and Black: The Seventeenth-Century Virginian* (Charlottesville, Va., 1971), p. 95. As a result, the average cost of training slaves to perform skilled crafts could have varied inversely with the proportion of Virginia's imports brought from the West Indies: If, as Craven believes, the share of slaves brought directly from Africa to Virginia rose in the last quarter of the seventeenth century, this average cost could have increased in this period. The issue raised by Craven points up the fact that the growth of the American-born proportion of the slave population in the Chesapeake, or other regions, need not have been a simple increasing trend over time. Yet the case noted by Craven must have been exceptional.
49 Phelps Brown and Hopkins, "Seven Centuries of the Price of Consumables," pp. 302–6.
50 Maryland slave prices are presented in Allan Kulikoff, "Tobacco and Slaves: Population, Economy and Society in Eighteenth-Century Prince George's County, Maryland" (Ph.D. diss., Brandeis University, 1976), pp. 485–8; the statement in the text is based on a conversion of these prices to sterling, using the exchange rates of John J. McCusker, *Money and Exchange in Europe and America, 1600–1775: A Handbook* (Chapel Hill, N.C., 1978), pp. 197–8, to eliminate some of the effects of Maryland's inflation. On English wages, see Phelps Brown and Hopkins, "Seven Centuries of the Price of Consumables," p. 313, and Elizabeth W. Gilboy, *Wages in Eighteenth Century England* (Cambridge, Mass. 1934), p. 220. To some extent, the rising slave prices probably overstate the real increase in labor costs, for they reflect the rising life expectancy and improving health of the increasingly American-born slave population in the early eighteenth century.

51 Other elements may also enter this explanation, and although the detailed evidence needed to settle the question remains to be collected, some suggestions can be offered. There may have been significant regional differences within the Chesapeake in the continuing importance of servants in the eighteenth century. Thus, unskilled servants may have virtually disappeared from the older areas of settlement on the lower Western Shore, where tobacco was grown on large plantations, relatively early in the eighteenth century, whereas servants may have continued in use longer for farm labor in the northern Eastern Shore counties that tended to engage in diversified farming on a generally smaller scale; for an indication of this, see Carr and Menard, "Immigration and Opportunity," p. 241. If servants were able to choose specific regions within a colony, the latter areas may have continued to attract servants for reasons similar to those discussed earlier for the Middle Colonies. Shipments of English convicts in the eighteenth century may also have provided an inexpensive source of indentured labor in the Chesapeake; see Smith, *Colonists in Bondage,* pp. 110–33.

Another possibility is that while large planters converted to slave labor, many small farms may have continued to use one or two servants; for evidence on the association between wealth and type of labor owned on Chesapeake estates in the late seventeenth and early eighteenth centuries, see Walsh, "Servitude and Opportunity in Charles County," p. 119; Paul G. E. Clemens, *The Atlantic Economy and Colonial Maryland's Eastern Shore: From Tobacco to Grain* (Ithaca, N.Y. 1980), pp. 85, 103–4, 148. The disproportionate use of servants on small farms could have resulted from differences in the interest rates faced by planters of differing wealth; if owners of small farms had faced higher credit costs, perhaps as a result of their higher default risks, this would have raised the relative cost of slaves to them, and could account for their continued reliance on servants after wealthier planters had switched to slaves.

52 Dunn, *Sugar and Slaves,* pp. 68–72; Sheridan, *Sugar and Slavery,* p. 136; Richard Ligon, *A True and Exact History of the Island of Barbados* (London, 1657), pp. 43–4; Alexander Gunkel and Jerome Handler, eds., "A German Indentured Servant in Barbados in 1652: The Account of Heinrich von Uchteritz," *Journal of the Barbados Museum and Historical Society,* 33 (1970):93.

53 Both differences are significant at the .10 level for two-tailed *t*-tests.

54 Tests of the hypothesis based on comparisons between the Chesapeake and Pennsylvania may be invalidated by the great quantitative importance of German relative to English immigration to Pennsylvania. It is likely that a larger proportion of the English than of the Germans were skilled; compare the shares of skilled among English servants bound for Pennsylvania in Table 6.6 with the figures for Germans in Robert Owen Heavner, "Economic Aspects of Indentured Servitude in Colonial Pennsylvania," (Ph.D. diss., Stanford University, 1976), p. 90. As a result, the skilled proportion of English servants bound for Pennsylvania overestimates the true skilled share of all white immigrants. The share of blacks in net immigration to the Chesapeake was of course higher than to Pennsylvania throughout the

eighteenth century. In spite of the bias just noted in measuring the skilled share of white immigration, the share of the skilled among English servants was virtually the same for the Chesapeake and Pennsylvania in the earlier eighteenth-century sample. By the 1770s, 89% of the Chesapeake's indentured immigrants were skilled, fully 20 percentage points greater than the skilled share of Pennsylvania's English servant imports. The latter result clearly supports the prediction of the hypothesis in spite of the bias.

55 Both differences in proportions skilled between the successive samples referred to are significant at the .01 level for two-tailed *t*-tests.

56 The difference in proportions is significant at the .01 level for a two-tailed *t*-test.

57 Menard, "From Servants to Slaves," pp. 378–80.

10. Indentured labor in the Americas: the experience of three centuries

1 Richard Ligon, *A True and Exact History of the Island of Barbados* (London, 1657), p. 43.

2 Richard S. Dunn, *Sugar and Slaves: The Rise of the Planter Class in the English West Indies, 1624–1713* (Chapel Hill, N.C., 1972), p. 247.

3 Abbot Emerson Smith, *Colonists in Bondage: White Servitude and Convict Labor in America, 1607–1776* (Chapel Hill, N.C. 1947), pp. 237–8, 264; Dunn, *Sugar and Slaves,* pp. 239–40. Edmund S. Morgan, *American Slavery, American Freedom: The Ordeal of Colonial Virginia* (New York, 1975), p. 312.

4 Alice Hanson Jones, *Wealth of a Nation to Be: The American Colonies on the Eve of the Revolution* (New York, 1980), pp. xxiv, 114–15. Separate estimates for Pennsylvania suggest that servants made up only between 6% and 12% of the total labor force of the city of Philadelphia during 1767–75, that in most of these years servants were outnumbered by slaves, and that servants accounted for smaller shares of the labor force in rural areas of Pennsylvania than in Philadelphia; Sharon V. Salinger, "Colonial Labor in Transition: The Decline of Indentured Servitude in Late Eighteenth-Century Philadelphia," *Labor History* 22, no. 2 (Spring 1981):165–91.

5 Russell R. Menard, "From Servant to Freeholder: Status Mobility and Property Accumulation in Seventeenth-Century Maryland," *William and Mary Quarterly,* 3d ser. 30, no. 1 (January 1973):37–64; Lois Green Carr and Russell R. Menard, "Immigration and Opportunity: The Freedman in Early Colonial Maryland," in Thad W. Tate and David L. Ammerman, eds., *The Chesapeake in the Seventeenth Century: Essays on Anglo-American Society and Politics* (Chapel Hill, N.C., 1979), pp. 206–42.

6 Cheesman A. Herrick, *White Servitude in Pennsylvania* (Philadelphia, 1926), p. 254.

7 Lewis Cecil Gray, *History of Agriculture in the Southern United States to 1860* (Gloucester, Mass., 1958), 1:350.

8 William Miller, "The Effects of the American Revolution on Indentured Servitude," *Pennsylvania History,* 7, no. 3 (July 1940):131–41. In Pennsylvania, an act of 1819 abolishing imprisonment of females for debt could

have reduced the attractiveness of servants to masters; Karl Frederick Geiser, *Redemptioners and Indentured Servants in the Colony and Commonwealth of Pennsylvania* (New Haven, 1901), p. 42.

9 Lewis Cecil Gray, *History of Agriculture in the Southern United States to 1860* (Gloucester, Mass., 1958), 1:351.

10 Jack P. Greene, ed., *The Diary of Landon Carter of Sabine Hall, 1752–1778* (Charlottesville, Va., 1965), 2:1055.

11 For nineteenth-century evidence and sources, see Richard A. Easterlin, "Influences in European Overseas Emigration Before World War I," in Robert William Fogel and Stanley L. Engerman, eds., *The Reinterpretation of American Economic History* (New York, 1971), pp. 384–95. A connection in the colonial period between migration to the Chesapeake and the region's economic prosperity has been drawn by Russell R. Menard, "The Tobacco Industry in the Chesapeake Colonies, 1617–1730: An Interpretation," *Research in Economic History* 5 (1980):109–77.

12 Robert E. Gallman, "The Pace and Pattern of American Economic Growth," in Lance E. Davis, Richard A. Easterlin, William N. Parker, et al., *American Economic Growth: An Economist's History of the United States* (New York, 1972), pp. 22–9; P. A. David, "New Light on a Statistical Dark Age: U.S. Real Growth before 1840," in Peter Temin, ed., *New Economic History* (Harmondsworth, 1973), pp. 47–9; Stanley L. Engerman and Robert E. Gallman, "Economic Growth, 1783–1860," *Research in Economic History,* in press.

13 On the pattern of immigration to the United States in the late eighteenth and early nineteenth centuries, see Marcus Hansen, *The Atlantic Migration, 1607–1860* (New York, 1961), pp. 53–145.

14 On nineteenth-century movements of indentured workers to destinations outside the Americas, see A. G. L. Shaw, *Convicts and the Colonies: A Study of Penal Transportation from Great Britain and Ireland to Australia and Other Parts of the British Empire* (London, 1966); Robert A. Huttenback, *Racism and Empire: White Settlers and Colored Immigrants in the British Self-Governing Colonies, 1830–1910* (Ithaca, N.Y., 1976), pp. 26–58; Katharine Coman, *The History of Contract Labor in the Hawaiian Islands,* Publications of the American Economic Association, vol. 4, no. 3 (August 1903).

15 On the history of the development of the form of contract used for immigrants to the British sugar colonies in the nineteenth century, see K. O. Laurence, "The Evolution of Long-Term Labour Contracts in Trinidad and British Guiana, 1834–1863," *Jamaican Historical Review,* 5, no. 1 (May 1965), pp. 9–27.

16 On the migration of Indians under indenture, see Alan H. Adamson, *Sugar Without Slaves: The Political Economy of British Guiana, 1838–1904* (New Haven, 1972); Donald Wood, *Trinidad in Transition: The Years After Slavery* (London,1968); Hugh Tinker, *A New System of Slavery: The Export of Indian Labour Overseas, 1830–1920* (London, 1974).

17 On Chinese indentured immigration, see Duvon Clough Corbitt, *A Study of the Chinese in Cuba, 1847–1947* (Wilmore, Ky., 1971); Watt Stewart,

Chinese Bondage in Peru: A History of the Chinese Coolie in Peru, 1849–1874 (Durham, N.C., 1951); Persia Crawford Campbell, *Chinese Coolie Emigration to Countries within the British Empire* (London, 1923).

18 For the estimate for the earlier period, see Chapter 1. On the nineteenth century, see Carter Goodrich, "Indenture," *Encyclopaedia of the Social Sciences* (New York, 1932), 7:644–7; W. Arthur Lewis, *Growth and Fluctuations, 1870–1913* (London, 1978), pp. 185–8; Kingsley Davis, *The Population of India and Pakistan* (Princeton, 1951), pp. 98–106.

19 These differences were noted by Stanley L. Engerman, "Coerced and Free Labor: Property Rights and the Development of the Labor Force" *Annales, Economies, Sociétés, Civilisations,* in press.

20 Goodrich, "Indenture," p. 647.

Appendix A. Servant registrations

1 Bristol Record Office, Bristol, "Servants to forraign plantations, 1654–1662," B.A.O. 04220(1), and "Servants to forraign plantacons, 1663–1679," B.A.O. 04220(2). I am grateful to the Bristol Record Office for providing a microfilm of these volumes.

2 Bristol Record Office, "Actions and Apprentices," B.A.O. 04355(6) and B.A.O. 04356(1). The Bristol servant registrations have been abstracted in Noel Currer-Briggs, "Indentured Servants from Bristol to America, 1654–1686" (MS, no date). I am grateful to Noel Currer-Briggs for making a copy of this manuscript available to me.

3 A printed copy of the parliamentary ordinance was also pasted into the first volume of the registrations. The texts of both acts are given in full in Appendix B.

4 This is also reproduced in Appendix B.

5 Richard S. Dunn, *Sugar and Slaves* (New York, 1973), p. 70.

6 The full text of the order is given in Appendix B.

7 Volumes XIII and XIV are held at the Corporation of London Records Office at London Guildhall. The servant registrations, together with the records of passes issued by the Lord Mayor giving individuals permission to travel outside England, have been abstracted in Michael Ghirelli, *A List of Emigrants from England to America, 1682–1692* (Baltimore, 1968).

8 The major part of this collection, consisting of 741 contracts, is held at the Greater London Records Office (Middlesex Section), as "Plantation Indentures," MR/E. These have been partially abstracted in Cregoe D. P. Nicholson, "Some Early Emigrants to America," *Genealogists' Magazine* 12, no. 1, through 13, no. 8 (March 1955 to December 1960), reprinted as *Some Early Emigrants to America* (Baltimore, 1965). An additional 70 contracts from the same series, now held in Washington, D.C., and Jamaica, have recently been found. They are abstracted in John Wareing, "Some Early Emigrants to America, 1683–84: A Supplementary List," *Genealogists' Magazine* 18, no. 5 (March 1976):239–46.

9 This has been transcribed by Elizabeth French, originally published in *New England Historical and Genealogical Register,* vols. 64 and 65 (1910–11),

reprinted as *List of Emigrants to America from Liverpool, 1697-1707* (Baltimore, 1969). For a description of the form of the list, see ibid., p. 3, no. 1.

10 On the possible sources of the registrations, see the comments of Abbot Emerson Smith, *Colonists in Bondage* (Chapel Hill, N.C., 1947), p. 355, n. 30. I am grateful to the Liverpool Record Office for providing me with a microfilm copy of the registrations.

11 Corporation of London Records Office, London Guildhall, "Memoranda of Agreements to Serve in America and the West Indies." The bulk of these are partially abstracted in Jack Kaminkow and Marion Kaminkow, *A List of Emigrants from England to America, 1718-1759* (Baltimore, 1964). An additional set subsequently found in the Guildhall among Court of Aldermen papers is abstracted in David Galenson, "Agreements to Serve in America and the West Indies, 1727-31," *Genealogists' Magazine* 19, no. 2 (June 1977):40-4. This set and the earlier Middlesex contracts from 1683-4 described above are the only large collections of servant contracts from the colonial period known to exist anywhere. Scattered contracts for individuals or small numbers of servants can be found, e.g., among the records of particular colonial estates. For a description of one such set of six contracts, with abstracts of the agreements, see David Galenson, "Servants bound for Antigua, 1752-56," *Genealogists' Magazine* 19, no. 8 (December 1978):277-9.

12 The text of the clause is given in Appendix B.

13 Examples of the two types are given in Appendix D.

14 These results are presented in Chapter 7.

15 These are contained in three folio volumes at the Public Record Office, London, Treasury 47/9-47/11. These have been transcribed by Gerald Fothergill, *Emigrants from England, 1773-1776* (Baltimore, 1964).

Appendix B. English laws and documents

1 Bristol Record Office, B.A.O. 04220(1).

2 Ibid.

3 Ibid.

4 There are a number of incomplete published versions of this order. The text given here is the full text as contained in the original proceedings of the Privy Council; Public Record Office, London, "Privy Council Registers," vol. 69, P.C. 2/69, pp. 595-6. What is apparently a contemporary copy, with some significant differences, also in the P.R.O., is contained in "Entries Relating to Plantations in General," vol. 2, C.O. 324/4, pp. 89-90. The transcription of the order given in W. L. Grant and James Munro, eds. *Acts of the Privy Council of England, Colonial Series* (London, 1910), p. 42, is an incomplete copy of P.C. 2/69, pp. 595-6; that given in A. S. Salley, *Records in the British Public Record Office Relating to South Carolina, 1663-1684* (Atlanta, Ga., 1928), 1:235, is an incomplete copy of C.O. 324/4, pp. 89-90.

5 Clause V of "An Act for the further preventing Robbery, Burglary, and other Felonies, and for the more effectual Transportation of Felons, and unlawful

Exporters of Wool; and for declaring the Law upon some Points relating to Pirates," in *The Statutes at Large, From the First Year of the Reign of King George the First, To the Ninth Year of the Reign of King George the Second* (London, 1786), 5:114.

Appendix C. Possible biases in age distributions

1 Full age distributions by sex for the sample are given in David Galenson, "The Indenture System and the Colonial Labor Market" (Ph.D. diss., Harvard University, 1979), Table III-5, p. 52.
2 This is the explanation given by Mildred Campbell, "Social Origins of Some Early Americans," in James M. Smith, ed., *Seventeenth-Century America* (Chapel Hill, N.C. 1959), p. 74.
3 Abbot Emerson Smith, *Colonists in Bondage* (Chapel Hill, N.C. 1947), pp. 78–9.
4 See Appendix B for the full text and references to this order.
5 Full age distributions by sex for the sample are presented in Galenson, "The Indenture System," Table III-4, p. 51.
6 Full age distributions by sex for the sample are given in ibid., Table III-7, p. 54.
7 Smith, *Colonists in Bondage,* pp. 80–1; M. Dorothy George, *London Life in the Eighteenth Century* (Harmondsworth, 1976), pp. 356–7.
8 The text of this clause is given in full in Appendix B.
9 It might also be noted that, as indicated in the passage quoted, the act provided for the registration only of those of age 15 or above. In practice, this lower limit appears to have been disregarded, as servants' ages of less than 15 were recorded from the beginning of the period of registration. As a result, it does not appear likely that ages would have been falsified on this account.

Appendix D. London registrations of 1718–1759

1 These amendments to the forms are not included in the abstracts published by Jack Kaminkow and Marion Kaminkow, *A List of Emigrants from England to America, 1718–1759* (Baltimore, 1964). This discussion is based on the manuscript agreements held at the Corporations of London Records Office, "Memoranda of Agreements to Serve In America and the West Indies." For further discussion, see David Galenson, "Agreements to Serve in America and the West Indies, 1727–31," *Genealogists' Magazine* 19, no. 2 (June 1977):40–4, and no.3 (September 1977):101–2.

Appendix E. Colonial destinations during 1697–1707

1 It should be noted that the results of these tests must be interpreted with caution because of the apparent changes in the seasonality of servant registrations, as seen in Chapter 6. Thus similar chi-square tests for the London registrations of 1718–59 indicate that the null hypothesis of no difference between the monthly percentage distribution of the Liverpool

registrants without recorded destinations and either that of the servants bound for the Chesapeake or that of those bound for the West Indies cannot be rejected at the .10 level.

Appendix F. Cash payments and salaries

1 Lewis Cecil Gray, *History of Agriculture in the Southern United States to 1860* (Gloucester, Mass., 1958), 1:364–5.
2 The dependent variable is the nominal value of the specified local colonial currency. Although most of the colonies' currencies were devalued somewhat relative to sterling, the differences in currency values across the principal American colonies in most of this period were small. See John J. McCusker, *Money and Exchange in Europe and America, 1600–1775: A Handbook* (Chapel Hill, N.C., 1978), Chaps. 3 and 4.

Appendix G. Categorization of occupations

1 For a relatively detailed example of such a listing, see David Souden, " 'To Forraign Plantacons': Indentured Servant Emigration c. 1630–1660" (B.A. thesis, Cambridge University, 1976), Table 3.1, pp. 17–20.

Appendix H. Estimates of migration by colony 1650–1780

1 The procedure followed here is similar to that used by Henry A. Gemery, "Emigration from the British Isles to the New World, 1630–1700: Inferences from Colonial Populations," *Research in Economic History* 5 (1980):170–231. Unlike Gemery's use of three regions, the present estimates have been made at more disaggregated levels. This investigation has also extended the procedure to the colonies' black populations, and provides estimates for most of the eighteenth century as well as the second half of the seventeenth.
2 Because the interest of this investigation is in estimating colonial immigration rather than European or African emigration, in contrast to Gemery's procedure, in the present study S excludes passage mortality and is defined as the proportion of those immigrants who survived the voyage to the colonies who died during their first year in the colonies as a result of exposure to the new disease environment.

Appendix I. Destinations of indentured servants

1 Separate tabulations of the destinations of the servants in each sample, also divided by sex, are given in David Galenson, "The Indenture System and the Colonial Labor Market" (Ph.D. diss., Harvard University, 1979), Tables VIII-1–VIII-12, pp. 216–28.

Selected bibliography

The following list represents a limited selection of significant published works that have influenced my interpretation of indentured servitude and the colonial labor market.

The literature on the economic and social history of England in the seventeenth and eighteenth centuries is vast. The works listed here include a few of the key studies that focus on English labor conditions and institutions of particular relevance to an understanding of the background to emigration and the adaptations of the colonial American labor market.

Ashton, T. S. *An Economic History of England: The 18th Century* (London, 1955).

Bridenbaugh, Carl. *Vexed and Troubled Englishmen, 1590–1642* (London, 1967).

Campbell, Mildred. *The English Yeoman Under Elizabeth and the Early Stuarts* (New Haven, 1946).

Clarkson, L. A. *The Pre-Industrial Economy in England, 1500–1750* (London, 1971).

Coleman, D. C. "Labour in the English Economy of the Seventeenth Century," *Economic History Review,* 2nd ser., 8, no. 3 (April 1956):280–95.

The Economy of England, 1450–1750 (London, 1977).

Davies, Margaret Gay. *The Enforcement of English Apprenticeship: A Study in Applied Mercantilism, 1563–1642* (Cambridge, Mass., 1956).

George, M. Dorothy. *London Life in the Eighteenth Century* (1925; reprint ed., New York, 1966).

Gilboy, Elizabeth, *Wages in Eighteenth Century England* (Cambridge, Mass., 1934).

Laslett, Peter. *The World We Have Lost,* 2nd ed. (London, 1971).

Family Life and Illicit Love in Earlier Generations (Cambridge, 1977).

Laslett, Peter, ed. *Household and Family in Past Time* (Cambridge, 1972).

Leonard, E. M. *The Early History of English Poor Relief* (Cambridge, 1900).

Notestein, Wallace. *The English People on the Eve of Colonization* (London, 1954).

Pound, John. *Poverty and Vagrancy in Tudor England* (London, 1971).

Schofield, R. S. "Age-Specific Mobility in an Eighteenth Century Rural English Parish," *Annales de Démographie Historique* (1970):261–74.

Thompson, Roger. *Women in Stuart England and America* (London, 1974).

Selected bibliography

Thirsk, Joan, ed. *The Agrarian History of England and Wales, Vol. 4, 1500–1640* (Cambridge, 1967).

Wrigley, E. A. "A Simple Model of London's Importance in Changing English Society and Economy, 1650–1750," *Past and Present*, no. 37 (July 1967):44–70.

Although the amount of attention American historians have devoted to indentured servitude has varied considerably over time, a number of older studies have done much to shape our knowledge of the institution. Many of the following works, which treat important aspects of the basis of colonial indentured servitude and its environment, are classics of American economic and social history.

Ballagh, J. C. *White Servitude in the Colony of Virginia* (Baltimore, 1895).

Bassett, John Spencer. *Slavery and Servitude in the Colony of North Carolina* (Baltimore, 1896).

Bidwell, Percy Wells, and Falconer, John I. *History of Agriculture in the Northern United States, 1620–1860* (Washington, D.C., 1925).

Bruce, Philip Alexander. *Economic History of Virginia in the Seventeenth Century*, 2 vols. (New York, 1907).

Campbell, Mildred. "English Emigration on the Eve of the American Revolution," *American Historical Review*, 61, no. 1 (October 1955):1–20.
"Social Origins of Some Early Americans," in James Morton Smith, ed., *Seventeenth-Century America* (Chapel Hill, N.C. 1959), pp. 63–89.

Davies, K. G. *The Royal African Company* (1957; reprint ed., New York, 1970).

Debien, G. "Les Engagés Pour Les Antilles (1634–1715)," *Revue d'Histoire des Colonies* 38 (1951):7–261.

Deerr, Noel. *The History of Sugar*, 2 vols. (London, 1949, 1950).

Geiser, Karl Frederick. *Redemptioners and Indentured Servants in the Colony and Commonwealth of Pennsylvania* (New Haven, 1901).

Gray, Lewis Cecil. *History of Agriculture in the Southern United States to 1860*, 2 vols. (1933; reprint ed., Gloucester, Mass., 1958).

Handlin, Oscar and Handlin, Mary. "Origins of the Southern Labor System," *William and Mary Quarterly*, 3d ser. 7, no. 2 (April 1950): 199–222.

Herrick, Cheesman A., *White Servitude in Pennsylvania* (Philadelphia, 1926).

Jernegan, Marcus Wilson. *Laboring and Dependent Classes in Colonial America, 1607–1783* (Chicago, 1931).

McCormac, Eugene I. *White Servitude in Maryland, 1634–1820* (Baltimore, 1904).

Middleton, Arthur P. *Tobacco Coast: A Maritime History of Chesapeake Bay in the Colonial Era* (Newport News, Va., 1953).

Miller, William. "The Effects of the American Revolution on Indentured Servitude," *Pennsylvania History* 7, no. 3 (July 1940):131–41.

Mittelberger, Gottlieb. *Journey to Pennsylvania* (Cambridge, Mass., 1960).

Moller, Herbert. "Sex Composition and Correlated Culture Patterns of Colonial America," *William and Mary Quarterly*, 3d ser. 2, no. 2 (April 1945):113–53.

Morris, Richard B. *Government and Labor in Early America* (New York, 1946).

Pares, Richard. *Merchants and Planters, Economic History Review*, Supplement No. 4 (Cambridge, 1960).

Selected bibliography

Riley, Edward M., ed. *The Journal of John Harrower* (Williamsburg, Va., 1963).
Semmes, Raphael. *Crime and Punishment in Early Maryland* (Baltimore, 1938).
Smith, Abbot Emerson. *Colonists in Bondage: White Servitude and Convict Labor in America, 1607–1776* (Chapel Hill, N.C., 1947).
Smith, Warren B. *White Servitude in Colonial South Carolina* (Columbia, S.C., 1961).
Wertenbaker, Thomas J. *The Planters of Colonial Virginia* (Princeton, 1922).
Williams, Eric. *Capitalism and Slavery* (1944; reprint ed., New York, 1966).

The past two decades have witnessed an intensification of interest in the study of colonial American economic and social history. The following list includes many of the most important of the recent works that have helped to illuminate the history of indentured servitude and the colonial labor market.
Bean, Richard N., and Thomas, Robert P. "The Adoption of Slave Labor in British America," in Henry A. Gemery and Jan S. Hogendorn, eds., *The Uncommon Market: Essays in the Economic History of the Atlantic Slave Trade* (New York, 1979), pp. 377–98.
Beeman, Richard R. "Labor Forces and Race Relations: A Comparative View of the Colonization of Brazil and Virginia," *Political Science Quarterly* 86, no. 4 (December 1971):609–36.
Breen, T. H. "A Changing Labor Force and Race Relations in Virginia, 1660–1710," *Journal of Social History* 7, no. 1 (Fall, 1973):3–25.
Bridenbaugh, Carl, and Bridenbaugh, Roberta. *No Peace Beyond the Line: The English in the Caribbean, 1624–1690* (New York, 1972).
Campbell, Mildred. "Response" (to Galenson), *William and Mary Quarterly,* 3d ser. 35, no. 3 (July 1978):525–40; "Reply," ibid., 36, no. 2 (April 1979): 277–86. (For references to my contributions to this exchange, see Preface, note 1).
Carr, Lois Green, and Menard, Russell R. "Immigration and Opportunity: The Freedman in Early Colonial Maryland," in Thad W. Tate and David L. Ammerman, eds., *The Chesapeake in the Seventeenth Century* (Chapel Hill, N.C., 1979), pp. 206–42.
Carr, Lois Green, and Walsh, Lorena S. "The Planter's Wife: The Experience of White Women in Seventeenth-Century Maryland," *William and Mary Quarterly,* 3d ser., 34, no. 4 (October 1977):542–71.
Clemens, Paul G. E. *The Atlantic Economy and Colonial Maryland's Eastern Shore: From Tobacco to Grain* (Ithaca, N.Y., 1980).
Craven, Wesley Frank. *White, Red and Black: The Seventeenth-Century Virginian* (Charlottesville, Va., 1971).
Curtin, Philip D. *The Atlantic Slave Trade: A Census* (Madison, Wis., 1969).
Davies, K. G. *The North Atlantic World in the Seventeenth Century* (Minneapolis, 1974).
Dunn, Richard S. *Sugar and Slaves: The Rise of the Planter Class in the English West Indies, 1624–1713* (Chapel Hill, N.C., 1972).
Fogel, Robert William, and Engerman, Stanley L. *Time on the Cross: The Economics of American Negro Slavery,* 2 vols. (Boston, 1974).
Galenson, David W., and Menard, Russell R. "Approaches to the Analysis of

Selected bibliography

Economic Growth in Colonial British America," *Historical Methods* 13, no. 1 (Winter, 1980):3–18.

Gemery, Henry A., and Hogendorn, Jan S. "The Atlantic Slave Trade: A Tentative Economic Model," *Journal of African History* 15, no. 2 (1974): 223–46.

Gray, Ralph, and Wood, Betty. "The Transition from Indentured to Involuntary Servitude in Colonial Georgia," *Explorations in Economic History* 13, no. 4 (October 1976):353–70.

Heavner, Robert O. "Indentured Servitude: The Philadelphia Market, 1771-1773," *Journal of Economic History* 38, no. 3 (September 1978): 701–13.

Economic Aspects of Indentured Servitude in Colonial Philadelphia (New York, 1978).

Hofstadter, Richard. *America at 1750: A Social Portrait* (New York, 1971).

Horn, James. "Servant Emigration to the Chesapeake in the Seventeenth Century," in Thad W. Tate and David L. Ammerman, eds., *The Chesapeake in the Seventeenth Century* (Chapel Hill, N.C., 1979), pp. 51–95.

Jones, Alice Hanson. *Wealth of a Nation to Be: The American Colonies on the Eve of the Revolution* (New York, 1980).

Kussmaul, Ann. *Servants in Husbandry in Early Modern England* (Cambridge, 1981).

Lemon, James T. *The Best Poor Man's Country: A Geographical Study of Early Southeastern Pennsylvania* (Baltimore, 1972).

Main, Gloria L. "Maryland and the Chesapeake Economy, 1670–1720," in Aubrey C. Land, Lois Green Carr, and Edward C. Papenfuse, eds., *Law, Society, and Politics in Early Maryland* (Baltimore, 1977), pp. 134–52.

Menard, Russell, R. "From Servant to Freeholder: Status Mobility and Property Accumulation in Seventeenth-Century Maryland," *William and Mary Quarterly,* 3d ser. 30, no. 1 (January 1973):37–64.

"From Servants to Slaves: The Transformation of the Chesapeake Labor System," *Southern Studies* 16, no. 4 (Winter, 1977):355–90.

Morgan, Edmund S. *American Slavery, American Freedom: The Ordeal of Colonial Virginia* (New York, 1975).

Mullin, Gerald W. *Flight and Rebellion: Slave Resistance in Eighteenth-Century Virginia* (London, 1972).

Sheridan, Richard B. *Sugar and Slavery: An Economic History of the British West Indies* (Barbados, 1974).

"The Role of the Scots in the Economy and Society of the West Indies," in Vera Rubin and Arthur Tuden, eds., *Comparative Perspectives on Slavery in New World Plantation Societies, Annals of the New York Academy of Sciences* (New York, 1977) 292:94–106.

Souden, David. " 'Rogues, whores and vagabonds'? Indentured servant emigrants to North America and the case of mid-seventeenth-century Bristol," *Social History* 3, no. 1 (January 1978):23–41.

Stiverson, Gregory A. *Poverty in a Land of Plenty: Tenancy in Eighteenth-Century Maryland* (Baltimore, 1977).

Walsh, Lorena S. "Servitude and Opportunity in Charles County, Maryland,

1658–1705," in Aubrey C. Land, Lois Green Carr, and Edward C. Papenfuse, eds., *Law, Society, and Politics in Early Maryland*, (Baltimore, 1977)
pp. 111–33
Wood, Peter H. *Black Majority: Negroes in Colonial South Carolina from 1670
through the Stono Rebellion* (New York, 1975).

As discussed in Chapter 10, the institution of indentured servitude survived the
American colonial period, and rose to considerable importance in a number of
areas outside North America in the nineteenth century. The following studies describe some important cases in which indentured servitude and other variants of
contract labor became a solution to labor market conditions.

Adamson, Alan H. *Sugar Without Slaves: The Political Economy of British
Guiana, 1838–1904* (New Haven, 1972).
Campbell, Persia Crawford. *Chinese Coolie Emigration to Countries Within the
British Empire* (London, 1923).
Coman, Katharine. *The History of Contract Labor in the Hawaiian Islands*,
Publications of the American Economic Association, vol. 4, no. 3 (August
1903).
Corbitt, Duvon Clough. *A Study of the Chinese in Cuba, 1847–1947*
(Wilmore, Ky., 1971).
Goodrich, Carter. "Indenture," in *Encyclopaedia of the Social Sciences* (New
York, 1932), 7:644–8.
Green, William A. *British Slave Emancipation* (Oxford, 1976).
Huttenback, Robert A. *Racism and Empire: White Settlers and Colored
Immigrants in the British Self-Governing Colonies, 1820–1910* (Ithaca,
N.Y., 1976).
Laurence, K. O. "The Evolution of Long-Term Labour Contracts in Trinidad and
British Guiana, 1834–1863," *Jamaican Historical Review* 5, no. 1 (May
1965):9–27.
Immigration Into the West Indies in the 19th Century (Barbados, 1971).
Nath, Dwarka. *A History of Indians in British Guiana* (London, 1950).
Shaw, A. G. L. *Convicts and the Colonies: A Study of Penal Transportation
from Great Britain and Ireland to Australia and other parts of the
British Empire* (London, 1966).
Stewart, Watt. *Chinese Bondage in Peru: A History of the Chinese Coolie in
Peru, 1849–1874* (Durham, N.C., 1951).
Tinker, Hugh. *A New System of Slavery: The Export of Indian Labour Overseas,
1830–1920* (London, 1974).
Wood, Donald. *Trinidad in Transition: The Years After Slavery* (London,
1968).

Index

Index

farmers, 34–5, 37, 38, 39, 45–6, 48, 51, 53–7, 60–3; length of indenture, 107; literacy of, 67, 70, 71–4, 76, 244n14; occupational category, definition, 211
farms, small, 126, 127, 145, 172, 272n51; in Middle Colonies, 157; in New England, 156
Fauquier, Francis, 129
female servants, 23–4; ages of, 26–8; destinations of, 82, 84t, 86, 94, 95, 224–7t; labor-force participation rates of, 259n5; length of indenture of, 112; literacy of, 66–7; occupations of, 94; requests for, 136; share of, in servant population, 23, 32; uses of, in colonies, 24–6, 32; as wives of colonists, 13, 234nn4, 5
Fiffet (servant), 132
Fitzhugh, William, 135
Fogel, Robert, 107, 109, 257n36
food and drink trades, 35, 51; literacy in, 67, 70, 71–2; occupational category, definition, 211
Forde, Thomas (servant), 135
fraud, prevention of, 65, 81, 238n12
free labor, 8, 95–6, 98, 126, 127, 141–9; initial colonization done by, 174–5; measurement of price and quantity, 146; reluctant to work in gangs, 145; skilled, 158
freedmen, 127; in Chesapeake, 154, 269n29; economic opportunity for, 110, 176, 178–9; emigrating from South Carolina, 155; lack of opportunity in West Indies, 138, 150, 151; in Middle Colonies, 176
freedom dues, 98, 99, 101, 102, 207, 253n17, 256n34
French (New World) colonies: contracts for bound workers in, 232n49

gang labor, 145, 150–1, 155, 176; disliked by whites, 145, 150, 265n16
gentlemen, 35, 38, 39, 61, 210
Georgia: as destination, 86; racial composition of, 118, 119t; transition to slavery, 270n32
German immigrants, 14–15, 157, 179; to Pennsylvania, 272n54
Gilbert, Sir Humphrey, 6
Glass, D. V., 239n17
Goodrich, Carter, 17
Gray, Lewis, 140, 158, 207

Haires, Francis (servant), 47
Haworth, George, 264n12
headright, 12
Helyar, Cary, 133–4
Hippy, William (servant), text of indenture of, 43f
hire rates, 268n23; effect on immigration, 147–9; in Middle Colonies, 157; servants and slaves, 146–9; skilled slaves/skilled servants, 159

Hoskins, W. G., 236n4
human capital, market evaluation of, 97–102, 103
husbandmen, see farmers

immigrant labor, 143; South Carolina, 155; supply curves for, 146, 147–9; West Indies, 150–1
immigration, 17, 142, 161, 167; change in levels of, 179–80; to Chesapeake and Pennsylvania, 178; and demand for labor, 126, 127; flows of black and white, 118–26, 139–40, 175, 176–7; of free/bound workers, 145–6; labor market as central mechanism in influencing, 174; and marginal productivity of labor, 174–6; to Middle Colonies, 156–7; relation of, to free labor, 174–5; variation among colonies, 149–57
indenture system, 171–80; base on which slavery was built, 4, 167; beginnings of, 3–19; and colonial market for skilled labor, 157–60; contemporary accounts of, 9, 10, 47–8, 107; as credit system, 8, 12–13, 97, 171; decline of, 4, 117, 172–80; economic risks in, 13, 14–15; end of (U.S.), 179–80, 182; enforcement in, 3, 8; exceptions to voluntary, 231n38; foreshadowed by Virginia Company's labor recruitment, 11–12; founding principle of, 5; was institutional accompaniment to labor mobility, 12; in nineteenth century, 180–2; principal function of, 178; relation to free and slave labor, 172, 174; relation to slavery in labor force, 139–40; relation to slavery in law, 3; role of, in colonial labor market, 117–40, 141–68; studies re, 16–17; as system of servitude, 181; see also redemptioner system
indentured labor, 34, 141, 143, 173–82; demand for, and abolition of slavery, 180–2; elasticity of supply of, 263n7; measurement of price and quantity, 146
indentured servants, 3–4, 51, 101, 127; American-born, 231n33; cash payments and salaries paid to, 207–9; changing economic skills of, 32 (see also occupations); characteristics of, 4, 91–6, 103, 112, 172, 173–4; choice of destination, 150 (see also destination[s]); choices facing prospective, 112–13, 175; compared with servants in husbandry, 6–10; custom of the country, 13, 249n23; demographic structure of, 23–33; economic and social status of, 45–50, 53–4, 61, 65, 66, 71–5, 76, 77–8; economic mobility of, 178–9; economic productivity of, 46, 47, 53–4, 98, 99, 246n23; expected present value of, 266n20; flows of, 163, 181; health/illness of, 89–91 (see also seasoning

Index

Liverpool registrations *1697–1707*, 87, 237n6; age in, 23–4, 26; destinations in, 82, 85; destinations of servants without recorded destinations in, 204–6; information in, 185

Lodge, Adam (servant), text of indenture of, 201f

London: Common Council, 11, 231n38; Lord Mayor, 65, 185

London registrations, 51, 184, 185; age distributions in, 195–9; female literacy in, 67; male literacy in, 67–70, 73–5, 76, 77; procedure in, 57; sex in, 23

London registrations *1683–86*, 30, 237n6, 254n22; ages in, 26, 92; recruiters listed, 97

London registrations *1718–59*, 107, 164, 208, 237n6, 254n22; ages in, 30, 31, 92; destinations in, 87; format of, 200–3; information in, 185–6; occupations in, 51–6, 61, 63; recruiters listed, 97; skilled men to West Indies, 92–3, 94, 95; surviving contracts, 102

London registrations *1773–75*; occupations, 51, 56–9, 63

Lynch, Sir Thomas, 128

Mack, Solomon, 231n33

mainland colonies: immigrant flows to, 120–6, 216–17t; labor costs in, 126–7; shortage of white servants in, 138–9

mainland colonies, southern: demand for skilled labor in, 126, 127; mortality rate in, 144–5; transition to slavery in, 177; *see also* specific areas, e.g., Chesapeake colonies, and colonies, e.g., Virginia

male servants, 23; ages of, 26–33; ages of, and presence/absence of occupational history, 45–7, 52–3, 56, 58t, 59, 61; destinations of, 82, 83t, 85–6, 95, 220–3t; economic background of, 60; economic productivity of, 46, 47, 53–4, 60, 94, 107–9; economic skills of, 60–6; literacy of, 46, 53, 67–74, 75–8; occupations listed, Bristol registrations, *1654–86*, 34–9; occupations listed, Middlesex registrations *1683–84*, 39–50, 61, 63; occupations listed, London registrations *1718–59*, 51–6; occupations listed, London registrations *1773–75*, 56–9; predominated in colonial period, 23, 31, 32; relative annual net earnings by age, 107–9; skilled, 92–5 (*see also* skilled labor); without occupations listed, 39–40, 45–7, 50, 51–6, 60, 61, 66, 75–8, 203

Martin, Samuel, 107, 129, 131–2, 135–6; *Essay Upon Plantership*, 131

Maryland, 4, 10, 24–5; demand for indentured servants in, 153; as destination, 85, 87, 95, 173, 178; importance of indenture system in, 139; imported English convicts, 157; as importer of servants, 124; length of

indenture in, 110, 111; racial composition of, 118, 119t; rise of slavery in, 151; skilled labor in, 166; slave prices in, 160, 268n23; slave/servant ratio in, 154; valuations of indentured servants recorded in, 100

Massachusetts, 156

masters, 8–9; obligations to servants, 97

Menard, Russell, 164

merchants, 86, 97–8, 101, 112; competition among, for recruits, 113; costs to, 100, 102, 111; profit made by, 250n3; protection from false kidnapping charges, 185–6, 187–8, 194, 198

metal and wood trades, 35, 51; length of indenture, 107; literacy in, 67, 70, 71–2; occupational category, definition, 211

Middle Colonies: attractive to immigrants, 176; composition of labor force in, 156–7; demand for labor in, 126; immigration to, 120, 167; proportion of blacks in, 118; role of white servitude in, 174

Middlesex (County) Quarter Sessions, 65, 184

Middlesex registrations *1683–84*, 30, 163, 207, 237n6, 254n22; age distributions in, 92, 194–9; information in, 184–5; literacy in, 67, 68–9t, 71, 73–4, 75, 77; occupations in, 39–50, 61, 63; procedure in, 44–5; recruiters listed in, 97; skilled men to West Indies, 92–3, 94; surviving contracts from, 102; types of printed forms used in, 40–4

migration, 143–5, 163; black, 163–4; decennial estimates of net migration, by colony, 212–18t; decline in, 266n16; magnitude of, 17; patterns of, 81–96, 173–4; role of indentured servitude in, 3–4; seasonal patterns in, 86–91; use of indenture to facilitate, 180; *see also* emigration; immigration

Miller, Perry, 6

minors, 186, 198, 208; form of contract, 200–3; length of indenture, 102–7, 112, 237n6; literacy of, 67, 71–3, 76, 244n11; without trades, 38–9, 45–6, 48, 50, 51–9

Modyford, Sir Thomas, 217

Montserrat, 177; racial composition of, 118, 120t

Morgan, Edmund, 9, 89, 267n20

mortality probability, 101

mortality rate, 111, 144–5; in Chesapeake, 152; in South Carolina, 155, 176, 269n30; in West Indies, 110, 144, 150, 151, 176, 264n13; *see also* seasoning mortality

Narragansett County, R.I., 156

Neuberg, Victor E., 245n19

Nevis: black population in, 126, 177; as destination, 85, 173; racial composi-

271n48; slaves in skilled positions, 134, 139; sugar production in, 91; transition to slave labor, 165, 167, 176, 177, 264n13; treatment of indentured servants, 172; white servitude basis for black slavery in, 128, 140; working conditions in, 110
Whaley, William, 133–4
Whistler, Henry, 48

white labor, 5–10, 141; costs of, 151; demand for, 147; elasticity of supply of, 150; relative productivity of, 158; search for cheap, 157; supply curves, 147–9, 160; supply of, 144–6, 246n23; unwilling to do gang labor, 151, 167
Williams, Eric, 4
Wood, Peter, 269n30
Wood, William, 10